THE RUSSIAN PEASANT MOVEMENT
1906–1917

THE RUSSIAN PEASANT MOVEMENT
1906–1917

BY
LAUNCELOT A. OWEN

WITH A FOREWORD BY
SIR BERNARD PARES, K.B.E.

NEW YORK
RUSSELL & RUSSELL · INC
1963

Andrew S. Thomas Memorial Library
MORRIS HARVEY COLLEGE, CHARLESTON, W. VA.
52358

FIRST PUBLISHED, 1937
REISSUED, 1963, BY RUSSELL & RUSSELL, INC.
BY ARRANGEMENT WITH THE AUTHOR
L. C. CATALOG CARD NO: 62-16196

PRINTED IN THE UNITED STATES OF AMERICA

FOREWORD

It can certainly be said that the most important of all the gaps in our direct knowledge of the historical details of the Russian revolution of 1917 is the subject of this book, the agrarian revolution of that year, in which the peasants created an accomplished fact by simply appropriating the whole of the land. The author is not exaggerating when he says that by so doing they contributed that basis on which the communist revolution in October of the same year rested, both for its achievement and for its permanence, which of course included the success of the Reds in the civil war. In this country, we knew practically nothing of all this, except for a number of lively personal records of very diverse value, and we know but little now except for the valuable work of Professor Geroid T. Robinson of Columbia University.

Mr. Launcelot Owen distinguished himself at the University of Western Australia in Perth by writing a dissertation based on such materials as were then accessible to him and was sent by his University to the School of Slavonic and East European Studies in London as the Hackett post-graduate research student to continue these studies. It was clear to me as his teacher that his dissertation was very remarkable in compensating for the comparative inadequacy of its materials by an unusual intelligence of what really counted and an exceptional soundness of judgment. In London he had the great advantage of the assistance of Dr. Alexander Meyendorff, formerly Lecturer in peasant land law in the University of St. Petersburg, a scholar of European scope and of an exceptional freedom from bias. He here had access to those materials of the first value which were saved for historical study by that admirable direction in research of Professor Michael Pokrovsky which secured that they should reach the world of scholarship intact. Of these materials Dr. Owen has made an excellent use. The most important were the daily reports sent in from the localities to the Provisional Government (March to November, 1917), recording the details of this colossal revolution, which in that short time changed property in land over a vaster surface than was ever covered by any previous movement of this kind. The story of this transformation is, among other things, the most lively revelation of Russian peasant nature that has ever been accessible.

Dr. Owen did not, of course, confine his researches to this period. He made a preliminary study of the whole history of serfdom (land bondage) in Russia, which does not appear in this book, except for a very short initial summary of his conclusions on the subject. But he concentrates in full detail on peasant history from the immediate antecedents of the first so-called "revolution" of 1905–7, and he later gives a full and critical account of the subsequent legislation of the last outstanding statesman of Russian Tsardom, Peter Stolypin, who, after he had driven off the revolutionary attack, set himself to create in the peasantry a new basis of support for the Government by the formation of a new population of landowning yeomen. Stolypin's success in this task was such as to cover a population of something like eight millions, and the tendency which he inaugurated must in all probability have gone very much further but for the world war and the final collapse of Tsardom. Then, in the absence of any controlling governmental authority, immediately followed the drastic action of the peasants themselves, to which allusion has already been made.

Dr. Owen rightly pauses, before describing this in detail, to give a full account of the views on the peasant question of the man who was not only to set the ball rolling but later, in phases not covered by this book, to inaugurate a completely new social régime in Russia.

And he shows how clearly Lenin saw into the whole question before his great opportunity came. The book is therefore rightly completed by the first land act by which Lenin, now in power, consolidated the agrarian revolution and directed it on its new path.

For the reasons which have been given, Dr. Owen's book should be in the hands of any reader of English who wishes to know what happened and how, in this great social question; and thus the reader will be able to follow with understanding the many further developments of it which have taken place in Russia since 1917.

BERNARD PARES.

PREFACE

THE original thesis of which this publication forms but a part, contained a somewhat extensive treatment of the period of Russian serfdom, if by that only partially accurate term the words *krepostnoe pravo* (bondage right) may fittingly be expressed. The conditions under which Emancipation (*Osvobozdenie*) was achieved in February 1861 by the privately-owned peasants were considered in some detail. The reasons why a "peasant question" existed at the outset of the time which is embraced in the following pages were briefly analysed. A cardinal feature of peasant social organisation—the land-commune (*mir*)—received the attention which is due to its historical importance.

But after a short historical introduction the reader of this volume will find him- or herself placed immediately in the revolutionary turmoil of 1905 which was a rehearsal, so to speak, of the catastrophic changes of 1917. The opening chapter illustrates the causes of a new Governmental policy in agrarian affairs—that known by the name of Stolypin—the last strong executive personality whom the old Russian régime produced. Stolypin's policy which caused acute controversy, especially in the new Russian Parliament (the "Duma"), is, together with its results, set out in the second chapter.

In view of Lenin's act in assuming responsibility for the aims of the peasant risings of 1917, the significance of the third chapter, "Lenin and the Peasant Movement," is obvious. From the fourth and fifth chapters one may gather in some detail how, after the fall of Tsar Nicholas II in the midst of the Great War, the widespread social dissolution in the villages played a fundamental part in what Russians call the October Revolution of 1917.

As a short epilogue the main achievement of the Peasant Movement of 1917, the Land Decree of October 26 (o.s.) is recorded, together with the post-revolutionary comments upon it of its political sponsor—the leader of the Bolshevist Council of People's Commissaries, Lenin.

Where possible original sources have been utilised in the preparation of this work. The publication of many collections of documents and also memoirs relating to the period 1906–17 has been invaluable in this respect. In addition to the benefit of the first-hand knowledge of Professor Sir Bernard Pares (Director of the London University School of Slavonic and East European Studies) and of Dr. A. F. Meyendorff (late of the London School of Economics and Political Science), the writer has been allowed the privilege of personal consultation with many of the chief actors upon the contemporary historical stage.

The following gentlemen have been good enough to express to the writer their ideas upon different aspects of the history of the period studied: A. Baikalov, N. Avksentyev, S. Bulgakov, A. Guchkov, A. Kerensky, A. Konovalov, M. Kritsky, Count Kokovtsev, A. Markov, P. Milyukov, P. Muratov, Baron B. Nolde, A. Onou, N. Savich, W. Safonov, C. Zaitsev, A. Zenkovsky.

Dr. G. Pavlovsky's seminar at the London School of Slavonic Studies provided expert guidance in the estimation of Russia's agricultural problems.

Both Professor Eisenmann and Professor Legras of the Sorbonne (University of Paris) were good enough to give advice upon available source-materials, as was also M. Lurat of the Bibliothèque de la Guerre, Vincennes, Paris.

To my wife, who has always encouraged me in my

researches and has assisted me in the preparation of this volume for the press, I must express my grateful appreciation.

Finally, I must thank the Senate of the University of London for its grant in aid of the publication of this book.

L. A. O.

CONTENTS

CHAP.		PAGE
	Foreword by Sir Bernard Pares, K.B.E.	v
	Preface	ix
	Introduction	xv
I.	Why the Government changed its Traditional Attitude to the Peasantry	1
II.	Tsar, Duma and Peasant: The Agrarian Legislation of Stolypin	22
III.	Lenin and the Peasant Movement	88
IV.	The Attempt under Lvov to Constitutionalise the Agrarian Movement (Feb. July, 1917)	132
V.	The Failure of Kerensky to Check the Rural Revolution (July–Oct. 1917)	196
VI.	Lenin and the Land Decree of October 26, 1917 (o.s.)	239
	Glossary	248
	Bibliography	251
	Index	259

NOTE

o.s. = Old Style. Unless otherwise stated, the Old Russian Calendar is utilised throughout. To obtain the corresponding date according to the Western Calendar, add thirteen days if the event occurred in the Twentieth Century and twelve if in the Nineteenth.

INTRODUCTION

To appreciate the agrarian problems of twentieth-century Russia as revealed in the following pages, it should be remembered that the formal abolition of serfdom took place as late as February 1861. On that date approximately ten million serfs belonging to some 103,000 squires (*pomeshchiki*) were officially set free from personal dependence upon their owners. It must be remarked also that another ten millions of peasants who were under the direct tutelage of the Government or of the Imperial Family were shortly afterwards given the status of tenants upon State lands. In both cases redemption payments, eventually made compulsory, were instituted to provide compensation to the former owners and the State for the freedom and land granted to those peasants. The final cancellation of these payments was one of the main achievements of the peasant disturbances of 1905.

The social dependence of the Russian peasant communities, while formally abrogated in 1861, and financially alleviated in 1905, left traces upon peasant character which were evident in the great land expropriation of 1917.

Whereas serfdom was a decaying force in Western Europe in the seventeenth and eighteenth centuries, in Russia that condition of social inferiority was then reaching its zenith.

Russian serfdom passed through three phases. First was the "personal contractual"—a kind of debt-bondage which tended to become "hereditary war-service," emerging under the Code of 1649. Registration of a peasant now tended to imply his formal enserfment in the military interests of the State.

At the end of the seventeenth and the beginning of

the eighteenth centuries Peter the Great's autocratic will strengthened this tendency.

By Katherine II's reign (1762–96) serfdom reached the "fiscal-police" stage. The peasant was a chattel—a slave of such type as the ancient Mediterranean had known and to which the contemporary Orient was no stranger.

Katherine's husband, the hapless Peter III, had, in May 1762, freed the Russian serf-owners from State service. Large numbers of peasants were "farmed out" to them in return for a revenue royalty.

When Alexander II, in February 1861, promulgated the Emancipation Edict and instituted his Great Reforms of the ensuing years, great hopes were raised for Russia's regeneration. But various features, such as the already-mentioned Redemption Payments and the strengthening under Alexander III (1881–94) of the legalised communal or collective ownership of the village land, served to remind everyone that, while much was changed, yet much remained the same.

Though the former squires sold a lot of their land and the peasant communities acquired increasing amounts, rural congestion was a menacing problem, causing a decline in that ratio of pasture to arable land so necessary to the maintenance of the balance of a primitive and extensive farming economy based upon draught animals and wooden ploughs.

Many famines occurred in the 'nineties. The condition of agriculture became a problem to the Government. Russia's industrial revolution gathered momentum in the early twentieth century. Was it the key to the peasant question or did it threaten to complicate it? It was difficult at that time to say.

An unsuccessful Far Eastern adventure leading to the Japanese War (1904–5) shook the Government's prestige.

The revolutionary outburst of 1905 was now at hand. In that movement, which affected the whole social life of Russia, there was an extreme diversity in the grievances of the various layers of the population.

What in brief was the background of the second *smutnoe vremya* (time of troubles) against which the flame of peasant insurrection assumed such a lurid glow?

War had as usual brought troubles in its train. Japanese tenacity had prevented the expected "short" and "victorious" outcome. The assassination of Plehve (Minister of the Interior) on July 15 (o.s.), 1904, opened a new chapter.

Prince Peter Svyatopolk Mirsky became his successor. The autumn of 1904 seemed to have become a spring of hope. It appeared that the gulf widening between Governmental and even conservative opinion was about to be bridged. The Chairman of the Moscow *Zemstvo* (Provincial Assembly) asked the new head of the Government to permit another Congress of the Provincial Assemblies of Russia.

This assembly, privately convened, opened its sessions on November 6 (o.s.), 1904. Disagreement immediately occurred upon the question of the powers of the proposed National Assembly. The Government was of course opposed to any diminution of its own prerogatives.

Official hesitation led to the emergence of the so-called "banquet" period, wherein the professional and business men of Russia commenced to form free associations. Among the working classes trade unions now became prominent as centres of anti-governmental policy.

Defeat stared the country in the face after the fall of Port Arthur in December of the same year. The Government lost its head when the well-known procession of Father Gapon tried to petition the Tsar on January 9, 1905, but was fired upon by the police. The period of peaceful aspirations was over. Mirsky, the liberal-minded, was replaced by the sterner Trepov who became Dictator of St. Petersburg.

The final disaster involving the destruction of the Russian Baltic Fleet at Tsushima, in the Sea of Japan, robbed the Russian Government of its prestige as the defender of the State.

A further Congress of Provincial Assemblies (this

time in conjunction with those of the towns) subjected the Administration to further criticism on July 6, 1905. In reply there was announced the scheme of a prospective consultative national assembly (August 6, 1905).

From the transactions of an Imperial Conference of the Tsar and his advisers at Peterhof, near the capital, it is clear that the peasant was still regarded as a firm bulwark of the old system. But had the Imperial counsellors read the signs aright? Had they not forgotten the disturbances of the spring of 1902 in Little Russia and the Central Agricultural Region of Great Russia? Were they not ignoring the agrarian disturbances which began in February of the very year in which the Conference sat?

During the summer of 1905 fully 60 districts, embracing 27 provinces, became unruly.

A comparative decline in peasant disturbances during August may have caused more optimistic feelings in governmental circles. But a dangerous political manifestation which appeared in May 1905 was a "Peasants' Union."

How far this Union was simply a socialist or liberal-inspired revolutionary organ it was at that date difficult to say. The Tsar's ministers certainly regarded the body as largely an agitator's device.

At the preliminary meeting held in Moscow the surrounding areas produced delegates who were partly "intellectuals" and partly peasants. An extension of operations followed. A congress including 100 peasants from 28 provinces held its opening sessions in the same city from July 31 to August 1, 1905.

What was the programme of the new association? The main points were: the abolition of private ownership of land; the free transfer to the cultivating class of lands belonging to the State, the Imperial Family and the Church; the expropriation of privately-owned land, some with compensation, some without. The detailed conditions of the reform were to be determined by a Constituent Assembly elected by universal suffrage. The agrarian claims of the ensuing revolutionary period were here sharply set forth. Russia's first Parliament—the Imperial Duma—was to split on this very rock—the land question.

What then were the characteristics of the peasant problem of 1905 which the foregoing programme raised to the political plane? That is the burden of the opening chapter.

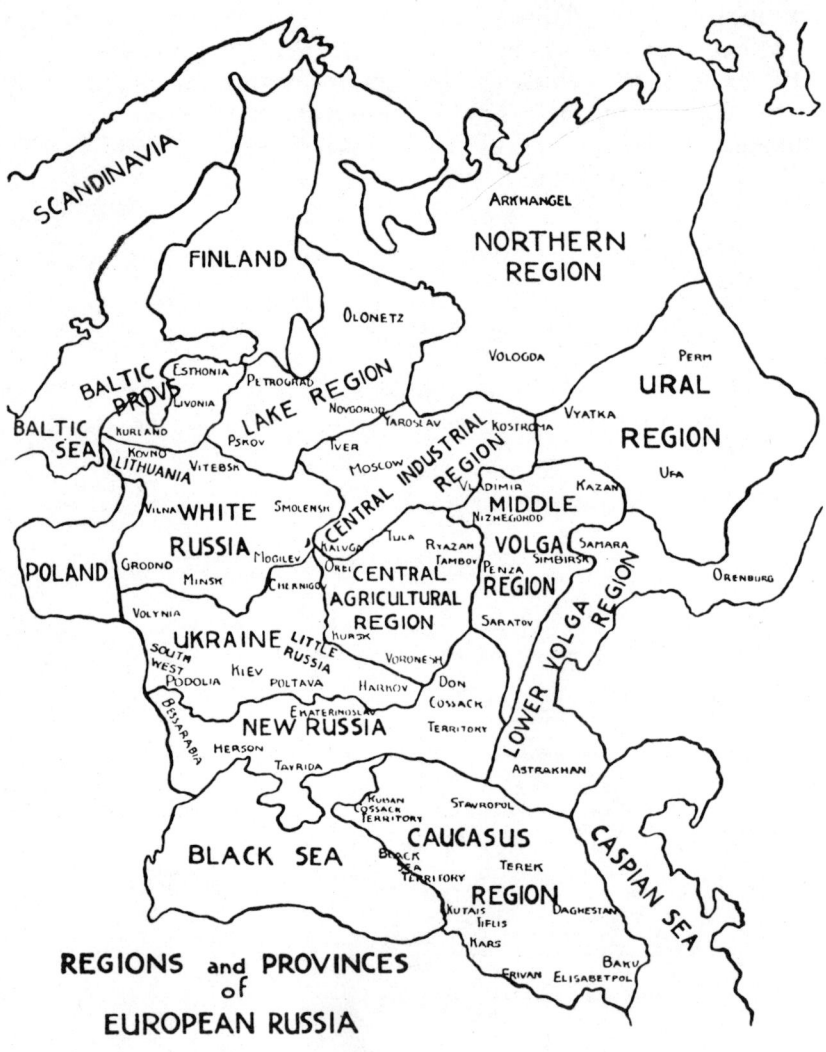

CHAPTER I

WHY THE GOVERNMENT CHANGED ITS TRADITIONAL ATTITUDE TO THE PEASANTRY

"I AM convinced that the peasant who is but half a person (*polu-persona*) in the eyes of the Act (of 1861) must nevertheless be made more like a complete individual (*persona*)." Thus wrote the legally-trained Procurator of the Holy Synod, K. Pobedonostsev, whose name will always in Russian history be associated with illiberal, unsocial and undemocratic theories, brilliantly expressed.[1] In view of the great numerical preponderance of peasantry as such in Russia, this sentence illustrates a significant fact in the social evolution of the country. It throws light upon the social and legal consequences of the "Emancipation Act" of 1861, and upon the change effected by the disasters of the Japanese War of 1904–5 upon the mentality of a typical exponent of Governmental beliefs, held with increasing tenacity during the 'eighties and 'nineties of the nineteenth century, and even reinforced on the eve of the Far Eastern adventure. Inspired by consideration for the general situation of anarchy, the Russian administrative machine spent much time in unravelling the tangled skein of policy—not least in the agrarian sphere. To guide the Central Government, reports were called for from many officials. Among them was S. S. Hrulov, Procurator of the Harkov Appeal Court, who composed a dissertation upon "The causes of the commencement and development of general peasant disorders and the measures for anticipating and suppress-

[1] Cf. Krasny Arhiv, *Perepiska S.J. Witte i K.P. Pobedonostseva*, 2620 (1905), Vol. XXX, p. 109.

ing them."[1] The significance of the document lies as much in its expression of an official view of the past history of the peasantry as in its foreshadowing of the agrarian changes inaugurated by Stolypin in 1906 which, with their later additions, were styled the "Stolypin Reforms." Hrulov himself (1860–1913) in his legal capacity had secured direct knowledge of the peasant risings in 1902 in the Harkov, Poltava and Chernigov Provinces of Little Russia, the Orel, Kursk and Voronesh Provinces of the Central Agricultural Region, and the Ekaterinoslav Province of New Russia.[2] The date of his remarks—September 1905—limits his survey to the period before the Tsar's Constitutional Manifesto of October 17 of the same year.

There is [he states] to be noticed almost universally among the peasant population a conviction amounting to a popular legend, of their having a kind of natural right to the land, which sooner or later must pass into their possession.[3]

This conviction, proceeded Hrulov, had frequently an historic basis. In ancient Russia, both before and during the Moscow Period, "peasants were free, and cultivated land either as actual owners or leaseholders." Gradually the Moscow State, from taxational and military reasons, at first limited and then abolished the right of peasants to move from one particular piece of land to another, and bound them to the soil, making them dependent upon the "service-gentry," who were themselves a "service-class" bound, on that account, to aid the State. But the binding of the peasantry for State ends did not shake their consciousness that the land which was in their possession belonged to them. "We are yours but the land is ours" was a common peasant refrain during the period of bondage. Furthermore, at the liberation of the peasants by the Act of February 19, 1861, considerably less than the total of the cultivable land which was actually in their possession, was given to them as an allotment,

[1] Krasny Arhiv, Vol. XXXIX, p. 76.
[2] op. cit., p. 80.   [3] op. cit., p. 80.

even excepting those with a "free allowance" (a diminished amount given in Black Earth Provinces, in lieu of redemption payment).¹

Therefore there did exist among the peasantry a real basis for considering that a certain amount of land, belonging to them under bondage conditions, had been taken from them and transferred to the squires. This circumstance, accompanied by the unsatisfactory economic position, appeared to Hrulov to be the source of any rumours of redivisions and additional grants of land, and of peasant disturbances.² Frequently deprecated by the administration, these rumours continually passed once more into currency. Alexander III, at his coronation in May 1883, had officially denied their validity before a gathering of peasant cantonal elders, when he had advised them

to follow the advice and guidance of their Marshals of Gentry, and to put no trust in idle senseless rumours concerning land redivisions and free supplementary land grants. Those rumours were, the Emperor said, spread abroad by their enemies. All property, including their own peasant property, must be inviolate.³

Nicholas II had similarly frowned upon such ideas, on September 1, 1902, in Kursk, when he addressed cantonal and village elders of the provinces of Kursk, Chernigov, Orel and Voronesh during military manœuvres. He referred to "the devastation of squires' estates in those areas in the spring of the same year." He said that

those guilty would receive punishment and the administration would not allow future happenings of the kind. Let them remember the words of his late father Alexander III and listen to their Marshals of Gentry and not believe idle rumours. Let them remember that people grow rich not by the seizure of others' property but by honest work, thrift and life conducted on righteous principles.⁴

These imperial words did not prevent the turmoil of 1905 with demands for increased free allotments. Indeed

---

¹ op. cit., p. 81.   ² op. cit., p. 81.
³ op. cit., note 3, p. 106.   ⁴ op. cit., note 6, p. 106.

Hrulov thought that the very character of the great Reform of February 19, 1861, with its "expropriation" of the private property of squires to allot land to the peasantry, created a hope among the same peasantry that their economic difficulties could be solved in a similar fashion. It was impossible not to see that the peasants could not acquire a very clear conception of private ownership of land. In earlier times, when land was plentiful compared with the population, anyone occupying a piece of land and cultivating it [1] was regarded as the owner of the land and, when he had exhausted it, left it and passed on to another. Thence was derived the so-called "labour-principle" (a principle advocated in the First Duma 1906 by the Trudoviki or Party of "Land-for-those-that-cultivate-it" and destined to play a great part in 1917 in the famous Land Decree of the Communist Government under Lenin, who thus adapted the ideas of the Labour Group and the Social Revolutionary Party to his own party objects). This principle, noted by observers of popular customs, implied that the land, which was considered to be common property, belonged to the person who actually cultivated it. The communal system, which since early times had been the basis of peasant order, obviously could not give rise to a concept of private ownership. The land on which it rested was transferred in strips at general redivisions from one household to another. Finally, with the definite crystallisation of bondage relationships, when (theoretically) "none was for himself but all were for the State," property distinctions, so far as they had existed before, gradually became confused.

The land of service-gentry and peasant community was usually not separately delimited, owing to the prevailing strip system. Peasant and squire had common pasture lands for cattle and common forest rights to timber. It was very difficult, as Hrulov points out,[2] for the peasant to acquire any idea of "private" ownership when he used

---

[1] "Zaimka," as in Siberia.
[2] Krasny Arhiv, Vol. XXXIX, p. 82.

the land in common with his social superior. From those facts emerged the constant (so-called) "illicit" timber-cutting, "illicit" pasturing of cattle and haymaking, which were relics of the old bondage conditions. Hrulov might here have added (one imagines) that the peasant, having been himself, not a person or even a "half-person" (as he became in 1861 in the eyes of the law; cf. Pobedonostsev, above) but simply a "thing," an "object of possession," under *krepostnoe pravo* (bondage), obviously could not be expected easily to recognise an abstract concept, without a considerable number of concrete "percepts" of the uses and advantages of individualised and separated property. It was the same difficulty that the *narodniki* or agrarian socialist "intelligentsia" of the 'seventies experienced in their *hozhdenie v narod* (going to the people), when they painfully comprehended that the concrete *zemlya*, or grip upon the means of existence, naturally represented a stronger influence in peasant minds than an abstract *volya* or socio-political freedom, revealed to peasants in illustrations which had comparatively little significance to a man or woman of little leisure, whose world was the village. "The unsatisfactory economic condition of the peasantry in our time [i.e. 1905] is acknowledged by representatives of all parties and opinions."[1] Such was Hrulov's deliberate judicial view. "Differences of opinion exist only as to the estimation of the dimensions of this phenomenon and of the way to meet the situation."[2] It will be illustrated later that it was with this idea that the First Duma (1906) assembled and promptly joined issue with the Administration. It was indeed owing to the peasants' faith in the Duma that peasant needs became a useful weapon for opponents of the old governmental methods. From the attempts to correct the peasantry's disabilities, the whole period from 1905 to 1917 derives a dark background for the socio-political constitutional struggle—the main features of which reflect the fact of their existence.

[1] op. cit., p. 82.   [2] op. cit., p. 82.

It was the peasants themselves [proceeded Hrulov] who felt, most of all, this need and insecurity. It was not surprising that, in the absence of their understanding of the inviolability of private property in land, and view of their general lack of education, they should violently seize squires' possessions at the slightest incitement from without.

As previously stated, a considerable proportion of the land which had been actually held by the peasantry remained, at the Emancipation, in the hands of the squires. Thus the area of actual peasant landownership was lessened, especially as in many cases "free" allotments were given to village communities (e.g. in the more valuable agricultural Black Earth Zone). Even in 1877, the well-known Professor Yanson,[1] having statistically investigated peasant allotments and payments, showed that the total of peasant payments exceeded the return from their land. While he did not accept Professor Yanson's conclusions as being right with regard to some localities, yet it was impossible for the Procurator of the Harkov Appeal Court to deny that "in certain areas there was a manifest insufficiency of land to satisfy their very pressing needs, both to secure their mode of life and to carry out their obligations to the Government"—the guiding principle of the 3rd Article of the General Act concerning the peasants.[2]

Owing to the growth of population for the period of more than forty years since the Emancipation, the average size of peasants' allotments had diminished by one-third.[3]

The peasant felt a special need not so much of arable or ploughland, as of meadows, pastures and woodland which, under the terms of the original statute charters of Emancipation, had been left to the squires, and often the situation was such that "there was not room to feed a chicken and still less a cow."[4]

---

[1] Professor Y. E. Yanson was an eminent statistician (1835–93) who superintended the St. Petersburg Statistical Department. His most important works included *The Comparative Statistics of Russia and Western European Countries*, *The Theory of Statistics* and his *Opyt Statistich. issledovaniya o krestyan. nadelakh i platezhakh*. The reference above concerns the last-mentioned book.

[2] Krasny Arhiv, Vol. XXXIX, p. 82.

[3] op. cit., p. 82.

[4] op. cit., p. 83.

The insufficiency of land compelled the peasants to supplement their earnings by renting land from the squires, by working on the squires' estates and by extra employment outside the confines of the village.[1] The low level of peasant development prevented ideas of intensive cultivation. It must be remembered, too, that the squire did not, after 1861, set a standard of " high farming " on a sufficiently universal scale to give the peasantry an example of technique. The Agrarian Revolution of 1917, in Great Russia at least, did not imply the disintegration of a series of highly-developed farms based upon a permanent agricultural labour. Such a situation would have implied a commercial-capitalistic management, which certainly was non-existent in Great Russia and only partially in being in the farms of the south-west of the Ukraine (based upon a relatively intensive beet-sugar culture). The Baltic Provinces, with their greater development in methods of production, had ceased to hold a peasantry in the Great Russian sense, but possessed a "proletariat" of permanent hired labourers whose problems were more akin to those of their urban fellows in cities such as Riga. Instead of cheap rents and increase of leased land, they desired higher wages.

Forced by the inadequacy of their "free" allotments, the peasants of the Black Earth Region who had accepted them, were compelled to lease extra land from their squires on very hard conditions—otherwise being condemned to hunger and poverty. Where they had not still retained their instruments of production—ploughs and draught animals, they were forced to become agricultural labourers and, though not nominally "proletarian," in the sense of a complete divorce from the soil and means of production—they rapidly became virtually of that social category.

According to Hrulov, the bulk of the peasant communities with "free" allotments were found in the vicinity of large squires' estates whose owners, owing to their usual

[1] This description compares with that of the Roumanian *latifundiary* cultivation of the soil described by Mitrany, *Land and Peasant in Roumania*.

absenteeism, gave the administration of their estates into the hands of managers who were often foreigners with no clear comprehension of the Russian peasant mentality.[1] These managers, operating on a commission basis, were naturally interested in getting as large a profit as possible from the estate: hence constant rises in land-rent, the diminution, or the maintenance at a low level, of wages for labourers, and the strict system of fines.[2] The peasant disorders which happened in the spring of 1902 and the winter and spring of 1905 in the Black Earth Provinces, occurred largely among peasant communities adjoining large estates and linked with them by lease or other economic ties.[3] It was in consequence of these conditions that the estate belonging to the Duke (Hertzog) of Mecklenburg-Strelitz, in Poltava Province (Little Russia), was devastated in 1902. In 1905, that of the Grand Duke Sergei Alexandrovich, in Orel Province (Central Agricultural Region), was treated similarly, as were also those of Tereshchenko and Baron Meyendorff. Kursk Province witnessed a like occurrence in regard to the estate of Volkov, while in Voronesh (New Russia) those of Count Sheremetev, Prince Vasilchikov, Count Mordvinov, Countess Panin, Prince Beloselsky and Princess Yusupov [4] met the same fate.

The burden of rent (as much as 30 roubles per desyatine in some cases) was augmented by the law of supply and demand, as much through the counter-competition of the peasantry themselves, as through the leasing out of the land in share-tenancy (*ispolu*). The low level of wages for labourers was still further depressed owing to the system of their advance-payment in winter. By this means the rate of wages was fixed at a much lower rate than it would otherwise have been, had the normal summer-rate been accepted. Consequently the advance-payment of wages amounted often to a usurious practice, although it bore a carefully veiled character.[5] In these circumstances it is comparatively easy to understand that

---

[1] Krasny Arhiv, Vol. XXXIX, p. 83. [2] op. cit., p. 83.
[3] op. cit., p. 83.   [4] op. cit., p. 83.   [5] op. cit., p. 84.

the system existing, particularly in the Black Earth Regions, might be termed one, if not of bondage-right (*krepostnoe pravo*), at least of semi-bondage (*polukrepostnoe*) as it came to be termed, and as Lenin termed it. Therefore, if socio-politically, the peasant in Pobedonostsev's words to Witte (in 1905) was a "semi-person" (*polupersona*), his socio-economic position, especially in the earlier developed portions of the Black Earth region, was in correspondence with it. It is evident that the "*osvobozhdenie*" of 1861 was a term capable of a very relative interpretation. If, as has been made clear by historical investigators, no one act reduced the "free peasant" or perhaps the "free peasant community" into a state of bondage, but a steady economic, political and social process resulted in a series of legal enactments which progressively effected a deterioration in the peasant class, it must be made clear once more that one set of legislation, such as that of 1861, certainly did not completely reverse matters. Whether it could have done so, it is not the place here to discuss. If bondage-right (*krepostnoe pravo*), as Klyuchevsky, Engelmann and Milyukov, among others, indicate, began to crystallise at the commencement of the Romanov Period and reached its climax in the eighteenth-century Petersburg epoch, it began generally to de-crystallise in Great Russia only in the second half of the nineteenth century (if we except Kiselev's earlier reform of the State Peasants' conditions). The years from 1861 to 1917, witnessing the gradual effacement of its relics, culminated in a rapid onslaught upon those relics, by the successors and representatives of a State system which had itself helped to create it. That onslaught was represented by the Reforms of Stolypin.

Despite the difficult economic position of the peasantry, the Report indicated that it was not solely the direct need of fodder that impelled the peasants to raid the squires' estates. Facts were adduced to show that during the "hungry years" such as 1872 and 1891–2, peasant disorders were conspicuous by their absence. Instead, there was evident a certain fatalistic resignation.[1] Furthermore, the years 1902 and 1905 witnessed harvests in the majority of the areas of disturbance either of average quality or above the average. Yet pillaging occurred, even in comparatively well-to-do villages with an allotment ranging from 2½ to 4 *desyatines* and with secure side-earnings at local works and town occupations.

Moreover, in many places there were not only illegal seizures of grain and fodder for cattle, but also removal of sugar, spirit and wine in refineries and shops, theft of domestic furniture—even clothes and—gramophones! Even comparatively wealthy peasants who had quite large stocks of grain did not refrain from participation.[2] Despite the "unsatisfactory economic position" of the peasantry, the Report claimed that much had been done for them by the Administration, since the Emancipation itself. The Government had adopted various, though insufficient, means to better the peasants' lot. But unfortunately little had been done for the previous forty years (1905) on the part of the Government, the Provincial Assemblies, or Society to raise the cultural level of the former "slaves"[3] after their freedom had created millions of "free citizens."[4]

Educationally, matters were at a low ebb. Schools were insufficient. Their curricula were unsatisfactory. Their staffs were poor, receiving a mere pittance as salary, thus giving grounds for the existence of revolutionary sentiments—a weapon in the hands of ill-disposed persons. Writing and arithmetic were taught in the schools but there was no instruction concerning the elementary bases of civic life—the idea of their native land, of patriotism, of the State, of law, of morality. "A People

---

[1] Krasny Arhiv, Vol. XXXIX, p. 84. [2] op. cit., p. 84.
[3] op. cit., p. 84.
[4] Does Hrulov here imply that the Act of 1861 made a "free citizen" of the former "bondman"? Both Maklakov and even stern Pobedonostsev thought differently. And the *nadel*, which, if a voluntary obligation, would have presented a spectacle of a really humanitarian piece of social legislation, by its perversion into a compulsory duty, vitiated the prospect of political freedom at its economic source.

which possesses a glorious history, and forms part of a great State with a unique structure, knows and hears nothing about it."¹ In such circumstances, literacy alone could not introduce anything into the cultural development of the people. The influence of schools was qualitatively completely absent. Sometimes indeed it appeared to be positively dangerous, when socialistic ideas, anti-state and anti-social, were spread abroad.

No better was the influence of the clergy, spiritually and morally, in regard to the peasantry. The priesthood, dependent materially upon the local population, tended to sink to its level. Drunkenness and immorality were condoned. Occasions were known when they even refused to teach Scripture in the schools. Moral and religious principles were frequently ignored. During peasant disorders, the priests, instead of restraining the riotous mobs of pillaging villagers, often themselves participated in the devastation!² Such evidence which, in the circumstances of a report from a reputable law officer of the Crown, was not likely to be unreliable, cast a very lurid light upon the intellectual and moral atmosphere of the village.

The influence of the district authorities upon the peasants' sense of legality and social discipline was not regarded highly by Hrulov. The cantonal administration, although elective, was distinguished by arbitrary conduct and was guilty of extortion. The local police were to be similarly criticised. The "Land Captains" (established in Alexander III's reign [1889] to control local government economically, legally and politically and regarded by some as indicating a virtual revival of bondage (*krepostnoe pravo*), especially as the *obshchina*, or communal system, was strengthened simultaneously) did not, unfortunately, have a beneficial influence upon the local population.³ They did not usually extort money. But their activity often contradicted the law; their attitude to the population was often coarse; the whole character of their action bore the imprint of personal considerations

¹ Krasny Arhiv, Vol. XXXIX, p. 84. ² op. cit., p. 83. ³ op. cit., p. 85.

and arbitrariness.¹ Such is the legally-trained Hrulov's harsh verdict upon a much-abused institution whose magisterial powers were vitiated by administrative features. Many of them, according to the writer of the Report, did not know their own districts and were hardly known to the people, thus possessing no moral authority. The learned lawyer goes so far as to impute that the usual areas of disturbance coincided with those of unsatisfactory Land Captains. This seems rather unfair, for, however bad they may have been personally, the Land Captains simply represented a system, and it has already been established that there were many social, economic and political causes behind the Peasant Movement. A solitary policeman however efficient, however popular personally, could not be expected to quell a riot emanating from circumstances beyond his control. The fault seems to lie in the fact that an official who was destined to be a magistrate, was a policeman as well.

The *Zemstva* (Provincial and District Assemblies) too received their meed of blame. The marshals of the provincial administrations were not in direct touch with the peasants, whereas the hired employees—medical, statistical and agricultural—were stated to be politically untrustworthy, being liable to disseminate socialistic views among the inhabitants. The only schools of legal ideas open to the peasant were the common law courts, where he appeared as juryman or as witness. Yet even this influence was not great. Being of the legal profession, Hrulov took heart at the fact that the courts, at least, did preserve among the peasantry a semblance of legal consciousness.²

Poverty and lack of education provided an admirable soil for the socialist anti-governmental propaganda which was continually increasing. Whether in verbal or printed form, such illegal propaganda was scattered far and wide and there was not a village that had not been subject to it.³ Proclamations were issued in simple peasant language and were even circulated in such separate local

¹ Krasny Arhiv, Vol. XXXIX, p. 85. ² op. cit., p. 86. ³ op. cit., p. 86.

tongues as Ukrainian. In the leaflets which the peasants were likely to see, land was treated as "common property" like light and air.[1] The peasants were told that their land hunger could be met by means of seizure from their "masters." The Report proceeded to complain that the source of these proclamations was not clear to the peasants, who were not aware of the political struggle proceeding in the towns over demands for freedom and the downfall of autocratic government. Indeed, owing to their still unbroken faith in the Tsar, the peasantry were ready to see "Imperial Decrees" in these revolutionary appeals. Such appeals were, according to Hrulov's information, scattered by *Zemstvo* surgeons, teachers and statisticians—the leading lights of the local *intelligentsia*. The revolutionary parties over the frontier were preparing to utilise the peasant disturbances, but (the Report stated) it was difficult for any strangely attired individual to appear among the local population without attracting attention from the police.[2]

Yet evidence showed that there was no "going to the people" (i.e. peasantry) (*hozhdenie v narod*) as in the old days of the 'seventies. The Report is a significant sidelight (it appears to the present investigator) upon the difference between the attempt of radicals and socialists in the early post-Emancipation days to overturn the Government by means of peasant risings, and the situation in 1905. When the *narodniki* (populists), filled with Chernyshevsky's economics and Dobrolyubov's logic, implementing Hertzen's messianic faith in the peasant mode of life at last moved among "the people," encouraged later as they were, from different angles, by the less active Lavrov or the more impetuous Bakunin, they met no resurrected Pugachovs or Stenka Razins as they hoped. Trust in the Sovereign Tsar baffled their dreams of a great peasant rising by which to change the existing constitution. In the 'seventies the old cleavage between "bond" and "free" induced by the long years of bondage (*krepostnoe pravo*), still prevented a united movement of peasant and revolu-

[1] op. cit., p. 86.   [2] op. cit., p. 87.

tionary *intelligentsia*. Possibly the *intelligentsia* had "too good a conceit of itself" to attract a slowly-moving yet firmly practical village brain. Even a dull uneducated peasant saw no reason to be "butchered to make a constitutional holiday". Then too the war-weary conditions of the third quarter of the eighteenth century that produced a military-Cossack-serf rising under a veteran officer, Pugachov (profiting by innovations in the laws of succession to the throne—the murder of a monarch—and the recent exemption of the ruling caste from civil or military obligations) had no parallel a hundred years later.

The Report of Hrulov presents other reasons why it was so hard to cause a general rising in the 'seventies of the nineteenth century. Yet such a rising occurred with apparent spontaneity at the beginning of the twentieth. An *intelligentsia*, such as went to the people in the 'seventies, was, in 1905, no longer necessary. There were already established in each locality permanent residents of that type, ready "to propagate socialist or anti-governmental ideas."

Secondly, the composition of the peasantry had changed considerably. A certain portion of the younger peasantry had become accustomed to seek extra work in the south, in the New Russian regions of the Black Sea littoral, where revolutionary ideas were very pronounced.[1] Such peasants were "spoilt by their comparatively large earnings, which led to display and independence of outlook." Having imbibed a revolutionary spirit, they represented a type of "home-grown nihilist-anarchist [2] denying faith, God and morality," appearing in their own villages with a kind of authority as "educated" people reinforced by their monetary support of local communities. The influence of the older people who remained at home naturally declined. Thence (said the Report) proceeded speeches about land, about the burdensome position of

---

[1] Not to mention the two capitals which certainly also affected such migratory workers.

[2] Krasny Arhiv, Vol. XXXIX, p. 87.

the peasantry, about the necessity of confiscating the squires' land and transferring it to the people who worked upon it. It was these propagandists from its own midst that the peasantry trusted. Thus (thought Hrulov) arose disturbances such as those in Kursk Province, where outside earnings (*othozhie promysly*) were now more developed.

Many of the younger generation went southwards to the Ekaterinoslav Province (New Russia) seeking work as miners or as carpenters. Some travelled further afield to the Crimea, the Caucasus and Odessa. Revolutionary organisations therefore took advantage of this seasonal or periodic migration to distribute leaflets or even funds. The discontent of the peasants was "capitalised by the various revolutionary groups among which the Social Revolutionaries were prominent." But what was more significant from the point of view of the stability of the governmental system, was the use which the parties of Liberal tendency were making of the agrarian disorders of 1905. Liberals were scattering ideas as to the necessity of convoking a Constituent Assembly to build up a new Constitution, to secure political freedom and to reorganise the situation of the peasantry with regard to land. Such a policy was regarded by the Report as being a reflection of the general Liberal movement among the *intelligentsia*—a movement which the history of the creation and progress of the Duma as a legislative organ amply illustrated. The dangers of the utilisation of peasant disabilities in the urban political struggle were shown by the various, generally-known, conferences of *Zemstvo* representatives and trades-unions. Their banquets and resolutions found an echo in the countryside. At the congress of town and provincial functionaries held in Moscow from the 6th to the 8th of July 1905, it had been acknowledged to be necessary to prepare the peasant population for political activity. Even the legalised periodicals, now temporarily largely freed from the previously strict censorship, assisted the revolutionary cause by their demand for representative government in a constitutional sense, for the convocation of a Constituent Assembly, for freedom of association, of meeting and even for the nationalisation of the land.¹ Agricultural societies such as those in the Province of Harkov and Poltava (Little Russia) gave scope for general discussions upon political topics. Outside people—particularly peasants—participated in these public meetings. The agrarian question and the position of the peasants led to consideration of measures for the nationalisation of land (whether privately-owned, Treasury, appanage or monastic) and of the necessity of converting to general ownership not only land but also factories, works and capital. Certainly there is evident here a foretaste of the radical socialist transformation of 1917. To the legally-minded Hrulov, it seemed desirable that there should be an amendment of the law, to forbid any discussions of such nature at meetings of nominally agricultural societies. One such meeting, on May 29, in the Sum district, when prohibited by the Governor, developed into an open-air assembly in a public square. Resolutions were passed regarding the necessity of additions to peasant holdings, at the expense of land possessed by other sections of the community and the State, and also regarding the desirability of changing the existing governmental system for one of elective type. Otherwise taxes ought to be withheld from payment.²

Profiting by the Tsar's Decree of February 18, 1905, many peasant assemblies took place during the spring of that year. Influenced (according to Hrulov) by the Liberal *intelligentsia*, they passed resolutions declaring that the convocation of a Constituent Assembly was necessary, as was also political freedom. It was further resolved that land should be added to the peasants' present holdings, from various sources already mentioned. In August of the same year was held in Moscow

---

[1] To prove his point as to the radical nature of contemporary Liberalism, Hrulov referred to the article of L. N. Tolstoy, "Veliky grekh," *Russkaya Mysl*," July 1905, Krasny Arhiv, Vol. XXXIX, p. 89.

[2] op. cit., p. 90.

a congress of peasant representatives from certain provinces to participate in the sittings of the so-called "Peasant Union," whose aim was evidently propaganda among the peasantry and a tendency towards agrarian reform on the basis of land expropriation.[1]

Even in *Zemstva* Assemblies, the inadequacy of peasant land-allotments was the object of discussion.[2] Characteristic of such activity, was the Harkov *Zemstvo* Board's report to the Special Provincial *Zemstvo* Congress of June 12, 1905 (when the annihilation of Russia's fleet at Tsushima in May had already illustrated the utter bankruptcy of the Russian Government's Far Eastern Policy). In it was a detailed consideration of the peasantry's economic position, and a decision upon the agrarian question on the lines of increasing the peasant holdings and nationalising the land. (When *Zemstva* voted for nationalisation of land, extreme revolutionaries like Lenin [one imagines] must have been embarrassed by such select company.) According to the Provincial Economic Committee's Report, the area of land held by landowners in Harkov Province was inadequate for that purpose. An increase of the area was essential. A special investigation in all provinces was required to reach a decision upon the problem. In one portion of this particular report (Hrulov declared) was a statement that nationalisation was a practical policy, while a supplementary (peasant) allotment was but a palliative; whereas, earlier, it was announced that nationalisation was not permissible.[3] While that particular meeting could not find a quorum for a decision on the subject, the report considered that such deliberations of public gatherings must inevitably affect peasant minds and induce disorder —which was probably very true.[4]

Among the causes of the Peasant Movement of 1905, Hrulov found it necessary to add that the "unfortunate war" was "misunderstood," and was "unpopular" among the peasant masses, and that the general troubles (such

[1] op. cit., p. 90.
[2] op. cit., p. 90.
[3] op. cit., p. 91.
[4] op. cit., p. 91.

as, presumably, the industrial-political strikes in St. Petersburg and Moscow during 1905, together with the cleavage among the various urban classes, generally affecting the country) found a ready response in their ranks. Mobilisation of bread-winners and labourers was reflected in the economic position of the population. It was the first time, too, that reserves of widely separated periods had been called up. War-news in papers and soldiers' letters did nothing to lessen the dissatisfaction. Such a large number of the troops being in the Far East, a belief arose that disorders could take place with impunity, because such troops as remained in European Russia were reservists who were not likely to move against the common people.[1] It was not necessary (the Report affirmed) to indicate the influence of the general dissatisfaction upon peasant disorders.

We are living through what might be called a second "Time of Troubles" [*smutnoe vremya*]. All classes and conditions of the population are to be found at loggerheads; a review of the basis of the whole existing structure is apparent; a mass of vital and fundamental questions is being raised; there is a struggle of parties; while the revolutionary movement hastens to adopt a terrorist system.[2]

The judicial temperament of Hrulov could not but lend weight to such a description of the situation with which opens the period considered in this work—a description even more applicable to the year 1917 with which it closes. The Imperial Decrees of December 6, 1904, and February 18, 1905, had led to a "national desire" to express popular needs. These discussions were being utilised for the purpose of agitation by anti-governmental elements. Such agitation was bound to have an effect on the peasantry, huge in its numbers, but uneducated. The prospective Duma with representatives from all the people, it was hoped would tranquillise society, and give

---

[1] It must not be imagined that reservists were not used in Manchuria. On the contrary, the War was largely fought by troops from the reserve (see Sir Frederick Maurice).

[2] Krasny Arhiv, Vol. XXXIX, p. 92.

a legal outlet to the tendency to regard as essential the transformation of the state and social structure.[1]

That Hrulov's beliefs in regard to the use of peasant assemblies as demonstrations against the Government were not without foundation, is shown by Sir Bernard Pares' account of a cantonal meeting which he attended on July 31, 1905 (o.s.).[2] Seventeen villages participated in the gathering upon the Squire Alexander Bakunin's estate in the Torzhok District. This meeting, occurring incidentally upon the same day as the initial Moscow Congress of the Peasant Union mentioned earlier, was itself directed against the Government's unpopular actions. Its resolutions asked for the spread of knowledge through real books; the abolition of legal class distinctions and the office of *Zemsky nachalnik*; the abolition of indirect taxation; the various "freedoms" in the *Zemstvo* programme; an eight-hour day for workmen, and a national assembly based upon universal suffrage.

To an eighth resolution demanding "the speedy cessation of this bloody and suicidal war," the meeting violently objected. The local peasant feeling had not ceased to be patriotic despite the approaching recognition of defeat. The question of peace was left to the future National Assembly. Lastly came a demand for a "full pardon for all exiles and prisoners who have suffered for the rightful cause of the People."

With this point still in their minds [proceeds Sir Bernard's account] all those present were asked to sign their names—which demanded courage at this stage of the movement—and this they did on the village street in the twilight, by the light of lamps or torches as the darkness closed in.

In the general conversation that ensued upon the closure of the meeting some interesting remarks were made. One peasant declared that if troops were quartered upon them, they would be treated like members of

[1] op. cit., p. 92.
[2] Cf. *Russian Memoirs*, pp. 94-5, and *Contemporary Review*, Jan. 1906.

the family. Another in confuting the *Zemstvo* men's doubts as to peasant ripeness for responsibility, asserted that the trouble was that they were "overripe." Still another when speaking of the effect of Pobedonostsev's church schools announced: "We should like to begin the Kingdom of Heaven here. We are promised a fine dinner in the next world. We should like to stand up now and have our first bite [*zakusit*]."

But it was October which, with its spectacle of Government impotence amid general disorder, brought matters to a climax. The peasants were certainly not backward in presenting their demands in a much more radical guise.

There began a general peasant rising which, during October, November and December, embraced 300 districts of 47 provinces. More than 1,000 manorial houses were ravaged and burned. Their distribution was as follows: Saratov Province, 272; Kursk, 146; Harkov (Volchansk district), 33; Ekaterinoslav (Verknedneprov district), 66; Tambov, 130; Simbirsk, about 50; Orel, 84; Tauris (Dneprov district), 20.

The peasant cry this time was reported to be: "Drive out the squires and transfer the land to the people." Among the "intellectuals" a demand was also raised for the political freedom of the people. In many places tax-payments were withheld and the cantonal authorities were displaced.

As a result of the increased strength of the peasant movement in the closing months of 1905, the Government under Witte's control found itself faced with a renewed and consolidated activity on the part of the Peasants' Union. The second conference of this body took place on December 6 and lasted until December 10. The Imperial Manifesto of October 17 envisaging a parliamentary constitution, and the declaration of the cessation of the Redemption Payment System (November 3), had deprived the revolutionary movement of some of its impetus. Even so, the Peasant Union reaffirmed its former programme, going as far as to advocate its attainment by exercising a "right of seizure."

This revolutionary body resolved to demand a new local self-governing institution on the basis of universal suffrage. No bargains were to be made with squires. No complaints were to be lodged through the usual local legal channels. No taxes were to be paid and no recruits provided. The new Duma was to be boycotted and a Constituent Assembly demanded.

Despite the development of the Union in 60 local conferences and the extension of the Duma suffrage by Witte on the day following the Moscow Conference, when the December rising in Moscow was in progress, the forward revolutionary movement was over. Reaction and repression began. The ensuing January of 1906 saw the Government no longer at the mercy of events. The Union was broken up and the Peasant Movement of 1905 crushed with no uncertain hand during the winter of 1906.

Despite the potential and even actual risings or disorders during the summer of that year (including a colossal agricultural strike in 25 provinces, lasting from May to June), the Peasant Movement had lost its unity. Its smouldering embers flashed up here and there. But the Government could face the future with more confidence even with the prospective Duma as a competitor for popular favour. It could proceed with its own agrarian policy.

That is the substance of the following section.

CHAPTER II

TSAR, DUMA AND PEASANT

THE AGRARIAN LEGISLATION OF STOLYPIN

THE Manifesto of October 17, 1905, was a landmark in Russia's history. Autocracy had, it was believed, officially abdicated and an avowedly constitutional régime was inaugurated. The concentrated legislative power of the Emperor was to be shared with representatives of the common people—including the peasantry. The peasant movement of 1905 had been a potent factor in this consummation. That this conclusion is correct Hrulov's analysis of peasant disabilities and A. Yermolov's letter to Nicholas II (1905)[1] have made obvious. If the October Manifesto was a landmark, it represented also the culmination of unified revolutionary activity. It was called forth not only by the dissatisfaction of pauperised working peasantry and ill-organised industrial and professional workers of the towns. What made the old Autocracy stand most in dread was the schism in the very squire class itself—a schism made clear by the rise of a new *Zemstvo* Party that was later to be the basis mainly of Octobrist and partially of Constitutional Democratic trends. As the very names of these two parties show, the October Manifesto presented a rallying point for moderate agrarian and industrial elements previously antagonised by Besobrazov's bankrupt Eastern imperialism and Plehve's Machiavellian police trade-union policy through Zubatov.[2]

[1] Krasny Arhiv, Vol. I (VIII), 1925, pp. 49–69.
[2] S. V. Zubatov, Head of the Moscow Police Department in the 'nineties, attempted to stem revolutionary agitation among the working classes and secure their support for the Government. In pursuance of this policy he

But despite the fact that it was even contemplated as a probability during the crisis that Nicholas and his family would have to flee abroad, every step was being taken under the Witte-Durnovo régime to prevent such a disastrous outcome and, if possible, to lessen the need to fulfil all the implications of the promises formally expressed on October 17. If the Administration could present the new legislature with a pacified countryside, the actual diminution of imperial prerogatives might be avoided. Before consideration is given to the significance of the agrarian question as revealed in the policy of the Government after October 17 it is interesting to illustrate the reverberations of 1905 in the punitive measures adopted in restoring order among the village communities. Concerning these measures there was an official conference held on January 28 and March 1, 1906.[1]

At this conference Lieutenant-General Kryzhanovsky's advice, presented on December 31, 1905, was examined. This officer, the Commander of the 2nd Cavalry Division, had reported to Witte's new Ministry on January 10, 1906. His policy was certainly not distinguished by sentimental weakness. The troops' mode of activity should be such that they could parody the old Cæsarian phrase and announce, "I came, I punished, I departed" ("Harakter etoy deyatelnosti voisk v obshchem dolzhen byt takov: 'prishel, nakazal i ushel' ").[2] The Chief-of-Staff, Palitsin, had approved of this statement of policy and had forwarded Kryzhanovsky's report to the President of the Council of Ministers with the words: "What he writes, we all feel" ("To shto on pishet, chuvstvuem

---

organised Workers' Unions such as the "Soviet rabochikh mekhanicheskovo proisvodstva" in Moscow and the "Obshchestvo vzaimopomoshchi fabrichno-zavodskikh rabochikh" in St. Petersburg. These associations received Government support in industrial strife provided they did not oppose the Administration in politics. The results were not what had been expected. The "Zubatovshchina" as it was termed, actually gave the first possibility of open organisation to the newly-formed factory class.

[1] Cf. *Borba S.J. Witte s agrarnoy revolyutsey*, Krasny Arhiv, Vol. VI (XXXI), 1928.

[2] Mosk. Voenno Ist. Arhiv, delo gl. shtaba, II otdel, 3 st., No. 63, 1906, ll. 40-4.

my vse"). Durnovo, Minister for the Interior, was not slow also in acquiescing.

It is generally known that the weakness of Russia's attempt to establish a legislative check upon the executive power was due to the Government's timely receipt of foreign financial resources and the successful return of the Army from Manchuria. But at the beginning of 1906 these two pillars of State were not yet placed firmly in position. Foreign loans were unlikely if domestic discord prevailed. An absolute Government which had no dependable military forces at its back was doomed.

At the Conference of January 28 and March 1 provision was accordingly made for the training of fresh units and the transfer of troops from the Far East. Definite results could be secured no earlier than the middle of March or the beginning of April. The troops would be ready only in August. It was not until the summer that the final blow could be given which should eliminate further agrarian insurrections. These facts are naturally interesting in view of the subsequent history of the First Duma and Stolypin's agrarian *ukaz* of November 9, 1906.

It was S. J. Witte's belief that March and August would see a recrudescence of peasant risings. To the arrangement of the military forces in Russia Witte makes reference in his Reminiscences [1] where he states that he did not agree with the removal of troops from the frontiers. Yet the January and March sessions of the Conference of 1906 belie his words. This change in the recognised objective of the Russian Army from a defensive force into that of garrison police, is believed to have affected its morale. The War Minister, Rediger, announced his disapproval to Stolypin (Sep. 13, 1906).

Even in 1910 when the Vilna military district reported "complete tranquillity among the peasants" and desired

---

[1] Witte, *Vospominaniya*, Vol. II, p. 115.
[2] Delo gl. shtaba, II otdel, 3 st., No. 199, ll. pp. 219–22; Krasny Arhiv, 1928, Vol. VI (XXXI), p. 86.

the abolition of the regional army system as established by the Conference in 1906, the general staff was still in favour of its maintenance as an insurance policy.

It appears from the *Zhurnal osobovo soveshchaniya* (January 28, 1906) that the provinces where a recurrence of peasant disorders was to be anticipated included (in order of probable outbreak) Voronesh, Ekaterinoslav, Kiev, Kursk, Mogilev, Nizhegorod, Orel, Penza, Perm, Poltava, Samara, Saratov, Simbirsk, Tambov, Harkov, Chernigov and Tula.[1]

While Witte was busily engaged in consolidating the Government's much-shaken power, the land question was keenly debated in the Council of Ministers. The October risings in 1905 had caused alarm among the supporters of the old régime. S. J. Witte has made this clear in his *Vospominaniya*. The *Agrarny Vopros v Sovete Ministrov v* 1906 g. (pub. 1924) also provides much material for the study of the question at that date. Even the all-powerful General Trepov was then a supporter of compulsory alienation of land for the peasantry. Migulin, a St. Petersburg professor, who was not noted for the liberalism of his opinions, presented to the Tsar, through Trepov, a report couched in generous terms (Oct. 1905). "I myself am a squire," said Trepov to Count Witte, "and I shall be very pleased to give away freely half my land, if only thereby I can preserve the other half."

Through Trepov's intercession, Professor Migulin received an Imperial Audience in November. His report had been sent to the Council of Ministers some time before. The Council (including Kutler, Minister for Agriculture) was hostile to the project, at least before the new Duma should meet. The Council nevertheless determined without delay to abolish Redemption Payments and, at the same time, to increase the Peasant Bank's powers regarding the acquisition of privately-owned land for sale to peasants. This policy was announced in the Manifesto of November 3, 1905. As far as the peasant movement of 1905 is concerned this

[1] op. cit., p. 89.

date represents its climax of achievement. The *Polozhenie* of 1861 and subsequent Acts had remodelled peasant conditions, but the compulsory redemption scheme had reinserfed the whole peasant mass, whether originally objects of possession to squire or Imperial Family or settled upon so-called State lands. Redemption dues already paid amounted to a sum which was estimated to be three times the original value of the lands allotted to peasantry at the *Osvobozdenie* of 1861.[1] Expressing this in another way, one may say that, for every rouble which the peasants paid for the land through their community or household, two more were paid as the purchase price of their personal emancipation from the power of the squire. (In the case of the State peasants, however, this alternative view is not admissible since they were not the private property of squires—some even having originally been squires themselves [e.g. *odnodvortsy*]).

In any event, on November 3, 1905, was removed the fiscal basis which had kept the mass of the formal *soslovie* (estate) of the peasantry in the position of a depressed and contributory debtor class. As is evident from the contents of *Agrarny Vopros v Sovete Ministrov* (1906), the squires of Simbirsk (Middle Volga Region) and Tula (Central Industrial Region) expressed their alarm at the change.

The Tsar's Ministers did not stop at this point. A projected law was drafted in the Council at Kutler's instructions. Its author was the well-known statistical and economic authority, Professor A. A. Kaufman, who was assisted by Rittikh (later Minister for Agriculture). Kaufman was later a supporter of the Kadet (Constitutional Democratic) Party, but Kutler's scheme even so was less far-reaching in its expropriation measures than that of the previously quoted Migulin, who became in course of time a supporter of the Octobrist Party.

On January 10, 1906, Witte reported to Nicholas II

---

[1] Cf. Ents. Slov. F. Pavlenkova, S.P., 1907, and Tcherkinsky, Agrarian Policy in Russia, *Inter. Rev. Agric. Econ.*, 1924.

the Council's majority against Kutler's measure. Hence
His Imperial Majesty wrote on the report: "I do not
approve" ("Ne odobryayu"). Kutler's expropriation
plan was dead. General Trepov ceased to sympathise
with a compulsory alienation policy and its sponsor the
Minister of Agriculture (Kutler) had to go. The
"crescendo" of peasant risings in the autumn of 1905
had become a "diminuendo" in the winter of 1906.
Punitive expeditions brutally inspired by Kryzhanovsky's
firmness were reducing the countryside to a fevered peace.

A. V. Krivoshein virtually replaced Kutler at the
Ministry of Agriculture despite the fact that Nikolsky
became its nominal head until the First Duma. While
the rejection of Kutler's project showed that the upper
administrative circles were breathing freely once more,
there was still the fear of the spring rising. That anxiety
is proved by the *Zhurnal osobovo soveshchaniya* (January
28, 1906).

The prevailing tendency in official circles was illustrated by A. Krivoshein's project, appearing in *Novoe
Vremya*, which suggested the liquidation of the agrarian
question principally by *zemleustroistvo* (land settlement
operations).[1] There was a movement among influential
circles against the *obshchina* (land commune) which
was considered to be a dangerous focus for peasant
discontents. This movement was typified by the
Letter of the Simbirsk Gentry already mentioned. The
portion of Count Witte's Report to Nicholas II (January
9, 1906) where it was stated that a means of exit from
the commune "may have a beneficent influence upon
peasant legal consciousness, and instil more wholesome
views among the peasantry concerning others' property
rights" received the Tsar's official approval.[2] A Special
Commission under the Head of the Land Department
in its sessions of January 31, February 7 and 10, 1906,
hastily received a project for the establishment of Land
Commissions. Krivoshein and Gurko were the principal
actors. On March 4, 1906, temporary rules were framed

[1] *Agrar. Vop. v Sov. Minist.*, p. 4.   [2] Ibid., p. 5.

for these Land Settlement Commissions. These rules formed the basis of P. A. Stolypin's legislation against the *obshchina* (*ukaz* of November 9, 1906, and Law of June 14, 1910). Generally speaking, in this respect, Stolypin simply moved along a continued and prearranged path. A V. Krivoshein completely understood the implications of the new policy—the very idea of the dissolution of the commune being finally recognised in ruling circles at the end of 1905. Stolypin of course as Governor of Saratov 1904–5 had "kept the bridge" on the Volga during the height of the agrarian storm. His report for 1904 helped to single him out as the ideal protagonist of the new official orientation.

Shortly before the opening of the First Duma (April 27, 1906) Count Witte was removed from office and Goremykin installed. This change of personnel was significant. The new Premier, at a Conference at the Imperial Residence of Tarskoe Selo, had developed the idea that, as the newly-elected members of the Duma would inevitably desire to discuss the question of "compulsory alienation" of squires' land, measures to prevent them must be adopted even at the cost of dissolution.[1] Witte had on December 11, 1905, made his last opportunist bid for the Liberal support. He had issued a regulation enormously widening the suffrage for the Duma elections —embracing thereby all taxpayers and almost all lodgers and factory workers. Preliminary election meetings had been permitted and the Duma was given control of the verification of its own constituency. The Prime Minister's edict was called forth by the Moscow rising of December 9–19 which might encourage, it was feared, a recrudescence of disorder in St. Petersburg, where Hrustalev-Nosar's "Soviet" had just been arrested on December 3. But Witte was never forgiven by Court circles for this action. It had made the Duma a stronger bulwark of popular feelings.

Despite Professor Migulin's record in 1905 as a supporter of compulsory alienation, he did not show much

[1] *Agrar. Vop. v Sov. Minist.*, p. 5.

consistency by his attitude in 1906 when he attacked (June 28) projects of the same type propounded by the new Legislature. In fact he incited the Tsar to dissolve the Duma on that very ground. In the following section the Duma's part in the agrarian struggle is more fully examined. But it is sufficient here to say that Migulin's vacillation from a policy of expropriation to one of stern rebuke of the Duma for giving similar advice, indicates how far the Tsar's Government had travelled between October 1905 and July 1906. The defensive Trepov-Witte-Kutler combination of the autumn of 1905 changed into the sturdier Durnovo-Kryzhanovsky-Witte offensive of January-February-March 1906. The new Fundamental Laws circumscribed the spirit of the October Manifesto.[1] The Goremykin-Stolypin policy foreshadowing the break-up, if necessary, of the new legislative institutions, took its rise in April and led inevitably to the supersession of Witte's pseudo-liberal Administration and the assertion by the Government of an independent agrarian programme.

The contest (Homeric it might certainly be styled in the full significance of a somewhat hackneyed term) passed from the stage of active revolution to the less strenuous battle of words in the legislative chamber of the First Duma. The Administration, it is true, was no longer in the position of acute distress that it had been when President Hrustalov-Nosar's "Soviet" had "exchanged compliments" in the Tsar's own capital with Witte, the new Prime Minister, and when it had been debated whether the Head of the "Soviet" would first arrest the Head of the Government or vice versa. That scene had been enacted in the closing months of 1905. Much water had flowed under the Neva Bridges when the Duma met on April 27, 1906. The revolutionary unity of parties had suffered a change during those selfsame months of the previous year. The class-cleavage which had become apparent in party alignments had

[1] Both the October Manifesto and the Fundamental Laws rapidly assumed an academic importance.

given great heart to the opponents of any policy of progress or violent uncompensated expropriation of property. The Witte-Durnovo combination of velvet glove and mailed fist was soon to be exchanged for one in which the first element was even less prominent. Such was the significance of Stolypin's advent to power after the Duma had revealed its radical composition.

The Government did not intend to allow the initiative in the peasant problem to pass irrevocably from its grasp. Stolypin's policy, later defined as "first pacification, then reforms," spurning the Western Parliamentary Responsible Government desired by Milyukov, indicated the weakness of the belief in the old-time loyalty of peasant for the "Tsar-Batyushka." That belief, already shaken severely by the peasant movement of the preceding year, was finally abandoned when the Government saw the newly-styled "Constitutional Democratic Party" (Cadets) angling for the support of the "Trudoviki" (Labour Party). The significance of the land question at the elections had been abundantly revealed by Yakushkin (Kursk) when he stated, "Vybory povsemestno proiskhodili pod edinodushnymi klikami: 'zemlya!' " ("The elections everywhere proceeded amid a universal cry of 'land!' ") [1]

In the "Address-in-Reply" to the Speech from the Throne, Nabokov, the Constitutional Democratic Opposition Leader, revealed the radical plans of his party which, even so, were less revolutionary than the " 'Trudovik' Bill of the 104."

The elucidation of the needs of the rural population and the adoption of corresponding legal measures form the most insistent task of the Imperial Duma. By far the most numerous portion of the country's population—the working peasantry—awaits impatiently for the satisfaction of its keen need of land, and the first Russian Imperial Duma would not fulfil its duty if it did not draft a law for the satisfaction of this insistent need, along the lines of the diversion to this object of the Treasury, Appanage [i.e. Imperial Family], Cabinet [i.e. Private Imperial], and monastic lands,

[1] Stenographicheskie Otchety Gos. Dumy, Sess. I, May 8.

together with the compulsory expropriation of privately-owned land.

Further he maintained that it was "necessary to draft laws affirming the peasant's equal legal status and removing from him the burden of arbitrary control and tutelage."[1] It devolved upon Professor Hertsenstein, the leading agrarian authority of Nabokov's (or Milyukov's) Party to propound such a scheme. In his measure[2] was involved an agrarian law whose only virtue, in the Government's eyes, was its payment of compensation "at a fair price" for the compulsory general expropriation of privately-owned estates. The further provision for uncompensated expropriation in cases of land leased for a money-rent, or in return for a labour-rent, or where peasant stock was used as the means of cultivation, showed the Government that even a normally property-respecting, commercial-manufacturing-professional party (such as the "Cadets" were primarily) could not refrain from flirting with a modernised *narodnik* (populist) doctrine. Shortly afterwards too, a land socialisation measure—"the Bill of the 104"—indicated the opinion of peasant members that land should be held by those that worked it.[3] This particular Socialisation Bill is of great interest as being an embryonic creation destined to reach maturity at the advent of Lenin to power in October 1917, when the Peasant Movement, that is being described, achieved the old ideas of the *narodnichestvo* (populism). In a sense this particular piece of suggested legislation was the spirit which the Land Decree of October 1917, by Lenin's aid, was to endow with flesh. It lends an artistic unity to the period which is treated here, since it is possible to trace the evolution of a basic idea permeating the years 1906 to 1917.

What were the provisions of the Land Socialisation Bill?[4] All land with its minerals and waters was to

[1] Ibid., Sess. I, Zased. 4, May 2, 1906.
[2] Ibid., Sess. I, Zased. 6, May 8, 1906. [3] Ibid., Vol. II, p. 561.
[4] Ibid., Ivo Soz., Sess. I, Zased. 13, May 23, 1906; Vol. II, p. 561.

belong to the whole people. Agricultural land was to be given only to those working it with their own labour. All citizens were to have an equal right to its use (Sect. 1). The Land Fund was to include Treasury, Cabinet, Monastic and Church lands. Privately-owned land was to be compulsorily resumed in so far as its dimensions exceeded the labour-norm fixed for the given district. *Nadelnaya* (allotment) land and private land not above the norm were to remain untouched. There was to be no engrossing of land in a single individual's hands (Sect. 3).

The State was to pay compensation for any land resumed, the amount and conditions of such compensation and also the cases of uncompensated expropriation being determined after the question and the whole agrarian reform had been decided by the people locally (Sect. 4).

Sale, mortgage and gift of land were to be immediately stopped (Sect. 5).

Mineral rights and waters, where not utilised by present owners, were to become general public property. A special law was to determine their handing over to social institutions and private individuals (Sect. 6).

There was to be a special law for the transfer to socialised ownership of mineral and water rights now privately-owned and exploited, and also for the land used for industrial undertakings and town settlement. Until this was effected, any increase of values due, not to labour and capital applied, but to social conditions, must be limited (Sect. 7). The remaining land, as far as it was fit for agriculture, was to be given to all those desirous of working it with their own labour. Local inhabitants were to be considered before newcomers and agriculturists. Each working person had a right to a homestead in the place where he lived and the right to an allotment in a place where free land existed (Sect. 9).

There was to be an allotment based upon a labour-norm. Any surplus was to be retained by central or local authorities to use for social needs—increase of population or migration (Sect. 10).

There was to be a right of State-aided migration if local land was insufficient for the consumption norm (Sect. 11). Labour and consumption norms could be varied if necessary. There could be internal community redivisions and migration at Government expense (Sect. 12).

Land not utilised was to revert to the land fund. There was to be State compensation for unused improvements. No private alienation of land was to exist (Sect. 13). The allotments were to bear a special graduated land-tax (Sect. 14).

Those who were unable to work the land received were to be recipients of State loans and assistance (Sect. 15). Any land other than of public significance was to be controlled by the local authority concerned. Such local authority would be based upon general, equal, secret and direct suffrage, and was to be self-sufficient (Sect. 16). Local committees were to be formed to arrange the land reform; provincial, district and cantonal or other, corresponding to local conditions. These committees were to be also based on the same democratic principles as in the preceding section (Sect. 17).

The committees aforesaid must (*a*) organise a free and broad determination (with the collaboration of the whole population) of the general bases and all details of the agrarian reform (Labour and food units, i.e. the working capacity of the peasant family and the needs of non-working dependants, were to be calculated); (*b*) fix, before the reform took place, rents of leased land, wages, the length of the working day and arrange any disputes of landowners and employees (Sect. 18).

The organisation of local committees and the plan of their work was to be determined by law (Sect. 19).

Elections for local committees and deliberations upon agrarian reform locally were to proceed on the permanent condition of complete freedom and personal inviolability (Sect. 20).

Such a programme revolutionising the agrarian (and incidentally socio-political structure of the country) was the alternative presented to the existing régime, if the present *trudovik narodnik* doctrine were to succeed in imposing its tenets upon the Administration. It was the apotheosis of the *mir* or land-commune, to which its sponsors desired to subject the existing private property relationships of Russia, as was in fact achieved by the Land Decree of October 1917.

A still more drastic socialisation measure introduced by Aladin and called the "Bill of the 33"[1] did not succeed in progressing as far as the previous two measures. It was thrown out and thus prevented from being used as material for the land legislation that the Agrarian Commission of the First Duma was then considering. Its provisions which are interesting as an expression of potential Social Revolutionary views will not be discussed here.

The Tsar's Government was by no means prepared to accept such fundamental changes. In fact, it has been previously seen that the Council of Ministers had discounted in advance any such revolutionary agrarian policy of the new Legislature. The correspondence between Nicholas II and Stolypin (1906–11)[2] has revealed Nicholas II's desire to receive direct credit for the inauguration of the land-settlement and migration schemes which history has associated with the name of the man who was soon to be his Prime Minister.

For a direct Government offensive the omens were now more propitious. The country was obviously tired after the revolutionary turmoil of the autumn, winter and spring preceding. It appears to the investigator that it was rather the fundamental cleavages of opinion among those opposing the Government that were the more potent causes of such passivity even when due weight is given to punitive expeditions, such as those of Riman, and the repressive measures chronicled in the reports of Dubasov and Panteleev.[3] The Government was disliked—indeed,

---

[1] Stenographicheskie Otchety Gos. Dumy, Sess. I, Zased. 23, May 8, 1906; Vol. II, p. 1142.
[2] Krasny Arhiv, Vol. V, pp. 102–8, 1924.
[3] op. cit., Vols. IV–V, pp. 182–92, 1925.

was detested, by many sections of society, but there was no "lowest common measure" of active anti-governmental feeling, or if there was, the "lowness" of the measure kept the more secure members of the community from venturing further into the complications which had almost wrecked the old order during 1905.

The Government having rejected popular proposals had perforce itself to produce an agrarian policy. Previous pages have illustrated that a policy had been elaborated during the preceding months under the impulse of the social war of 1905 and the prospective radicalism of the First Duma. The ideas behind it were indeed "in the air" even at the end of the preceding century—one of its pioneers, Stolypin's uncle, having already evolved a practical agricultural philosophy whose aim was similar.[1] Sir Bernard Pares has published his notes of conversations with the Russian Premier Stolypin, who was the already destined sponsor of the change.[2] They give some guide to the characteristics of the new land policy of the Government and of the man who was to set it in motion and secure its legislative approval before he perished by an assassin's hand in the Tsar's own presence in September 1911.

Even before Stolypin became President of the Council of Ministers, the Government through his predecessor, Goremykin, explained rather vaguely its new attitude upon the agrarian question. The occasion was its answer to the Duma's Address-in-Reply to the Speech from the Throne and incidentally to Hertsenstein's proposal of May 8. This enunciation of agrarian policy was delivered on May 13, 1906.[3]

With particular attention does the Council of Ministers regard the suggestions of the Duma for the immediate satisfaction of the urgent needs of the peasant population and for the enactment of a law which will institute equal rights for peasants with persons of other classes.... With regard to the solution of the peasants'

---
[1] Cf. *Ob organizatsii nashevo selskavo byta*, D. A. Stolypin, Moscow, 1892.
[2] Cf. *Russian Review*, Vol. II, i, 1913.
[3] Stenographicheskie Otchety Gos. Dumy.

land question, as suggested by the Duma—by handing over for this purpose, appanage, crown, monastic and church lands and by the compulsory expropriation of the land of private owners, *including that of peasant proprietors who have redeemed their land by purchase*—the Council of Ministers feels it to be its duty to announce that the solution of this question, on the principles proposed by the Imperial Duma, is absolutely inadmissible.

The State cannot recognise the right to property in land for some and, at the same time, take away this right from others. The State cannot refuse to admit the general right of personal ownership of land, without at the same time refusing to admit the right of ownership in any other kind of property. The principle that property cannot be seized, that is inviolate, is the corner-stone of public well-being and development the world over and at all stages of evolution in civic life. It is the basic support of social life, without which the very existence of a State is unthinkable. The conditions of the situation do not call for the proposed measures. With the extensive, and far from exhausted, resources which are at the disposal of the State and with a broad application of all legal methods at hand, the land question can, without doubt, be satisfactorily solved without destroying the very foundation of our State interests and without undermining the vital forces of our country.

Further, the Premier added,

The strength of the Russian State is built up first of all on the strength of its agricultural population. The well-being of our country cannot be secured so long as the necessary conditions for the prosperity and development of agricultural labour, the basis of our whole economic life, are not guaranteed. Considering, therefore, the peasant question as—in view of its all-embracing public significance—the most important now brought up for solution, the Council of Ministers thinks that proper care and caution are necessary in seeking ways and means of solving it. Caution is here needed to avoid any sudden shock to the conditions of the peasantry which have had an historical development of their own. But in the opinion of the Council of Ministers, the recent reform of our system of government, which has given to persons elected from the peasant population a share in the work of law-making, defines in advance the main principles of the peasant reform which is before us. Under these conditions, the distinctiveness of the peasants as a class must give way to their junction with other classes in relation to civil law and order, administration and justice.

All those limitations on the rights of ownership in communal land, which were instituted to secure the punctual liquidation of the redemption debt, must also disappear.

The giving to the peasant of equal civil and political rights with the other classes should not, however, deprive the State of the right and obligation to show particular solicitude for the needs of the peasant agriculturists. Measures in this field should be directed toward *improving the conditions of peasant land-tenure within its existing limits* and towards increasing the area of land of that portion of the population which has insufficient land, at the expense of unoccupied crown lands and by obtaining possession of land of private owners through the Peasant Bank.

The field of work which here presents itself to the public authorities is extensive and fruitful. The improvement of *conditions of agriculture, which are now at a very low level of development,* will increase the measure of productiveness of the country and thus raise the standard of well-being. Vast expanses of land, suitable for cultivation, now lie unoccupied in the Asiatic possessions of the Empire. The development of migration will, therefore, be one of the most immediate tasks of the Council of Ministers.

In the above address to the First Duma, it is evident that there appears in a generalised form the policy afterwards enforced by Stolypin, Goremykin's successor in the office of Prime Minister. Five parts of the speech have been underlined by the investigator, who would like to emphasise their importance. First there occurs the statement that compulsory expropriation of land would include that of peasant proprietors who had redeemed their land by purchase. This point is very important when it is considered that it was a means of driving a wedge into the apparently solid peasant "bloc" in order to rout the supporters of the idea of the *trudovik* or peasant-labour doctrine. This wedge was symbolic of much of the subsequent Governmental agrarian activity. The point was driven home when Gurko (Minister of the Interior) resisting the "Bill of the 104" desiring land socialisation, categorically announced that "expropriation must lead to the nationalisation of peasant land" (May 23, 1906) and declared that Hertsenstein, the Constitutional Democratic sponsor of the earlier bill for expropriation of land "at a fair price," had himself expressed the same view a year previously. One is reminded of Lenin's treatment of the question in his review of the Social Democratic Agrarian Programme in 1902, when the more timorous element in his party feared the effect upon certain potential peasant allies of a declaration of nationalisation. It was again to be the *bête noire* of Maslov the "municipaliser" against whom Lenin thundered in his Agrarian Programme of 1907 discussed elsewhere. Much of the party manœuvring of these fateful years before 1917 (and even later) is explained by this one question of the implications of the term "nationalisation" which must be distinguished from "socialisation."

Secondly, there is the reference to discrimination in property rights. Why should certain kinds of property only be recognised as ethically just? If landed property were declared illegal, why should any other property be sacrosanct? It is precisely here that is to be found the cross-road of both 1905 and 1917. It was the cause of schisms in the advanced parties such as the "Constitutional Democratic" and even the "Social Democratic" Party. The Menshevik Social Democrats with Maslov's "municipalisation" scheme were admittedly on the horns of a dilemma. Could peasant property be recognised if the squires' were confiscated? Lenin (and his Bolsheviks) who would have been astounded to be seen "in the same galley" as Goremykin ("Que diable allaient-ils faire dans cette galère?") for once would have agreed with him. Once the revolution abolished some landed property rights, there was no turning back. Ethically, there could be no defence of any property. It was here that the Constitutional Democrats, flirting with peasant aspirations, realised, too late, that they were playing with fire. Even the radical Social Revolutionaries eventually in 1917 found themselves also in the same position. One could not revolutionise rural without revolutionising urban property rights. The French Revolutionaries in 1789–93 had technically saved themselves by officially confiscating at first only the possessions of *émigrés* and the Church, which peasants subsequently bought at a low price. That salvation was not possible in Russia if a general land expropriation were effected on behalf of the peasants. It is a most interesting phase in the development of the revolutionary mind from 1905 to 1917 and warrants serious attention.

The third point is instructive as revealing the official *raison d'être* of the "communal system." It is clear from the Government's statement that this system had been definitely related to the redemption of bondage conditions. When the redemption dues ceased or were abolished, it was frankly announced here that the Administration was no longer interested in the *mir* as a special unit. In fact, it feared it.

Lastly, the conditions of agriculture were admitted to be at a very low level of development. It will be seen later how far the Government's Land Policy, after 1906, cured that national ailment, and whether it was capable of cure by the methods which were adopted.

Convinced by the appearance of the Land-Socialisation Measure of the "104," that Goremykin's declaration had evoked no response in the new Chamber, the Tsar's Government, determined to maintain the initiative in the handling of the vital peasant land question, issued a "Public Communication" on June 20, 1906, reiterating its definite refusal to permit confiscation of private lands, or any form of nationalisation, but stated that it would utilise the Peasant Bank to aid the peasantry to secure land.[1] This announcement was a definite challenge to the Duma as a legislative authority. It was regarded as such by that body. The Duma's Agrarian Commission was consequently appointed on June 26, 1906. Its President was Mukhanov who gave reasons why Duma ought to meet the Government's action.[2]

It was an historic moment. The sands of time of the first modern Russian legislative chamber were fast run-

---

[1] Cf. Stenographicheskie Otchety Gos. Dumy, Sess. I, Zased. 38, July 4, 1906; Vol. II, p. 1953.
[2] Ibid., Sess. I, Zased. 38, July 4, 1906; Vol. II, p. 1953.

ning out. Unknown to the members, unless they had dim presentiments, their last hours were at hand. The dissolution decree was already prepared and Stolypin was soon to supersede Goremykin as Premier and assume his historic rôle on July 8 ensuing. Obninsky, the Commission's Reporter, detailed the process through which the Commission had passed in reaching its determination "to appeal to the people" against the Government. He reviewed the important dates—May 5, when the Duma's Address-in-Reply had demanded land for working peasants—even private land; Goremykin's statement of May 13, with its theme—"No expropriation": lastly the Government's Public Communication of June 20, over the Duma's head. The Duma, in anger, had proceeded to formulate new legal projects by means of the Special Commission of 100 members. These projects involved expropriation of all land except "allotment" land or that in small ownership. By the Manifesto of October 17, the Sovereign had promised that no proposal of the Administration was to have the force of law except after ratification by the Duma. In that respect the Government's Public Communication of June 20 was unconstitutional. The Duma was now going to take the step of a direct Appeal to the People, stating that as a regularly-drafted law was necessary, it hoped the population would remain quiet pending its passage.[1]

Kusmin-Karavaev, member for Tver, supporting the idea of an Appeal to the People on the agrarian issue, referred to the successive weakening of the Duma's position.[2] "In nearly two months of its existence, its real results have been nil. . . . Constitutional mechanism is slow to move. . . . People think we cannot act. . . . We are extraordinarily unanimous on negations: are we as unanimous in positive ideas?"

The general principle of the Report was agreed to, notwithstanding Professor Petrazhitsky's qualms as to the wisdom of venturing upon such uncharted seas.

---

[1] Stenographicheskie Otchety Gos. Dumy, Vol. II, p. 1955.
[2] Ibid., p. 1960.

Stakhovich, too, thought that "the Appeal to the People" on the land question was "the most important step of all that the Duma has taken till now."[1]

The suggested "Appeal" was issued on July 6, promising the peasants compulsory expropriation of land.

On July 8, the Stolypin axe fell. The Duma was closed and its 230 radical members had to be content with the fatuous Vyborg Appeal from the safe distance of the Finnish Coast.

So ended the First Duma.

Nor was the Second long in following in its footsteps, when Stolypin, emboldened by his previous success and having already on November 9, 1906, issued, by virtue of Article 87, his Agrarian Decree, perceived the danger that once more the popular representatives would take up the peasant cudgels. There is a graphic description, in President F. A. Golovin's correspondence, of the fate of Russia's second attempt to combine popular power with the Tsar's prerogatives.[2] There is an air of pessimism that pervades the chamber. "Gospoda, my sidim zdes tri mesyatsa. Shto my dali strane?" ("Gentlemen, we have sat here for three months. What have we given to the country?") plaintively asks Volk Kacharevsky. There is the question of the Arrest, not of the Five, but of the Fifty-five (Social Democratic) Members. Stolypin entered to demand their expulsion. "His birds," unlike those of British Charles I, had not "flown." They were still there. It was June 2. The Duma had considered the question of the arrest. The old Russian question again arose, "what was to be done?" The Constitutional Democrats in their private conference were hard put to it.[3] Said Milyukov, the unofficial leader, "We will protect the Duma and give up the delinquents." Said Nabokov, the official leader, "Either

[1] Ibid., p. 1952.
[2] Krasny Arhiv, Vol. XLIII, 1931, Is Zapisok predsedatelya II Gos. Dumy, F. A. Golovina; Osoby otdel Moskovskovo Tsent. Istoricheskovo Arhiva.
[3] Cf. Protokol zased., fraktsii part. narodnoy svobody, June 2, 1907; Krasny Arhiv, Vol. XLIII, p. 69, 1931.

give up all or none." The party decided to surrender the members.

Meanwhile in the House itself, in its 53rd (and last) sitting, Tsereteli, leader of the band of proscribed Social Democratic members, had moved a motion to fix for the next day a discussion on the treatment of projected laws introduced according to Article 87 (Emergency Power) and also on the question of the Budget. Now the Agrarian Decree of Stolypin had been promulgated in the interval between the dissolution of the First Duma, July 8, 1906, and the meeting of the Second, February 20, 1907 (o.s.). The Tsar's Government saw itself again challenged by the new deliberative body upon the most vital question of the hour—agrarian law. The Legislature's expressed opinions had long been regarded with disfavour by the Tsar who, on March 31, 1907, wrote as follows to Stolypin: "The extreme speeches on the agrarian question broadcast over the whole of Russia, and also the letters printed in the names of members, form a serious menace to the peace of the country."[1] Such words coming from the Emperor himself could foreshadow only one result. They could not fail to be a definite indication of the Imperial will, although two months elapsed before they affected the life of the Second Duma. For the Prime Minister they were mandatory. Brooking no delay, such as would have been involved in a protracted legal enquiry into the alleged guilt of the accused members, Stolypin's axe once more fell. In the night of June 2–3 the Second Duma was dissolved. A revised electoral law was issued. Tsereteli and many of his companions went to Siberia.

So ended the Second Duma.

A survey of the Government's agrarian legislation involves a study of three enactments, the last amplifying and supplementing the preceding two. There is first the *ukaz* of November 9, 1906; secondly there is the Law of June 14, 1910; and thirdly the Law of May 29, 1911 (the Statute of Land Settlement, Vol. X, Part 3 of the Code).

[1] Krasny Arhiv, Vol. V, p. 110, 1924.

Clause 1 (Section I) of the *ukaz* of November 9, 1906, provided that "every head of a peasant family holding allotment-land (*nadel*) by right of communal tenure is entitled at any time to claim the appropriation, as private property, of his due share of the said land."

Clause 2 provided that in village-communities where there had been no general redistributions of land in the course of the last twenty-four years, the peasant desiring to withdraw from the commune was entitled, besides his homestead, to all the land that was in his actual possession, as a member of the village commune at the time when the request was made. In other cases (as, for instance, in communities where redistributions had occurred in the last twenty-four years) Clause 3 allowed any individual peasant to claim his share of communal land. In addition, if at any time of separation, his actual holding exceeded his share, the excess had to be purchased by him from the community and paid for at the average price of land fixed for the purpose of redemption at the Emancipation of 1861.

By Clause 4, the peasant who had his share of communal land appropriated to him, preserved his right of use over those parts of the village land which were not divided among the members of the community, but exploited jointly, such as forests, meadows or pastures. Clause 12 allowed a seceding peasant to claim the allocation to him of his share of communal land "as far as possible" in a single plot. By Clause 13, the community could redeem the land in question at an agreed or judicially-determined price if the enclosure of the land claimed was found to be technically impossible. But under Clause 14, the village community was bound to grant a request for enclosure, made at the time of a general land-redistribution. There was no possible alternative of money compensation.

Clause 1 (Section III) struck at the root of customary peasant law when it announced that "individual peasant holdings . . . are the private property of heads of households, in whose possession they are." The old idea that the allotment was in the tenure of the whole *dvor* (peasant family) was thus definitely assailed. It was in some ways a greater innovation than the attack on communal property itself. By Section IV, the *ukaz* stipulated that

> whole village-communities, whether holding land in common or by heritable tenure, can effect the enclosure of the holdings of their members by a majority of two-thirds of all the peasants possessing the right to vote in the village-assembly.

It is clear that two acts were involved in the operation of the above *ukaz*. Firstly, where communal tenure existed, *ukreplenie* (appropriation of holding) must be the preliminary stage. If "enclosure" of the land concerned into *otrub* or *hutor* was desired, that was a further process. Where *obshchinnoe* (communal) tenure did not exist, but simply *podvornoe* (heritable household tenure), "enclosure" could be proceeded with immediately under the newly-legalised personal property-right of the "head of the family."

Clauses 2 and 3 (Section I) seemed to favour the more fortunate members of the land-commune, the third clause in particular. It really subsidised seceding peasants at the expense of those remaining. However, it being the Government's policy to reorganise on new lines the rural life of Russia, the fact is not surprising.

Individual secession (*vydel*) was one means of implementing the new legislative measure, while another was a general communal dissolution to secure the division of the land of the whole village (*razverstanie*). The second course was necessarily preferable in every respect, as it lessened a possible sense of inequity.

It is interesting to note that the Government's method of agrarian reform was introduced as a decree (*ukaz*) and not as law (*zakon*). A "law" now required, as a result of the October Manifesto of 1905 and the subsequent creation of the Imperial Duma, legislative assent on the part of the elected representatives of the people. The revolutionary spirit abroad in the country (of which the earlier sections have given some indication) prevented this "consummation devoutly to be wished." It was, however, argued by supporters of the Government that Clause 87 of the new Constitution (promulgated before the session of Russia's first modern parliament) allowed the Executive to legislate by direct *ukaz* provisionally, pending subsequent legislative ratification. But to the investigator it seems that it was regrettable that such a course was followed here. It could not have been contemplated that the emergency power of an administrative decree should have sufficed to vitalise a measure which was intended to change "root and branch" the economic and social conditions of the overwhelming majority of the population. If the new measure had been announced before the creation of a legislature there would have been no moral objection. But the October Manifesto of 1905 was a milestone in Russia's modernisation of her political structure. And the means adopted by the Government in enforcing the new agrarian measure undoubtedly prevented its securing its deserts if only on the ground of its attempt to improve farming technique, as, for instance, the abolition of *chrezpolositsa* (intermingled strips). When, too, it became necessary to disfranchise sections of the community to secure the assent of the new legislative instrument (the Third Duma), much encouragement was given to its opponents after the February Revolution of 1917 to declare that it was not worthy of acceptance by a revolutionary democracy.

The momentous significance of a land policy that was to affect the destiny of the majority of the population of an empire of 182,000,000 people was not lost upon the Russian Sovereign.

Nicholas II's personal interest in his Prime Minister's agrarian policy is indeed emphatically expressed in his correspondence. In the *Novoe Vremya* of January 8, 1911 (No. 12,509), Arcady Stolypin, the Russian Prime Minister's brother, wrote an article entitled "Oktyabristkaya Gosudarstvennaya Duma i ee Kritiki." Reviewing the services of the Third Duma he said: "The Third Duma placed a sword in the hands of unarmed Russia"—

referring evidently to Guchkov's attacks upon the inefficiency of the old Army Command as revealed in the Japanese War (1904–5). Further he proceeded: "The Third Duma passed and ratified the administrative law which heralded for the economic situation of Russia an epoch similar to that established for the country by the civil law concerning the Emancipation of the Peasantry (1861)."[1] Stolypin's brother of course had in mind the *ukaz* of November 9, 1906, which was approved and even extended by the Duma in the Law of June 14, 1910. The Tsar did not like this assertion of the popular participation in the Government of the country of even that definitely conservative body.

Your brother's article in yesterday's number of the *Novoe Vremya* [wrote Nicholas to his Premier (January 10, 1911)] did not please me. Consider the places marked by me—with regard to the Army and the Law of November 9th (1906). Does he mean to say that both measures came from the Imperial Duma?[2]

In the previous year the Tsar's keen interest in the new policy was also directly expressed.

I learned with pleasure [he wrote to Stolypin (September 22, 1910)] of your written report and that of Krivoshein (Minister for Agriculture) about all you have seen and the proposals for further migration measures. Durable resettlement of peasants inside Russia and similar settlement of migrants in Siberia—those are the two fundamental questions upon which the Government must unceasingly work. It does not follow of course that we should forget other needs—schools, means of communication, etc., but those two (points) must be kept in the forefront.

Yet the legislation represents a truly ambitious attempt to change the encrusted habits of generations. Enclosure movements there have been in other countries. England, for instance, in the last third of the eighteenth century and the first half of the nineteenth finally abandoned the open field system and fundamentally changed her agrarian appearance. Yet it was not achieved by a

---

[1] Krasny Arhiv, Vol. V, p. 128, 1924.   [2] op. cit., p. 122.

general Enclosure Act. There was a series of private Enclosure Bills, each of which required the sanction of the national legislature. It was only towards the end of the process that general legislation was passed (1845). Koefoed's careful survey of the open field system in Europe and in Russia[1] starting with England and Algau (*Bavaria*) and describing France, Denmark, Sweden, Finland, Norway, Prussia and the remaining German countries, provides much food for thought in this regard. It is a work which was accompanied by a briefer handbook *Hutorskoe Rasselenie* (*Settlement on Self-contained Farms*), both being "text-books," so to speak, for the guidance of the new Land-Settlement officials. The chapter on England in the first of these works is instructive as to the methods described, which were certainly not subsequently adopted in Russia. Koefoed, one notes on page 6, says, "Tak delo (i.e. ogorazhivanie) prodolzhalo razvivatsya v techenie stoletiy c harakterno dlya Anglii postepennostyu i posledovatelnostyu" ("Thus the task (i.e. enclosure movement) continued to be pursued in the course of centuries with the graduality and sequence characteristic of England"). On the same page he mentions that "from 1709 to the 'forties of the nineteenth century there were issued more than 4,000 special acts (Enclosure Acts) for dividing commons at the intercession of large landowners." On page 7 he refers to the "chrezvichayno medlennoe razverstanie chrezpolositsy v Anglii" ("the extraordinarily slow dissolution of the intermingled strip system in England").

What a task, then, did his official superior and, even more, the head of Nicholas II's ministry, Stolypin, take upon themselves in 1906! Klyuchevsky's apt allusion to the fact that Peter the Great's reforming zeal raised a wind against it in inverse proportion, has its modern application to Nicholas II and his supporting ministers. The decay of villages in England too was assisted by the old customary mode in southern and western England of living in separated farms. Even in Central

[1] *Borba s chrezpolositseyu v Rossii i za granitseyu*, A. A. Koefoed.

England[1] villages were intermingled with separated family-holdings. There was thus an example to be followed when enclosures tended to predominate in the late eighteenth and early nineteenth century. Nevertheless, enclosure was impeded by its great expense and complication. Each complete enclosure, unless unanimously desired, was subject to the passing of a private Parliamentary Act, which involved a large legal expense and also needed considerable influence.

Between 1700 and 1760 there were only 200 English Enclosure Acts, involving as yet only 300,000 acres. But in the period 1760–1800, when the agrarian and industrial revolutions (really, as in the case of Russia, two facets of the same phenomenon) were gaining momentum, there were 2,000 Enclosure Acts, involving 3,000,000 acres. Between 1800 and 1850 a further amount of 2,500,000 acres was affected, consisting, it is stated, mostly of reclaimed land. Whereas the sixteenth-century Tudor enclosures, which were non-legalised evictions to create sheep pastures, amounted only to 2 per cent, the late eighteenth and early nineteenth-century enclosures, which were mainly for the purpose of wheat production, represented 20 per cent of the land. Parliament avoided a unified agrarian policy during the English enclosure movement, there being during the process no real "general Enclosure Acts."

It is not the desire of the investigator to labour the point, but it is evident that there are no analogies in English agrarian history to the methods of transforming a communal system or commonage rights such as were adopted in 1906–10 by the Administration of Stolypin. And it must be remembered that the communal system of Russia was unique in Europe for its type, tenacity and prevalence. The delayed commercialisation of Russian life, developing rapidly in the late 'nineties of the eighteenth and the first decade of the twentieth centuries shook the whole pre-existing edifice to its very foundations. Like the effect of

[1] Koefoed, op. cit., p. 7.

new wine in an old bottle, there was possibility of catastrophic result.

When another Western European country, France, is examined, it is again realised how ambitious the agrarian efforts of the Tsar's Government undoubtedly were. How far an incipient process of enclosure led to the French peasant movement of 1789–93 may be gathered from the *cahiers* (or Instructions) of representatives of members of the "Tiers État."[1] On page 12 of Koefoed's work, it is stated that

> the chief obstacle in France to the passing of a rational law effecting complete enclosure is regarded as being due to the hostility of the rich peasants who now utilise the extensive communal pastures to the detriment of the poor. And the rich peasants have great influence in Parliament.

It is strange that such a sentence should appear in a text-book prepared by an official of the Russian enclosure movement which admittedly was to strengthen the Government by "betting on the strong" as the expression went! In France it was apparently the more prosperous peasantry, in Russia the less prosperous who saw advantages in the drawbacks of the old system.

The progress of the movement against the strip-system was most successful on the Continent in Holstein, Denmark and Old Prussia. Inside the Russian Dominions, Finland and the Baltic Provinces were the leaders. The French Revolution, Koefoed indicates, hampered the process in districts which adopted the Code Napoleon, because the principle of inviolability of private property inevitably prevented any radical or general change in the direction of consolidation of allotments. That was why France, the Netherlands and the Southern German States found legal obstacles in the way. These legal obstacles were reinforced by the attractions of the social life of the village. The ordinary "stay-at-home" German had the same aversion to separation from the society of his fellow-men as had his Slav neighbour. The willingness of

[1] Cf. Herbert, *Fall of Feudalism in France*.

German colonists in Russia to live on separate farms was an acquired rather than instinctive characteristic.

To return to the Russian Dominions it is clear that Swedish example affected Finland, as it did also the (so-called) Baltic Provinces, of which Latvia had the oldest tradition of separate farms.

It is shown by Koefoed that even in Russian Poland, save upon Treasury estates, the strip-system still prevailed. When it is comprehended that Poland and the Baltic States had older traditions of what conduced to good farming, the magnitude of the issue at stake in the interior of Russia among the more purely native population is more easily grasped. Indeed, upon the information derived from Koefoed's research, it would appear that *chrezpolositsa* ("the strip-system") itself had not prevented considerable advances in technique, e.g. in France and Belgium. Manuilov too stresses this point.[1] But it is one of the advantages of such study that surprises are always in store for the student.

The attack on *chrezpolositsa* commenced in the Western regions of Russia where Polish, German, Czech and Lettish influences assisted. The conditions however of the Baltic Provinces where *chrezpolositsa* was finally abolished during the second half of the nineteenth century are not typical of Russia as a whole. In the Baltic Provinces it must be remembered that the Emancipation of the Peasants (1816–19)[2] had been a landless liberation. There were in consequence the relatively large farms of the squires, the somewhat smaller farms of the richer peasants, no villages in the Great Russian sense of the word, but, in addition, an agrarian proletariat of *batraki* which tended to join forces with the growing industrial population of the ports such as Riga.

The Great Russian "communal" provinces presented a very different aspect, especially in the excessively populated agricultural centre whose poverty at the beginning

[1] *Russian Review*, Vol. I, No. 4, Oct. 1912.
[2] The peasants were emancipated in 1816 in Esthonia, in 1817 in Kurland and in 1819 in Livonia.

of the twentieth century was one of the basic causes of the Peasant Movement.

The Ukrainian Provinces of Poltava and Chernigov were in a peculiar position. They were at a stage where the communal system had decayed but a hybrid heritable household-allotment system prevailed. There was much confusion between squire and peasant land which, interesting to relate, the *Polozhenie o razmezhevaniem* (Delimitation Act) tried to cure while insisting upon the preservation of the very conditions against which, later, Stolypin's legislation was directed. There was to be no breach of the compulsory sowing-rotation and no formation of separate farms (*hutors*). Thus in the region of Russia where *chrezpolositsa* meant a petrified system of petty family holdings, no change had been effected even in July 1906, the date of the publication of Koefoed's work.

It is advisable to consider the reasons given by Koefoed for the changes introduced in peasant agrarian organisation by the Stolypin Acts. Further evidence of the proposed changes in the peasant's economic and social life may thus be obtained. The aim, as expressed on page 95 in the *Zaklyuchenie* (conclusion), was "farming conducted upon a single well-rounded holding," as opposed to that upon many scattered strips.

The reform has now been set in its niche of international relativity and some idea has been gained of the magnitude of the undertaking. What were the objections a peasant *skhod* (assembly) might raise when the project was placed before it?

Firstly, common pasture of the whole village cattle was alleged to be better for the cattle and much cheaper than separate stock-farming. Secondly, the scattered nature of the existing type of farming was an insurance of the individual agriculturist against blight (*gradobitie*), because the whole allotment was rarely affected at once. Thirdly, the social spirit of emulation in the commune prevented any individual from allowing his holding to go to ruin. This control would be lost under an individualistic system. Finally, it was objected that individualised farming was advantageous only for holders of a large amount of land, the petty landholder being rapidly ruined. One reason for this belief was that before the final redivision, the poor peasants' cattle could be pastured on the common land which, after redivision, would disappear.

Koefoed, as an agricultural expert acquainted with the *hutor* system in Denmark and Scandinavia in particular, was prepared to answer all these complaints. He considered the most substantial objection to be the question of stock-raising. But he thought it was obvious that the improvement of dairy-cattle, for instance, was much more likely under an enclosed system. He instanced Holstein and Jersey. He might too have instanced England, pre-eminent for its cattle breeding since the eighteenth century. It is indeed the chief virtue of an enclosure system.

As regards insurance against a total loss of crops through blight, Koefoed thought the best protection was careful farming—one of the results of the *hutor* system. He thought the diminution of transport problems caused by the strip-system was a countervailing advantage which outweighed the possible insurance benefits of the unenclosed fields.

The agricultural expert thought it was ridiculous that the communal spirit of emulation should be required to spur on the less energetic members of the community— "the ballast of the village," as he calls them.[1] It was more significant that communal cultivation impeded the tendency of the more active farmers to improve their methods.

But the gravest question, Koefoed admitted, was that of the peasants who had little land. Actually these peasants would lose by enclosure, unless they were recompensed for their loss of the right of common pasture they previously possessed *de facto*, yet to which they had, Koefoed declared, no claim *de jure*.[2] These "little

[1] Koefoed, op. cit., p. 97. [2] Koefoed, op. cit., p. 97.

brothers" must be compensated as they had been in the West of Europe. However the "little brothers" were going to express themselves rather forcibly in 1917. In some ways, this point seems to the investigator to be the "crux" of the reform—the weakest link in the economic and social chain. The agricultural expert recognised that legislation would be needed to correct any such abuses likely to arise.

Next, was the peasant settled on a *hutor*, likely to "go wild," neglect his children's education, forget his religious duties and all his social relationships? Would the formation of co-operative societies be frustrated by the enclosed farm system? Would the new system lead to the accumulation of land in the hands of *kulaks*? On the other hand, would the system lead to a subsequent parcellation of territory in which the last stage would be worse than the first?

To these questions, it was Koefoed's answer that it was possible that temporarily the new independent farmer (*hutoryanin*) would see no further than his own plot, and would neglect his social functions. But Latvia and Finland, where the *hutor* prevailed, seemed in the long run to negative such ideas. The development of a social and educational sense was also pre-eminent in Denmark and Sweden, where enclosed farming was in vogue. The co-operative movement was certainly not backward in Denmark, where there was no *chrezpolositsa*. Its strength there was known generally.

There was, it was further stated,[1] no ground for the fear that there would be an "engrossing" of petty peasant property in the hands of the richer, who would find it cheaper to buy land elsewhere, in view of the increased price enclosed land was bound to obtain. While some peasants who were no longer farmers at heart were bound to sell their allotments, there was no need to fear that the *kulak* would take advantage of the situation to form excessively large *hutors*. It is appropriate to state here that large numbers of non-farming peasants did ulti-

[1] Koefoed, op. cit., p. 101.

mately sell their allotments, and the question of "engrossing" of peasant land was debated in the Third Duma before the final elaboration of the Stolypin legislation in 1911. The Danish remedy[1] was to prevent the removal of homesteads from the individual farm. On the other hand, "parcellation" of *hutors*, noticed in Scandinavia, might require legislative interference.

After again enumerating the various advantages which *razverstanie* (dividing up) would bring, Koefoed reflected upon the question of the need of raising the peasant's cultural values, while remarking that cultural needs are widely spread only among those whose physical needs are satisfied. (Cf. Danton's declaration carved beneath his monument near the Odéon, Paris: "Après le pain, l'éducation est le premier besoin du people.") If the new scheme, one imagines, preserved the peasantry from a repetition of the "hungry 'nineties," then it could be accounted a success.

The agricultural expert, however, revealed that he was not entirely a theoretician. " It is impossible to judge life and village development on city ideas"—a truth which many people, not alone in Russia, are apt to forget.

Physical conditions certainly required to be favourable as, for instance, water supplies, and there must be an area of cultivable ground to sustain a complete peasant-family through the whole year. He was not prepared to affirm definitely that the peasant land of Russia fulfilled those conditions.[2] In the east and south were areas where water supply rendered separate farms impossible. Reasons of safety also precluded them in frontier districts. Land-shortage was, Koefoed admitted, a fatal obstacle to the transfer of many peasant families to the *hutor* style of farming. It was impossible to obtain side-earnings on an isolated farm.

The size of the *hutor* would necessarily be determined by the district in which it was situated. It might range from 10 *desyatines* in the non-black earth region to 7 or 8

---

[1] Koefoed, op. cit., p. 102.   [2] Koefoed, op. cit., p. 105.

in the central black earth region and be even larger upon the "steppe" country.

In the case of the under-allotted *darstvenniki* (the recipients of the "beggarly" free land-grants at the Emancipation of 1861, of whom there were 600,000, mostly in the black earth regions), Koefoed offered no hope of advantage from land-settlement. Consequently, one must remark, these *darstvenniki* represented a definite revolutionary factor of discontent both in 1905 and in 1917.[1] It was important that the peasantry should be prepared and educated to accept the new idea. They were believed to be ready to do so in the western regions. It was desirable that the Peasant Bank should take an active part in the actual creation of *hutors* out of land which came into its hands and these *hutors* should preferably be sold to newcomers. Both of these points were adopted and had peculiar results among the peasantry who regarded the local squires' land as being their own reversion. The time was propitious (Koefoed thought) for the transfer of the village dwellings to the isolated farms, seeing that rural Russia was still a "wooden" edifice, stone being little used throughout the country. He thought that the Western German tendency to crave for social intercourse had not yet taken a hold in Russia. (Did events show that he was right?) Next it had to be decided what proportion of the village population would be needed to enforce the innovation: should it be two-thirds or less? This point was one of the chief questions which were deliberated during the elaboration of the Stolypin legislation.

It was desirable to include in the dividing up (*razverstanie*) all land whether communal or subject to "servitudes," and whether it was *nadel* (allotment) or purchased.[2]

These were the views officially published in July 1906, and adopted as the Government's aim and method in promoting agrarian change to save the political situation and strengthen the country's economic position by the

[1] Koefoed, op. cit., p. 107.   [2] Koefoed, op. cit., pp. 113–14.

establishment of a yeomanry of small holders, each possessing in his own right a self-contained farm. (The condensed description of the principles of the anti-communal legislation expressed to the writer by A. Savich, A. Guchkov's right-hand man in the Third Duma.)

From A. Tyumenev's carefully-compiled and statistically-exact description, *Ot Revolyutsii k Revolyutsii* (Leningrad, 1925), much may be gathered concerning the effects of the new decree of 1906. In his second chapter ("Revolyutsya 1905 g. i rassloenie selskovo naseleniya"), the author gives evidence that, before 1905, differentiation, which Lenin's *Razvitie Kapitalisma* (Development of Capitalism) had shown to be increasingly undermining the communal principle, was an unequally distributed phenomenon. It was confined, generally, to the less-congested areas of the "steppe" provinces, while leaving the danger zone of the peasant problem, the Central Agricultural Region and the Ukraine, practically untouched. In fact, these two regions exhibited a general decline of all types of peasant farming. The fringes of the "steppe"-country were those which were most clearly tending to capitalist accumulation.[1] But, until Stolypin's decree, the process was confined to extra-allotment leases and purchased property. Tyumenev, as a Marxian economist, valued the Stolypin Reforms because of their capitalist features and declared that it was through the liquidation of the old *nadel* that "differentiation," or the creation of capitalistic and labour groups in the village, became finally possible. The *obshchina* (commune) began to break up and *bourgeois* relationships began to spread over the countryside.

Before the revolution of 1905, the land commune (*obshchina*) had been predominant in Russia, save only in the western White Russian and Ukrainian Provinces. *Podvornoe vladenie* (heritable household tenure) represented 22·8 per cent of the *nadelnaya zemlya* (allotment land). This relatively small amount was concentrated solely in the western regions—Baltic Provinces (100 per

[1] A. Tyumenev, *Ot Revolutsii k Revolutsii*, p. 24, Leningrad, 1925.

cent), Lithuania (100 per cent) and Ukraine (90–100 per cent), White Russia (25–50 per cent). Generally speaking, the remainder of European Russia—Great Russia in particular—was predominantly communal. There were a few islands of "podvornoe" landownership representing the results of differentiation effected outside communal bounds (Herson, 6·7 per cent; Tauris [Crimea], 7·9 per cent; in Ekaterinoslav, only 0·8 per cent and Samara, 0·9 per cent). It was clear that communal ownership was not a purely nominal affair. In more than 70 per cent of all the communes general redivisions were still effected. In still more of the others partial redistributions were still in vogue. Only in 17 per cent of the communes had there been no redivisions at all. The *obshchina* was weak in functioning only in the north-west —the Lake Region and in the western areas. In the Lake Region, cases of non-functioning or weakly functioning communes amounted at the end of the nineteenth century to 55·9 per cent.[1] In the Western Region these amounted to 60 per cent. In the Central Industrial (Moscow) Region such cases equalled 25 per cent; in the Central Agricultural 27 per cent; in the Volga Region nearly 20 per cent. In New Russia (Black Sea Area) these instances were only 15 per cent (less than anywhere else). In the Eastern Region nearly 30 per cent and, finally, in the Northern Area 25–30 per cent. Lest one should draw the obvious conclusion that the land commune was especially strong in the most recently developed areas—those of New Russia and the Volga—Tyumenov was anxious to state that it was especially here that the greatest break occurred in the communal idea as a result of Stolypin's decree. One might add, naturally, because it was exactly on the Black Sea littoral and in the Volga interior that the suction of the Western European market for grain was acutely felt. They were to be fateful regions even after 1917.

The policy of Stolypin already decreed in November

[1] Kachorovsky, *Narodnoe Pravo*, 1906g., and Veniamonov, *Krestyanskaya Obshchina*, 1908, Tyumenev, op. cit., p. 25.

1906 was definitely reaffirmed before the new (Third) Duma a year later on November 10, 1907.[1]

By setting on its feet the numerous rural population and giving it an opportunity of achieving economic self-sufficiency, the legislative institutions will establish the basis upon which a sure transformation of the structure of the Russian State will be attained. There will be no indiscriminate bestowal of land, no pacification of sedition by gifts—sedition will be suppressed by force—but, instead, an acknowledgement of the inviolability of private property and, as a consequence ensuing therefrom, the creation of petty personal land-ownership, a real right of exit from the land commune and the decision of questions concerning the improvement of land-cultivation. Those are the tasks the realisation of which the Administration has considered and will consider as questions concerning the very existence of the Russian Realm.

Here it is obvious is a very definite exposition of the new State policy—a policy later discussed in the correspondence already mentioned between the Tsar and his Prime Minister when there was a dispute as to the authorship of the reorganisation scheme—the Tsar fearing that the Third Duma might claim credit for having ratified what the bureaucracy had put into force.[2] Reliance upon a potentially strong layer in the peasant world —"*stavka na silnykh,*" as the expression went—was to be the cardinal point in the new agrarian policy. Count S. Witte, indeed, mistrusted the violent methods instituted by the Stolypin decree[3] while approving and having himself already partially inaugurated some of its features.[4]

In the Second Duma—the "Duma of popular wrath" —Stolypin in the course of his battle to save the old order, now recovering confidence after the Viborg fiasco of the First Duma's appeal to the revolutionary instincts of the people, elaborated the basic principles of his Reform. He realised—as did, of course, the Govern-

[1] Stenographicheskie Otchety Gos. Dumy, Sess. I, Part I, p. 310.
[2] Krasny Arhiv, Vol. V, p. 122.
[3] Cf. Witte, *Vospominaniya*, Vol. II, p. 313.
[4] Cf. Witte, op. cit., Vol. I, pp. 404–5, and also S. Witte's Report on the Agrarian Question, January 10, 1906—*Agrarny vopros v Sovete ministrov* 1906g., M.L., 1924g., p. 80.

ment of which he was the spokesman—that to attain the frankly avowed political aim of the Reform, there must be economic self-sufficiency in the new class of "yeomen" who were to be the pillars of a rejuvenated agrarian system. In his speech on this occasion (May 10, 1907) he contrasted the socialist (*trudovik*) levelling of the "cheloveka lenivovo i trudolyubivovo, cheloveka tupoumnovo i trudosposobnovo" ("the idle and the industrious, the unenterprising and the capable") with the emergence of the "chelovek darovity, silny, sposobny opirayushchiysya na pravo sobstvennosti i na resultaty svoikh trudov" ("the talented, sturdy, capable man depending upon the right of ownership and on the results of his own labours"). Continuing, he stated that

the Administration's aim was quite definite: it desired the support of peasant landownership, it desired to see the peasant wealthy and satisfied since, where sufficiency existed, there must ensue education and real liberty.[1] But to attain that end it was necessary to give the capable, work-loving peasant (the salt of the Russian earth) the possibility of bursting those shackles in which he was then bound. The peasant must be given the means of securing for himself the fruits of his own labours and of keeping them as his inalienable property.[2]

"Secure individual ownership" was set in opposition by Stolypin to the "land-commune," as the chief "stimulus to toil" and as the "incentive which makes men work."

Compare the speech of the Minister of Land Settlement and Agriculture, Prince Vasilchikov, before the Second Duma (March 19) when he gave utterance to the following sentiments: referring to the definite intention of the Government to "spread abroad the benefits, resulting from the principle of property, over the huge territory of peasant landownership which so far had been deprived of such benefits," he adapted Arthur Young's words to the situation.

[1] Cf. Danton, "Après le pain, l'éducation est le premier besoin du peuple." Convention, Aug. 13, 1793.
[2] Stenographicheskie Otchety Gos. Dumy, Vol. II, pp. 437–41, 442.

The principle of property fertilises the labour of the agriculturist and it is only in combination with this principle that the agriculturist's work acquires that marvellous force which is capable of turning barren sands [*sypuchie peski*] into gold, and a howling desert [*goluyu skalu*] into a smiling garden [*svetushchy sad*].[1]

Before an examination is made of the extent to which the land commune diminished in influence or might be said to have been undermined by the *ukaz* of November 9, consideration must now be given to the increased pressure brought to bear by the Law of June 14, 1910. This law was certainly more drastic than the original measure. The Government felt more secure both at home and abroad. It had obtained the confidence of the Third Duma—somewhat lessened in value, it is true, as an indication of popular feeling. Nevertheless, the legislation which had been entirely bureaucratic in its origin, now acquired a constitutional form more in consonance with the spirit of the October Manifesto of 1905. Clauses 1 and 2 of the Act of June 14, 1910, made a distinction between village-communities which had redistributed their holdings since the original Emancipation Allotment and those that had not done so. Land communes whose land had been allocated before January 1, 1887, and which had never effected a general distribution since that date (i.e. for at least twenty-three years), were considered to have tacitly adopted a system of heritable tenure. Therefore all such villages became automatically in the eyes of the law identical with those under *podvornoe vladenie*. To achieve the physical enclosure of their land, individual holders in such cases were relieved of the necessity of obtaining titles to their land.

It might be objected here that there were "partial" as well as "general" redistributions of communal land and that the efficacy and virtue of the communal system lay precisely in the first type. Was there not here danger of the Administration's going ahead of popular consciousness? Did it give vogue to a "paper" creation of private

---

[1] Stenographicheskie Otchety Gos. Dumy, 2vo sozyva, Vol. I, p. 755; Tyumenev, op. cit., p. 72.

property? Did it deceive the Government as to the actual strength of the communal habit? One has to ask these questions in view of subsequent events.

The Government pressure in favour of enclosure was increased by the provision under Clause 45 for villages under *podvornoe vladenie* to enclose their holdings on the motion of a simple majority of the village assembly. Consider the effect of this clause in conjunction with that of Clauses 1 and 2 and one perceives the cumulative effect. It was a frontal attack upon the communal principle. Where, however, general redistributions had taken place during the preceding twenty-three years, a two-thirds majority was still required to secure *razverstanie*—a general separation of holdings.

The Law of May 29, 1911, codified the whole process and the Stolypin agrarian system was legislatively complete. The codification introduced several new principles —one especially being important concerning what must be regarded as the most desirable aim of the whole scheme —the actual enclosure of the lands nominally appropriated. It was the only way in which a real change in peasant life could be effected. Otherwise there was a danger that titles of private and personal property might remain utterly devoid of significance. Provision was now made for the immediate enclosure of any appropriated land.

The Act of 1911 allowed compulsion upon one party in certain cases, where enclosure was impeded. By Clause 35, any number of individuals could require enclosure at a general redistribution if their application had preceded the decision of the assembly to redistribute holdings. Clause 36 provided that apart from general redistributions, enclosures could be enforced if the applicants amounted to at least one-fifth of the families in a commune (of which the total membership did not exceed 250) or to at least 50 (if the membership of the commune did not exceed that number). Where injury to the rest of the village was unlikely even a single member could ask for it (Clause 36). Clause 37 allowed enclosure at the request of a simple majority of peasants of a communal village, where portions of arable land had been permanently appropriated. No agreement at all was needed under Clauses 23–7, with regard to parts of arable land which were appropriated as private property. Again, under Clause 37 no single peasant was allowed to prevent the technical perfection of a neighbour's farm by refusing to exchange strips to allow of consolidation.

With the addition of one provision of the Act of June 14, 1910, the survey of the relevant portions of Stolypin's legislation will, as far as this work is concerned, be concluded. That provision was meant to prevent undue engrossing of peasant land which, while being preserved as peasant land *in toto*, was to be redistributed among members of the class upon very strict lines. By Clause 56 an individual peasant was allowed to possess only 6 peasant allotments (*dushevoy nadel*) in any given district (*uyezd*). Such allotments were not to exceed in size the maxima fixed for Great and Little Russia at the Emancipation. Thus the belief which many people held that Russia had embarked upon a new policy of peasant capitalistic farms was, so far as the statutes were concerned, not substantiated. Even in its new and apparently *laisser-faire* policy, the Administration still preserved some of its old paternal ways of peasant control which seemed reminiscent of Alexander III's régime. If a *kulak* class were to develop it would have to do so, as of old, in a subtle and half-invisible manner—not assessable in terms of broad *desyatines*.

What, one may now ask, were the results of this legislative and administrative activity? The ideas of the expert Koefoed have revealed the setting of the new enclosure and private property movement. How far did the peasant rally to the new ideas and what strength was the Government likely to obtain in its struggle with subversive forces?

Some statistics concerning the movement in favour for private ownership among the peasants are instructive. They are as follows:

Tsar, Duma and Peasant

Years.	No. of Heads of Families asking for Appropriation of Land as their Private Property.	No. of Heads of Families finally leaving the Land Commune.
1907 (incomplete)	211,922	48,271
1908	840,059	508,344
1909	649,921	579,409
1910	341,884	342,245
1911	242,328	145,567
1912	152,397	122,314
1913	160,304	134,554
1914	120,321	97,877
1915	36,497	29,851
Total	2,755,633	2,088,432 [1]

As far as *nadelnaya* land was concerned 14,000,000 *desyatines* became private property. Compared with the number of communal holders of land, the number of applications for personal appropriation of allotments amounted to 30 per cent. The number of those who were ultimately successful in securing the ownership of their occupied area was about 20 per cent, while the quantity of land separated from communal tenure equalled 14 per cent. It was the less self-sufficient and the less fortunately situated as regards land that took advantage of the new Stolypin policy. They had lost hope of gaining a supplementary allotment and hastened to abandon their farming operations. The period between 1907 and 1910 was the climax of the separation movement. It coincided with the climax of the movement among a large number of squires to liquidate their own estates and leave rural pursuits.[2]

Furthermore (excluding the war-years 1914–15), it is evident that from 1910 the movement of separation began to decline. That fall was of course influenced by the Act of June 14, 1910. However, in connection with the issue of deeds allowing separation, there is the same

[1] Tyumenev, op. cit., p. 14.   [2] op. cit., p. 14.

tendency towards a rapid diminution in the numbers of those leaving the land commune. (May this fact be construed as a sign that the *obshchina* having, so to speak, jettisoned its excess cargo was once more on an even keel? This is Kachorovsky's belief).[1] Compare the following table:

Years.	No. of Communities and Villages Applying for Separation Deeds.		No. of Heads of Families Applying for Separation Deeds.
	Villages.	Heads of Families.	
1910	676	18,487	35,281
1911	4,024	111,350	140,841
1912	1,115	35,923	85,126
1913	676	19,295	82,898 [2]

It is Tyumenev's opinion that the decline in the number of "dissidents" from the commune could not be linked with the fact of the distribution of deeds of separation, since the two phases were prevalent over very different provinces and localities. According to the statistics of separation from the land commune, the following were pre-eminent: Samara, Ekaterinoslav, Kursk, Herson, Orel, Harkov, Saratov and Tambov, i.e. especially the central and southern areas. But according to deeds of separation the outstanding provinces were the western and (partially) central-industrial (Moscow):—Kaluga, Vitebsk, Mogilev, Moscow and Smolensk.[3]

To Tyumenev it seemed that the separation from the land commune resulted in the exit of two village elements —the pauperised layer giving up farming and thus securing its allotments simply for sale, and the more prosperous

[1] Cf. Article, *Slavonic Review*, 1929.
[2] Tyumenev, op. cit., p. 15. Extract from Minister of Finance's Report of Expenditure, 1915, Part 2, p. 17.
[3] Cf. Provincial data in Dibaylov's article in Agricultural and Land Settlement Department's publication for 1913, and also A. Kaufman's article, "Land Settlement and Land Policy," *Ezhegodnik Rech*, 1914; Tyumenev, op. cit., p. 15.

members who were freed from communal restrictions. The applications for general deeds of separation (relatively few) gave evidence rather of the relatively decadent structure of the redistributory commune in the area concerned.

The figures representing secessions from the *obshchina* were of a catastrophic character when compared with the numbers of peasants who left it between 1861 and 1906. While for the seven or eight years of the operation of the Decree of 1906 and the Act of 1910, the number of those leaving the commune and also of those receiving deeds of separation exceeded 3 million, the whole preceding 45 years gave as the total of such abandonment, only 140,000. The number of hereditary (*podvornoe*) holders of allotment (*nadelnaya*) land comprised 2,800,000 in 1905 and was thus less than the number of those leaving the commune after the Decree of November 9, 1906.[1]

A phenomenon of considerable interest as affecting the fate of the land which was removed from communal control is indicated by the data collected by the Free Economic Society concerning the years 1910–11. It is evident that the majority of those seceding from the *obshchina* desired to continue farming operations rather than to leave the countryside. Between 1907 and 1910 3,723,000 *desyatines* of allotment land was subjected to sale, there being a consistent rise in the yearly figures, the rate however decreasing certainly in 1911 and showing a slight actual decline in 1914.[2]

There was a rapid increase in the number of communal holders who sold their allotments, such cases amounting to 1,072,687—a slight actual decline occurring in the last year of the period from 1908 to 1914.[3] It may be noted that the Report upon Expenditure for 1915, Part 2, p. 18, gives a diminished figure both for land sold and for individual sellers—2,830,269 *desyatines* and 767,412 sellers respectively.[4] According to official figures at the

[1] Tyumenev, op. cit., p. 16.
[2] Cf. Table on p. 16 from *Statistical Year Book of Minister of Justice* and for 1907 *Statistics of Landownership*, Abstract XXIII.
[3] Statistics of Ministry of Justice.
[4] Tyumenev, op. cit., p. 16.

commencement of 1910 only 10 per cent of those seceding from the commune had sold their allotments ; but by the beginning of 1915 the number of sellers exceeded one million, a figure including particularly communal holders who had appropriated their land. These numbered 900,000, i.e. about 40 per cent. of all those leaving the commune at that time. Consequently, the quantity of land sold by them equalled 20–25 per cent of the total quantity of appropriated land. The excess of the percentage of sellers over that of the land sold by them was sufficient evidence to Tyumenev of the tendency for petty farming to decrease.[1]

It is clear to the investigator that the rapid "mobilisation" of peasant allotments and the simultaneous sale of squire estates were two aspects of the same phenomenon. "Latifundiary" and "communal" land-holding were declining in parallel. The *pomeshchik-krepostnik* (former serf-owning squire) and the *krestyanin-poluproletary* (semi-proletarian peasant) were each in turn leaving the stage for new actors to come upon the scene—the enterprising squire (*hozyaistvenny pomeshchik*) and the enterprising tenant (*hozyaistvenny muzhichok*).[2]

The growth of peasant wealth presages the final liquidation of large landownership in the near future. If already large landownership is as scarce as prehistoric animals [*kak zubry*], it will rapidly become a rare museum specimen and ultimately pass away.[3]

This change in rural relations naturally affected the old system of *otrabotki* (lease of land in return for labour), since the districts particularly affected by squire and petty peasant "evacuation" of the agrarian field were those where it had been strongest.

The new situation developing in rural Russia, which was to reinforce the Peasant Movement of 1917, had two aspects. Firstly, there was the squire who remained to manage his own estate, refusing to proceed by the old method of lease to the communal peasantry. "He was

[1] Tyumenev, op. cit., p. 17.
[2] Cf. Prince E. Trubetskoy, "Novaya Zemskaya Rossiya," in *Russkaya Mysl*, Dec. 1912.   [3] Tyumenev, op. cit., p. 17.

considered a fine farmer and as forwarding cultural aims." [1] On the other hand it is important to note the effect of the cessation of the old "latifundiary" methods upon the members of the land commune who had previously depended upon them partly for their own subsistence. There was such an instance in Petrovsk district, Saratov Province.

Before the estate of the Duke of Leykhtenberg was bought by the Peasant Bank, the peasants of surrounding villages, Danilovka, Stary Slazkin, Kamaevka, Marevka, Sinodskoy and others, used to lease it. That land, together with the land of Usov, adjacent to it, began to be divided into separate farms (*otrubs*) of 16, 18 and 20 *desyatines*. Previously, all those lands were utilised on lease by the peasants of the surrounding villages, who took one or two *desyatines* per household. Now, however, that land was to pass into the hands of 60 holders of separate farms (*hutors*) and all the remaining villagers had to be satisfied with their original allotments. But these allotments were such that "ovtsu ne prokormish, ne tokto—semyu" ("you could not feed a sheep upon them, not to mention a family"). A hopeless position was thus created for many villagers. There was no help but to leave the village community, sell one's allotment and find work of some kind elsewhere.[2]

Besides furnishing a vivid picture of the old system prevailing before the inauguration of the Stolypin Reforms of 1906, such cases make it abundantly clear that there were dangers ahead while peasant life was passing through such a difficult transition. Statistics indicating the progress of a new scheme such as that of Stolypin, inevitably cause one to overlook the fact that it was human beings with their complicated mental assortment of hopes and fears that were the raw material of the process of evolution.

Before 1905, how far could it be said that the peasants

---

[1] Cf. *Vestnik Evropy*, 1909, February, p. 727.
[2] Cf. I. Konovalov, "Na hutorakh," *Russkoe Bogatsvo*, 1910, January, pp. 35-6. There is a similar picture of the peasants' lack of land in the Orel Province in the same periodical for February.

were developing into two mutually differentiated layers? Lenin in his *Razvitie Kapitalisma v Rossii* (Development of Capitalism in Russia), 1898, studied the statistics relating to the 'eighties. But it is evident that the process of such differentiation was practically confined to the border steppe-lands with their wide expanse of unused territory rather than the congested areas of the Central Agricultural and Ukrainian Regions, with their relatively small land reserves.[1] But even in the border regions of the south, it was not upon the allotment land that this cleavage in the economic structure of the *obshchina* was being effected. It was rather upon purchased and leased land that the process had its chief field of action, that is for the more prosperous layers of the community.

The question whether the Stolypin legislation with its attempted limitation of the purchase of peasant holdings and of the excessive concentration of land in the hands of a few peasants, succeeded in its aim, is denied by Tyumenev who asserts, on statistical grounds, that "engrossing" did occur.[2] He is inclined to believe that the Peasant Bank assisted the process, principally by its direct sale of land to the peasants. Its policy was definitely one of favouring individual purchase as opposed to the pre-existing policy of collective ownership. Its activity too was no longer spread equally over the whole of the provinces of European Russia, but was almost exclusively confined to the Central Agricultural and Volga regions.[3]

Between 1906 and 1914 the amount of land purchased through the Peasant Bank reached the total of 3,321,789 *desyatines* of which an increasingly large proportion, amounting in all to 2,644,609 *desyatines*, was purchased by individuals. These figures afford some indication of the change in the Government's policy of collective purchase which was prevalent before the revolutionary period culminating in 1905.[4] The land commune was definitely

---

[1] Cf. Statistical Tables of Lenin, *Razvitie Kapitalisma*; Knipovich, *K voprosu o differentsiatsii russkovo krestyanstva*, 1912; Tyumenev, op. cit., pp. 20–3.
[2] Tyumenev, op. cit., pp. 42–9.   [3] Tyumenev, op. cit., p. 49.
[4] Tyumenev, op. cit., p. 50.

limited to its existing area—an additional factor in the pressure brought to bear upon its members to desert it and seek other avenues of activity. The year 1907 led most of the peasantry to abandon hope of *prireski* (supplementary lots) and buying of Bank-land proceeded rapidly thereafter. Whereas during the twenty-five years of the Bank's operations from its foundation (1883) to 1907, its assistance in the transfer of land had been confined to 207,000 *desyatines* for individual purchase and 9,525,000 for collective purchase, in 1908 alone, the year of obvious change, 152,000 *desyatines* were transferred to private use and 867,000 *desyatines* to collective use. The four years between 1909 and 1912 showed that separate individuals purchased 2,910,206 *desyatines*, while groups purchased a lesser amount of 2,353,000 *desyatines*.[1] It is clear from the above figures how fundamental was the cleavage between the old and new policies effected by the events of 1905. The Bank's activity was certainly galvanised very considerably, while, as mentioned earlier, the encouragement of individual appropriation of land corresponded with the spirit of the Decree of Stolypin of November 9, 1906.

An interesting phenomenon in relation to the Bank's promotion of land "mobilisation" is the contrast between its almost equally distributed operations in the years before 1905 and the concentration solely upon certain regions afterwards. It was in the Central Agricultural region (i.e. Provinces of Voronesh, Kursk, Orel, Ryazan, Tambov, Tula, in the Bank's classification) and the Volga areas (i.e. Eastern: Kazan, Penza, Saratov, Simbirsk, Ufa, and South-Eastern: Samara, Astrakhan, Orenburg [2]) that 60 per cent of the land purchased through the Peasants' Bank was to be found. If the amounts of land transferred in the Ukrainian region (i.e. Provinces of Poltava, Harkov, Chernigov, Volynia, Kiev and Podolia) and the New Russian (Black Sea) region (i.e. Bessarabia, Don,

---

[1] Tyumenev, op. cit., p. 53.
[2] N.B.—In the last two provinces little was sold. Tyumenev, op. cit., p. 54, footnote.

Ekaterinoslav, Tauris [Crimea] and Herson) are added to the preceding percentage, 80 per cent of the total is obtained. Consequently the Peasants' Bank's work was practically confined to those areas where both communal and squire-land were being placed upon the market, as a result of the new movements in social life.

The data concerning land settlement upon separate farms (*hutors*) also confirm the fact of the concentration of the Bank's influence in the above localities. The following provinces each possessed more than 100,000 *desyatines* devoted to *hutor* or *otrub* types of farming: Saratov (527,441 *des.*), Samara (359,962 *des.*), Penza (186,867 *des.*), Simbirsk (186,501 *des.*), Voronesh (134,728 *des.*). Those with more than 75,000 *desyatines* under such types of cultivation included Orel (99,666 *des.*), Harkov (90,172 *des.*), Ufa (89,537 *des.*), Tambov (79,365 *des.*), Herson (77,172 *des.*). Provinces with from 50,000 to 100,000 *desyatines* of such undertakings included those of Ukraine and New Russia.[1] Land settlement and land sale evidently went hand in hand.[2]

How far did the Peasants' Bank fulfil the object of its creation—the cure of peasant congestion and the provision of land facilities for the pauperised peasantry? The statistics of the Bank seem to imply that "landless" peasants were the most fortunate in securing farms and subsequently, according to the figures for 1906–11, becoming superior to all other purchasers in the dimensions of their holdings (average for "landless" 9·2 *des.*, for remainder 5·1 *des.*). There is evidently some misunderstanding as to the use of the term *bezzemelnye* (landless). S. N. Prokopovich[3] pointed out that in view of the prices required by the Bank and the considerable resources needed for the conduct of farms on purchased land, these *bezzemelnye* represented not the poorest but the wealthiest section of the village, having acquired their money either

---

[1] Tyumenev, op. cit., p. 54.
[2] Cf. N. Pershin, *Uchastkovoe zemlepolzovanie v Rossii*, 1907–1916, M., 1922, pp. 46–7.
[3] S. N. Prokopovich, *Agrarny Krisis i meropriyatiya pravitelstva*, M., 1912, p. 157.

in trade or service outside it. There were no village *batraki* (labourers) among them.

Furthermore, from the figures on pages 60, 61, 62, Tyumenev has secured much evidence that the separate farming (*hutor*) system encouraged by the Bank was a comparatively costly undertaking which flourished more upon Bank-land than upon land recently separated from the commune. In addition, the value of the farm stock and implements upon the separate farms (*hutors*) was much greater on the first than the second.[1] It is obvious that if a peasant were poor before 1906 he was not likely to become richer as a result of the Bank's policy. One must, of course, give the Bank credit for its work in helping to transform the stagnant villages into centres of commercial activity. But, socially at least, it is to be gathered that there was a residue of population in the rural areas, which gazed longingly on the new improvements but was powerless to share in them. Did that not have reverberations in the Peasant Movement of 1917?

Many peasants were unable to carry on their farming operations owing to financial demands upon them as a result of the new system. Details of such difficulties were revealed in articles of such periodicals as *Rech* (1910, November 10), *Russkoe Bogatsvo* (1910, February, p. 17, "Na hutorax," by Konovalov), not to mention the work of Finn-Enotaevsky (*Sovremmenoe Hozyaistvo Rossii*, p. 458). Economic differences were creating a certain amount of social tension in the village which might in the future require careful handling. The "amorphous peasant mass,"[2] as it had appeared through urban spectacles in 1905, was taking shape (or rather shapes), even as the *oblomov* (dilettante) element in the old *dvoryane* (squires) was being supplemented by new commercialising forces. The growth of production, particularly in the two or three years preceding the War of 1914, was creating not only a class of well-to-do peasantry but also a new class of urban business men who might be expected to

[1] Tyumenev, op. cit., p. 62, a ratio of 166 to 83 after purchase.
[2] Cf. Trotsky, *Russian Revolution to Brest Litovsk*, p. 2.

exert more influence as the years went by. Certainly it is true that the peasant element that was evolving into an embryonic class of rich farmers had stronger roots than the corresponding type of business man in the cities, who was dependent in many cases upon foreign firms or direct Government support. Industry subsidised, though to a less extent after 1910, by a succession of Government orders, was not in a position to assume a very independent political rôle. The simple fact of the great area of the country and its still relatively inadequate system of communications prevented a spiritual coalescence of these two forces. Thus is explained much of subsequent events. The village community was dissolving, but it took, like Charles II, "an unconscionable time in dying"—that is in the eyes of those enthusiastic supporters of the new policy of Stolypin who regarded the land commune as the chief evidence of Russia's economic backwardness.

The division that was changing socially and economically the content of the village community was most noticeable in the Southern and Eastern border regions (where it had scope even before 1905), besides the Central Black-Earth regions where congestion had impeded any such process before the Reform Decree of 1906. In the Northern and Industrial Provinces, the Decree of 1906 did not have such a fundamental effect. It involved a shaping and perfecting of long-standing relationships. The sections of the peasant element affected here were the semi-proletarian mass of those who worked in the towns but were still nominally of peasant condition. There were difficulties here, but they were not of the same type as those in the other regions. These areas were influenced more closely by the country's industrial evolution.

The existence of economic distinctions among the peasantry could be detected in an analysis of the returns of the Agricultural Census of 1917. (Cf. Table below.) The least change was evident in the Northern (Vologda Province), the White Russian and the Ural regions. In the Lake (Petrograd) and Industrial (Moscow) regions there was a one-sided extension of the pauperised elements, while there was no corresponding growth of large farming enterprise on peasant land. Any capital that was accumulated here usually left agriculture and was withdrawn to the urban areas. Greater variation in the size of peasant holdings was to be seen in the Central Agricultural region. The most obvious differentiation was evident in the Lower Volga region (Astrakhan, Saratov and Samara) which resembled the "steppe"-country and offered more scope than the others for extended farming.

CENSUS OF PEASANT AGRICULTURE, 1917 [1]

Regions.	Unsown.	Very small. Up to 1 des.	Small. 1–4 des.	Average. 4–8 des.	Large. 8–22 des.	Very large. Over 22 des.
Northern	8·9	14·4	68·2	8·2	0·3	—
Lake	15·5	18·0	55·2	10·2	1·1	—
Central Industrial	13·8	15·5	56·4	12·9	1·4	—
White Russian	8·3	4·8	50·0	30·0	6·9	—
Central Agricultural	8·0	10·8	45·8	24·6	10·3	0·5
Ural	8·0	4·5	36·6	34·9	15·6	0·4
Middle Volga	9·8	7·2	45·2	27·0	10·6	0·2
Lower Volga	30·9	3·5	17·3	20·7	23·6	3·7

A stage has now been reached when to complete the picture of the work of Nicholas II's Prime Minister, Stolypin, in trying to turn the country from a revolutionary path, a description must be given of the degree of success of the establishment of isolated (*hutor*) or self-contained (*otrub*) farms. For they are the touchstone of the success of the Stolypin Reforms. The simple assertion that a certain number of strips in an open-field state (*chrezpolositsa*) belonged to a particular peasant would have been valueless as a sign of progress. The right *de jure* had to be validated *de facto*. Technical change must reinforce statute law if there was to be a creation of a new conception of property among the mass of the

[1] Hryashchev, *Vestnik Statistiki*, 1920, Sept.–Dec., p. 36.

peasantry. Again it must be remarked that the year 1917 tested in a very drastic fashion the foundations of this new technical betterment—the most essential feature in the changes initiated on November 9, 1906.

In the *Russkaya Mysl* of December 1913, Prince E. Trubetskoy described the new Russian countryside (*novaya zemskaya Rossiya*). Two new facts struck him as being worthy of chronicle. One was the growth of prosperity and the noticeably rapid development of a new social spirit. On the other hand, it was evident "that in the village was being created a powerful petty *bourgeoisie*."[1] This new class was quite alien "both to the ideals of the united gentry and to socialist dreams." It seemed to the author that the general transfer of the peasantry to personal ownership of separate farms, and the increase of prosperity among the rural population, must in the future prevent any repetition of the terrors of a general rising (*pugachovshchina*). But (an investigator may ask) was the time that elapsed between the inauguration of the new policy (November 9, 1906) and the Russian military defeats of 1915 sufficient to consolidate such a fundamental change affecting the vast mass of the population? Could the habits of long years be transformed in a decade? How far was this apparent progress of the Government's ideal of peasant personal property simply nominal?

It has been shown previously that 30 per cent of those that left the land commune did so in order to sell their holdings and abandon farming. Others left the village community to take advantage of the virtual subsidy granted by the Government where an approaching redivision threatened to reduce their allotment, which was in excess of the village normal, owing to decline in the numbers of their households. According to the rural correspondents of the Free Economic Society, such cases represented the majority. It was, it seems, only a section of the comparatively well-to-do village class which separated from the land commune in order to live

[1] Tyumenev, op. cit., p. 73.

like "miniature squires" (*malenkimi pomeshchikami*) on their permanently separated territory. The larger number preferred to remain in the commune.[1] It seemed to be evident that the solution of "the most difficult and colossal question of our time" [2] was that of the areas of congested population (the problem termed "land-shortage "). "No one imagines that one means alone can solve it," continued Petrunkevich in his address to the First Duma. There was indeed a "mass of questions linked up with the peasant question" as Rodichev, the well-known Liberal member for Tver, rightly remarked to the same legislative body.[3] Between the First and Second Dumas there had been effected an extension of peasant landownership through the Peasant Bank. Stolypin in his speech to the Second Duma had announced the necessity of assisting the peasant land deficiency by use of the "existing land reserve."[4]

After the convocation of the Third Duma with its majority favourable to the Government, the policy of extending peasant communal landownership was gradually abandoned, and an insistence was made upon personal ownership and completely separate farms (*hutors*), especially upon land bought from the squires. The policy of November 9, 1906, caused greatly increased mobility in land purchase, but corresponding technical progress represented by the development of the self-contained farms had relatively insignificant results. The great difficulty in the way of the adoption universally of the *hutor* or *otrub* forms of farming was exactly the difficulty which the old communal system was finding it so hard to face, i.e. lack of sufficient land per peasant family. Russian agriculture was of the extensive type. The methods of farming were largely primitive. Therefore, separate, self-contained holdings needed abundant acre-

[1] Cf. Chernyshev, *Obshchina posle 9 Noyabrya 1906g.*, 1907g., Vol. I, p. 48; also pp. 133, 169, and Vol. I, p. 167; Vol. II, p. 140; Tyumenev, op. cit., p. 74.
[2] I. I. Petrunkevich, member of First Duma. Stenograficheskie Otchety Gos. Dumy, Sess. I, Zased. 13, May 23, 1906, Vol. I, p. 569.
[3] Ibid., Zased. 4, May 27, 1906, Vol. I, p. 81.
[4] Ibid., 2 sozyva, Part II, pp. 442–3.

age. The average area required naturally varied, but almost everywhere it considerably exceeded that of the peasant allotment in the different regions.[1] According to *Zemstvo* and "Free Economic Society" enquiries the minimum required for a separate farm was as follows (the average peasant "allotment" [1905] is placed in parentheses following the Provincial figure):

Orel Province 15 *des.* (7 *des.*), Tula Province 15–50 *des.* (6·3 *des.*), Ryazan Province 10–50 *des.* (6·6 *des.*), Voronesh 15–30 *des.* (6 *des.*), Tambov Province 8–50 *des.* (7 *des.*), Nizhegorod Province 13 *des.* (7·4 *des.*), Kazan Province 16 *des.* or (according to the data of the *Zemstvo* Correspondent) 30 *des.* (8·6 *des.*), Samara Province 25–30 *des.* (19·8 *des.*), Ekaterinoslav Province 20 *des.* (9·3 *des.*), Chernigov 10–15 *des.* (6·3 *des.*).[2]

It is clear from the above figures what a gulf yawned between the required area for a successful individual farm and that of the average existing peasant holding. When it is remembered that a great number of those farms, even of the desired dimensions, on Peasant Bank land were forced into subsequent liquidation, the significance of the above situation becomes manifest.

Yet the process of consolidated individual farms proceeded apace in the southern and Black-Earth provinces, even exceeding the capacity of the existing Land Settlement Staff. The peasants themselves realised the advantages of the new system.[3] Their chief objections were the prevailing land-shortage and the absence of cattle-pastures—a vital item in a system of cultivation relying upon natural fertilisation of the soil and the use of draught-animals (with hardly any mechanical power) for the labour involved in farming.

[1] Tyumenev, op. cit., p. 75.
[2] Chernyshev, op. cit., Vol. I, pp. 24, 54, 67, 84, 110; Vol. II, p. 12. Also *Ukreplenie nadelov v lichnuyu sobstvennost v Kazanskoy gubernii 1911g.*, p. 84, and *Podvornoe i hutorskoe hozyaistvo Samarskoy gubernii*, Samara, 1909, Vol. I, p. 77. *Otchet po issledovaniyu hutorskovo hozyaistvo v Verkhnedneprovskom uyezde*, 1908g., Zemsky Sbornik Chernigovskoy gubernii 1909 goda, Vol. XII, pp. 82–3. Tyumenev, op. cit., pp. 75–6.
[3] Cf. Sir Bernard Pares, *Russian Memoirs*, Chap. XI, "Stolypin's Land Settlement, 1910–1911."

If there were more land, then, of course, the self-contained enterprise would be a good thing, since it would be possible to fertilise the land when necessary, and conduct rational agriculture.[1] The self-contained farm system is acknowledged to be better than the communal, on theoretical grounds, but there must be sufficient land and, under conditions of land-shortage, it is impossible to conduct separate farming.[2]

Similar expressions emanate from Ryazan, Tula and Orel. "Horosho na hutore, u kovo semya bolshaya, da zemli desyatin 30" [3] ("Settlement on a self-contained farm is satisfactory for a person with a large family if the area of land is equal to 30 *desyatines*"). There is an epigrammatic flavour, which smacks of Roman Martial in his less vindictive moods, in the remark from Penza, "Obshchinnoe vladenie polezno dlya skota, a podvornoe dlya poryadka" ("Communal land-tenure is good for cattle pasturing, but individual (family) tenure for law and order").

Tyumenev, for all his criticisms of the methods of the policy, believed that the Government was acting in response to necessity in embarking upon the course it took. The *obshchina* he thought was a decrepit institution even in the central Black-Earth regions, not to mention the western and south-western districts. In the seven or eight years after Stolypin's Decree had been officially issued, great changes occurred, especially upon the newly-created separate farms. Nevertheless, such opportunities of improvement were open mainly to the already fairly prosperous groups.

To the poorer members of the land commune the expenses of conducting a separate farm (*hutor*) were a great strain. Some of such owners allowed their husbandry to decline to the same level as that of their old communes.[4] There was a particularly sharp distinction

---

[1] Voronesh, Chernyshev, op. cit., Vol. I, p. 23.
[2] Tambov, Chernyshev, op. cit., Vol. I, p. 51.
[3] *Ukreplenie nadelov v lichnuyu sobstvennost v Kazanskoy gubernii*, Kazan, 1911g., p. 84.
[4] Cf. I. Konovalov, "Na hutorakh," *Russkoe Bogatsvo*, 1910g., Jan., p. 36.

between the two types in the Orel Province.¹ Another significant statement is made in the same periodical of the same date.² Wealthy owners of *hutors* were rich peasants long before the laws about Land Settlement. If the information ascertained by certain *Zemstva*, at the request of the Ministry of Land Settlement, is soundly based, then it seems that the line of distinction between successful and unsuccessful farming peasants was not equivalent to that separating individual and communal holders. A pauperised section of independent farmers (*hutoryane*) was also evident. Out of 142 investigated cases in the Pskov and Ostrov districts of the Pskov Province (with a separate farming tradition dating from the 'seventies and 'eighties of the nineteenth century), nearly 25 per cent of the holders had been compelled to abandon their enterprises between 1885 and 1906. A number of less well-endowed farms in the Moscow Province were either abandoned or leased to other people.

Information from Kiev seems to indicate that the cost of the transfer to the new type of farming was such as to ruin many—the repayment of the Peasant Bank's advances playing no small part in the process.³ Information contained in the *Zemsky Sbornik Chernygovskoy gub* (1909g., pp. 83–5) definitely describes the separate owners as employing technical methods no different from those of their neighbouring *obshchinniki*. The "quality and quantity of the livestock"—a strong point, one would imagine, on an enclosed farm, "remained on a low level." ⁴ Koefoed, whose views at the initiation of the Reform have previously been discussed, is quoted by Tyumenev as stating that, despite the cessation of *chrezpolositsa* (the strip system), the cardinal fact of land shortage was a fatal obstacle to successful maintenance of separate farms (*hutors*) by the poorer peasantry. The absence of adequate pasture affected the numbers of

---

¹ Cf. *Russkoe Bogatsvo*, 1910g., Feb., p. 5.
² *Russkoe Bogatsvo*, 1910g., Feb., p. 5.
³ Cf. *Hutorskoe hozyaistvo Kievskoy gubernii*, Kiev, 1911g.
⁴ Tyumenev, op. cit., p. 87.

live stock. The consequent lack of draught animals and fertilising products made it impossible for them to proceed.[1]

The next question—and a very serious one for the success of the Reform of 1906—is: did actual farming improve generally in such critical nerve-centres as, in 1917, the Central Agricultural and Middle Volga regions became? (The provinces included are Voronesh, Tambov, Ryazan, Tula, Orel, Kazan, Nizhegorod, Penza, Simbirsk and Saratov.) In the words of I. Chernyshev, who reviewed the results of the Free Economic Society's Enquiry of 1911, "At the time of the investigation, the abandonment of the land-commune had not noticeably changed the character of cultivation either in the case of those who remained communal-holders or in the case of those who had left it." Betterment of farming methods was a universal phenomenon.[2] The question of maintenance of stock—the cardinal point one must again insist, of such cultivation as Russia knew—was the chief difficulty of those who left the commune.[3]

In 1915 were published the results of a survey of the autumn of 1913 conducted by the Land Settlement Department itself. It embraced twelve districts situated in different regions. Its conclusions showed the relative prosperity of the northern *hutors* and the comparative degeneration of those in the south.[4] The *Kievskaya Mysl* of 1910, No. 153, revealed the Governor-General of Kiev as asserting that peasant land-shortage was the principal obstacle to the widespread development of the *hutors*.[5] Certainly one may note Kiev did not lead in regard to *hutors*, despite its high farming culture. According to the *Ezhegodnik Rechi*, 1914, p. 99, the Agricultural Con-

[1] Koefoed had of course made remarks of a similar character in those works which have already been discussed. See earlier, and also "Opyty samostoyatelnovo perekhoda krestyan k hozyaistvu na otrubnykh uchastkakh nadelnoy zemli," *Izvestya Russkovo Geogr. Obshchestva*, Vols. I and II, pp. 220–1. Tyumenev, op. cit., p. 88.

[2] Tyumenev, figures on p. 89.   [3] Chernyshev, Vol. I, pp. xxiv–v.

[4] "Svodnye dannye o zemleustroitelnom hozyaistve v 12 uyezdakh." Tyumenev, op. cit., p. 90.

[5] Tyumenev, op. cit., p. 90.

ference at Kiev in 1913 adopted a negative attitude towards Land Settlement, although it was not opposed on principle to individual enclosed farming.

Relying upon the statistics and information he had conscientiously collected and assessed,[1] Tyumenev was of the opinion that the transfer to enclosed farming methods which, in the southern and central Black-Earth regions, was a widespread phenomenon, did not justify the expectations of the authors of the Decree of November 9, 1906. Yet, the successful adoption of enclosed farming was, he thought, a touchstone of the individual peasant's self-sufficiency—a kind of "natural selection." Many peasants on enclosed farms who did not possess adequate financial backing or were paralysed by their paucity of pasture-land were in a hopeless position. The Peasant Bank's policy of building up enclosed farms from the lands vacated by the squires after 1906, assisted considerably the already well-to-do layer in the commune. Those members of land-communes who simply took advantage of the new legislation to secure title-deeds to an area which a subsequent redistribution might have diminished, and who did not cease to be farmers of unenclosed land (*cherespolosniki*), exhibited the defects and not the advantages of both the communal and the enclosure systems. Their farming retrogressed.[2]

What effect did the new legislation have upon those who remained in the *obshchina*? It must be remembered that these communal peasants were still in the majority, even after ten years' Land Settlement work. The mode of utilising the land of those of the gentry who forsook their country estates inevitably influenced the *obshchinniki* (communal-holders), who generally relied upon *otrabotki* (labour-leases) as an additional means of livelihood. Such diminution of available local land reserves was emphasised by the exodus from the commune, which further removed the "very ground from under their feet." The system of *otrabotki*, with all its drawbacks, and the

[1] Tyumenev, op. cit., p. 103.
[2] Cf. Chernyshev, Vol. I, pp. 52–3; Vol. II, p. 70.

possibility of securing leases beyond the village boundaries played a large, even if unsatisfactory, part in the poorer peasants' budget. Such petty leaseholders were inevitably ruined. A case in point occurred in the Saratov Province—on the Ogarevka Estate. There were 2,000 *desyatines* of arable land on the estate and a few hundred *desyatines* of woodland. The estate was offered to the Peasant Bank, but a transaction was not effected, because the owners wanted 140 roubles per *desyatine* and the Bank offered 120 roubles. Then the owners offered the land to the peasants of those villages which had previously cultivated it themselves, i.e. Chernavka, Tuguska, Sorokino, Danilovka and others. The land was secured by the peasants, either for a cash payment of 25–30 roubles, or alternatively cultivated on a somewhat original *metayage* or *mezzadria* system, giving two-fifths to the peasant and the remainder to the squire, all work in connection with ploughing or harvest being incumbent upon the leaseholders. Meadows were subject to the same conditions. Tuguska and Sorokino were in a particularly difficult position, since it was they who primarily depended upon the land now for sale. Their allotments were small. There was no additional land elsewhere. Tuguska, indeed, was surrounded by squires' land on three sides, on one by that of Aplecheev, on another by that of Danilov and on a third by that of Ogarev. The Danilov estate however was also for sale. If the villagers did not secure the Ogarev Estate they were inevitably subjected to the economic dominion of the remaining squire, Baron Aplecheev. "Zemlya eta vot kak neobkhodima, shto tolko nu! . . . Bez nee nam kaput . . . Pryamo nado govorit, shto esli zemlya eta uydet iz nashikh ruk—lozhis i pomiray! Odno slovo!" ("You see how necessary this land is, come now! Without it we are ruined. . . . We must say, without beating about the bush, that if this land passes out of our hands —lie down and die will be the only thing to do.") But while discussion raged in the village *skhod* (assembly), the more prosperous peasants bought the estate. The peasants of Ogarevka, Sorokino, Danilovka and Tuguska "upustili zemlyu iz-pod nosa", ("let the land go under their very noses"), and "ne uspeli rta razinut", ("could not even open their mouths"), as they saw it belonged to *novym pomeshchikam* (new squires). Tuguska thus remained in the complete control of the remaining Squire Aplecheev. Some peasants abandoned their holdings, others entered into agreements with the new owners of the estate.[1]

Furthermore there ensued the gradual wreckage of the machinery of redivision. This process, whatever its many defective sides, and discounting any sentimental idealisation, did play a practical part in the less fortunate peasants' economy. Dissension invariably arose. "U nas ukreplyalas zemlya na umershie dushi" ("among us land has been appropriated for 'dead souls' [non-existent persons"]), wrote peasant correspondents. "Eto nam ochen obidno, umershy i poluchil, zhivomu cheloveku net".[2] ("It is very annoying to us that a dead man has received land while there is none for the living.") Such expressions might have been neglected if subsequent events in 1917 had not rendered them significant. A definitely expressed hostility to seceding members was evoked. This feeling was to be a strong weapon in the hands of revolutionary parties after Nicholas II's downfall in February 1917.

From the enquiries of the Free Economic Society, it appears that there was little actual "free agreement" evident in the loosening of the communal bond. It is rather striking to find that 75 per cent of the secessions were obtained without the local communities' consent by officials who frequently relied upon force.[3] If this state of affairs is correctly reported, then Koefoed's advice at the initiation of the Reform was being ignored. The Kazan *Zemstvo's* enquiries present corroborative testimony on this score.

[1] Cf. Konovalov "V derevne", *Sovremenny Mir*, 1909, Feb., pp. 26, 31.
[2] Tambov Province. Chernyshev, Vol. I, p. 47.
[3] Cf. Chernyshev, Vol. I, p. 165; Vol. II, p. 137.

Hostile manifestations towards separating members of communes often assumed bitter and barbaric forms. Fires, murders, and conflicts involving bloodshed were by no means rare occurrences. There was even a case of almost unbelievable atrocity in the drenching with oil of a departing member by his fellow villagers, who burnt him like a live torch.[1]

One is reminded of the rioting of Luddites against the implications of the newly industrialised England of the late eighteenth and early nineteenth centuries or of the agrarian outrages in Ireland. The less fortunate peasantry, seeing their village *nadel* land shrinking, and their former squires' estates parcelled out into *hutors*, which they had not the money to buy, were driven to migrate "across the Volga." Such cases happened in the Saratov Province, if Konovalov's account is reliable.[2] Some peasants in Penza Province, unable to purchase the new farms on Peasant Bank Land, still hoped for "ot tsarya nadeleniya zemley" ("land allotments from the Tsar").[3]

Whereas in eight years after the initiation of the new policy, communal landownership increased by one million *desyatines*, there was an area of 14 millions to be subtracted on account of seceding members. While in 1907 the amount acquired by communes was 350,000 *desyatines*, the year 1912 saw it decline to 36,169 *desyatines*.[4]

The Russian village like a disintegrating chemical compound was capable of producing electric currents of high potential, disastrous in the "short circuit" of 1917, when other factors which commenced to operate in 1915 assisted the explosion. The intensity of feeling was accumulating most noticeably in the Central Black-Earth and the Little Russian regions where relics of old bondage conditions were still prevalent. In the western and south-western regions, where the changing conditions harmonised to a greater degree with earlier tendencies,

---

[1] Cf. Alekseev, "Ocherki novoy agronomicheskoy politiki," *Sovremenny Mir*, 1909g., Sept., pp. 236–9.
[2] " Zemleustroiteli," *Sovremenny Mir*, 1909g., Oct., pp. 8, 9, 21.
[3] Chernyshev, op. cit., Vol. II, p. 142.
[4] Tyumenev, op. cit., Table, p. 110.

the results were not so deleterious. The Central Industrial region likewise presented a more fertile field for innovation, seeing that the peasantry who left the commune (*obshchina*) and could not become independent farmers (*hutoryane*) were possessed of commercial outlets of activity. The northern regions were more adapted to the new conditions than those of the centre and south.[1]

If one sums up the results of the Agrarian Reforms of Stolypin together with their extension at the hands of the Third Duma, one finds that the technical development of *hutor* and *otrub* did not correspond with the advance in the assertion of rights of peasant private ownership. This weakness was due to land-shortage—the old bane of Russian extensive agriculture—and to peasant poverty. The degree to which enclosed farming was successful corresponded to the resources possessed by the more fortunate peasants. These fortunate peasants were able to profit, particularly by the disintegration of the old communal allotment system, and partially by the breaking up of such squires' estates as had been previously rented by the respective village communities. It may be clearly understood therefore how the hostile feeling of the less fortunate members of the village communities came to express itself during the agrarian revolution of 1917.

At the conclusion of this section is to be found a statistical analysis of the results achieved by Land Settlement (*zemleustroistvo*). What were its effective achievements before it was submerged in the social cataclysm of March–October 1917? The labours of the Land-Settlement staff led to no inconsiderable results, despite the immensity of the undertaking. Even as early as the beginning of 1912, the Land Department could proudly proclaim[2] that its operations had already embraced an area equal to 32 per cent of Austria-Hungary, 39 per cent of Germany, 40 per cent of France, 43 per cent of Spain, 48 per cent of Sweden, 67 per cent of Norway, 69 per cent of Great Britain, 76 per cent of Italy, and exceeded

---

[1] Tyumenev, op. cit., p. 113.
[2] *Itogi Zemleustroistva*, Izd. 1912, St. Petersburg, Table 4.

that of any of the remaining individual countries of Europe. Out of a total of almost 12,000,000 holdings of peasant *nadel* land, 1,303,300 were enclosed and consolidated. Out of the total area of 118,156,900 *desyatines* of such land, 12,652,300 *desyatines* were thus reorganised. The proportion of enclosed and consolidated holdings equalled 10·9 per cent, and that of area, 10·7 per cent.

But great as had been the work of the Settlement Staff, there still remained unconsolidated 89·1 per cent of the holdings and 89·3 per cent of the area. Almost 90 per cent of both area and holdings was untouched. When the great convulsion occurred, the "vested interest," so to speak, of the *otrubniki* and *hutoryane* (individual peasant owners) on allotment land involved only 1 in every 10 peasant holders. And when one remembers that the aim of the Reforms of the Stolypin period was the creation of absolutely separate and enclosed farms (the *otrub* being only an intermediate stage to that ideal), it is clear that the physical disruption of the old communal village occurred in an amount of 3 per cent, at most, of the original allotment-holdings.

There were provinces which considerably exceeded the general Russian average of enclosed and consolidated farming. Ekaterinoslav (33 per cent holdings, 32·6 per cent area), Taurida (32 per cent holdings, 24·9 per cent area), both in the Southern Black Sea region; Vitebsk (31·6 per cent holdings, 26·1 per cent area), Petrograd (31·3 per cent holdings, 27·7 per cent area), both in the north-west of the country, were the provinces which achieved the greatest progress in Land Settlement (*zemleustroistvo*) as far as the actual number of holdings was concerned. In addition, Stavropol (in the Northern Caucasus region) showed the greatest progress in area (35·4 per cent) under Land Settlement despite the fact that its ratio of enclosed holdings was less (24·9 per cent). It should be noted that the new system met with the greatest success in all cases where the provinces concerned were not far removed from maritime trade-routes. In addition

Ekaterinoslav, Taurida and Stavropol possessed relatively less densely populated fields of activity. Vitebsk and Petrograd, too, could copy the example of the neighbouring Baltic Provinces where self-contained farms were universal.

As a safeguard against a peasant revolt the agrarian schemes of the inter-revolutionary decade were obviously quantitatively inadequate. That a large section of Russian public opinion regarded them as qualitatively insufficient helped to reinforce the revolutionary wave which determined their fate. This revolutionary wave forms the subject of the remaining sections of this work.

But before the peasant aspect of the Revolution of 1917 is considered, it is desirable to listen to the diagnosis of Russia's agrarian problems by an historic figure who was destined soon to seize the Government of a disintegrating State. What then were the views of Lenin? How did the International Socialist analyse his native country's cardinal social problem?

RESULTS OF THE FORMATION OF ENCLOSED HOLDINGS OF THE "HUTOR" AND "OTRUB" TYPES ON ALLOTMENT LANDS FOR THE DECADE 1907 TO 1916

Provinces.	Total No. of Holdings.	No. of Holdings Enclosed and Consolidated.	Percentage of Enclosed Holdings.	Total Area of Allotment Land (in *des.*).	Total Area of Enclosed Holdings (in *des.*).	Percentage of Area in Enclosed Holdings.
Archangel . .	55,100	300	0·5	334,800	1,900	0·5
Astrakhan . .	67,000	5,800	8·6	1,902,300	182,600	9·5
Bessarabia . .	284,600	23,900	8·4	1,864,000	142,000	7·6
Chernigov . .	367,400	14,600	3·9	2,329,200	94,100	4·0
Don Territory	130,700	13,000	9·9	577,800	120,000	20·7
Ekaterinoslav .	270,800	90,500	33·0	2,531,100	825,300	32·6
Grodno . .	91,700	11,100	12·1	1,517,200	94,400	6·2
Kaluga . .	172,000	10,200	5·9	1,391,600	84,200	6·0
Kazan . . .	374,600	20,500	5·4	3,205,400	135,400	4·2
Kharkov . .	364,100	87,800	24·0	2,662,100	534,300	20·0
Kherson . .	294,300	70,700	24·0	2,291,200	529,900	23·1
Kiev . . .	383,500	35,400	9·2	2,106,800	163,600	7·7
Kostroma . .	239,800	8,400	3·5	2,136,400	76,900	3·5
Kovno . . .	110,400	24,600	22·2	1,610,400	326,000	20·2
Kursk . . .	335,300	28,000	8·4	2,455,400	172,100	7·0
Minsk . . .	213,900	14,400	6·7	1,946,000	188,000	9·6
Mogilev . .	198,300	29,800	15·0	1,619,300	305,200	18·2
Moscow . .	120,600	20,000	16·5	1,584,600	126,900	8·0
Nizhni-Novgorod	264,700	20,600	7·7	1,970,200	119,500	6·0
Novgorod . .	214,200	20,400	9·5	2,886,900	275,600	9·0
Olonets . .	66,600	1,000	1·5	4,335,600	66,900	1·5
Orel . . .	287,200	17,000	5·9	2,009,100	122,300	6·0
Penza . . .	241,000	23,500	9·7	1,814,000	158,800	8·7
Perm . . .	520,500	12,500	2·4	8,337,500	34,800	0·4
Petrograd . .	106,500	33,400	31·3	1,031,000	287,500	27·7
Podolsk . .	458,800	11,300	2·4	1,754,200	34,800	1·9
Poltava . .	446,900	50,100	11·2	2,195,500	229,700	10·4
Pskov . . .	158,900	29,000	18·2	1,460,600	274,700	18·8
Ryazan . .	280,900	15,200	5·4	1,885,000	77,400	4·1
Samara . .	337,100	87,400	25·9	6,712,300	1,927,300	28·6
Saratov . .	351,100	64,900	18·4	3,349,000	739,800	22·0
Simbirsk . .	244,900	21,000	8·5	1,658,300	148,600	8·9
Smolensk . .	215,900	39,100	18·1	1,936,100	393,000	20·2
Stavropol . .	140,200	34,900	24·9	1,788,000	633,400	35·4
Tambov . .	406,000	26,900	6·6	2,848,200	178,100	6·2
Taurida . .	132,900	42,600	32·0	1,957,500	487,500	24·9
Tula . . .	214,100	26,300	12·2	1,350,300	136,700	10·1
Tver . . .	302,900	26,600	8·7	2,641,600	264,600	10·0
Ufa . . .	318,700	18,700	5·8	6,251,800	344,800	5·5
Vyatka . .	482,500	4,700	0·9	7,718,000	50,100	0·6
Vilna . . .	94,400	12,600	13·3	1,278,700	120,000	9·3
Vitebsk . .	138,600	43,900	31·6	1,593,100	416,300	26·1
Vladimir . .	243,000	13,600	5·5	2,162,500	109,700	5·0
Vologda . .	238,000	8,400	3·5	3,699,400	104,400	2·8
Volhynia . .	292,400	37,400	12·7	2,298,900	272,000	11·8
Voronezh . .	388,600	35,000	9·0	3,746,400	246,000	6·5
Yaroslavl . .	198,600	14,000	7·0	1,420,600	120,000	8·4
Total . .	11,950,000	1,303,300	10·9	118,156,900	12,652,300	10·7

N.B.—Figures concerning enclosed holdings are taken from the collection *O Zemle*, Vol. I, Moscow, 1921, Appendix II; those for the total number of farms and the total area of allotment land refer to 1905.

The above table is reproduced in *Russian Agriculture during the War* (Antsiferov and Bilimovich), published by Carnegie.

CHAPTER III

LENIN AND THE PEASANT MOVEMENT

To link the name of Lenin—an industrial internationalist —with a peasant rebellion—a congeries of localised village risings—may seem paradoxical to many. Yet without peasant participation the revolutionary outbursts of 1905 and 1917 would never have achieved any great social significance. If manorial *usadbas* had not been burning in the cantons and the peasant soldiery had not broken with the disciplinary traditions of the past, it would have been ridiculous for a combined Left-Wing Social Democratic and Left-Wing Social Revolutionary Group to have hoped to achieve their objectives in 1917. The failure of the Bolshevist "coup" in July could not but have been duplicated in October.

There were indeed many factors operating upon the political situation of Russia at the end of 1917. Village disintegration was certainly not the least. And Lenin was not the first Russian revolutionary who relied upon peasant discontent to effect a radical transformation of the existing order. If he was an internationalist whose ideas transcended frontiers, he was, too, pre-eminently Russian in his revolutionary pedigree—a kind of inverted Pobedonostsev.

It must not be forgotten that a temporary political alliance between Left Social Revolutionaries and Bolsheviks effected the final downfall of Kerensky and put the seal of ratification upon the peasant rebellion. The Bolshevik attitude to the contemporary agrarian question therefore requires elucidation. That elucidation is best given in the words of the Party Leader himself.

It is interesting to find that in estimating the agrarian

side of Lenin's policy his own colleagues had diverse views. Some like Zinovyev, Kamenev and Trotsky were inclined to regard it as a sort of modernised *narodnichestvo* and even clothe it in sentimental garb. Others, such as Stalin, saw it purely as a means to an end—the socialisation of the world's activities and the dictatorship of the class which alone could secure that aim.

According to one of them (G. Zinovyev, 1924) "the first new idea that Lenin introduced [into Marxism] was his outlook upon the peasantry . . . the union of a working-class revolution with a peasant war." Further, the same Marxian colleague on another occasion during the same year asserted that "the question as to the rôle of the peasantry is the fundamental problem of Bolshevism, of Leninism." [1]

Another colleague possessed of the same Marxian view of world problems (L. Trotsky) thought that it might be surprising to characterise Lenin as *narodnik* (a peasant socialist). Yet he considered that to direct a revolution such as had occurred in Russia, obviously required "an organic connection that sprang from the deepest roots." [2] Trotsky, it is interesting to note, thought that Lenin "outwardly resembled a peasant" and indeed had something about him which was "strongly suggestive of a peasant." There was, facing Smolny, "a statue of Karl Marx wearing a black frock coat . . . but it was quite impossible to imagine Lenin wearing a black frock coat." [3]

Further Trotsky asserted that "the peasant element was the basis of Leninism so far as it was the basis of the Russian 'proletariat'." He was even prepared to regard Lenin as leader of the *populist* (peasant) element. In his eyes Chernov—the leader of the peasant element in the Constituent Assembly—"embodied the epigone of the old intellectual revolutionary tradition," while Lenin on the other hand was "its consummation and complete victory." [4]

[1] Pravda, Feb. 13, 1924.   [2] Ibid., No. 86. April 23, 1920.
[3] 7th All-Russian Party Congress, April 5, 1923.
[4] *Lenin*, Trotsky, p. 155.

The above opinions, written after the close of the Civil War (1917–21) in a period of party strain and stress, seem strange upon the lips of avowed Marxian Internationalists. They heralded the well-known post-revolutionary party cleavage—a cleavage made abundantly clear by the next quotation. Its author is Stalin.[1]

Some think that the essential foundation of Leninism, its starting point, is the peasant problem, the rôle of the peasantry, the importance of the peasantry. This is absolutely wrong. The essential foundation of Leninism, its starting point, is the question of the dictatorship of the proletariat, the question how that dictatorship is to be established and strengthened. The peasant problem, the question how the workers in their struggle for power are to secure the support of the peasants, is a subsidiary one. . . . Lenin would have been nothing more than a peasant philosopher that literary wiseacres are fond of depicting had he been content to study the peasant problem not on the basis of the theory and tactics of the dictatorship of the proletariat but independently of this base and apart from it.

According to the last quotation, Lenin's treatment of the peasant problem was based upon tactical considerations. There was to be a struggle for political power in the Russian State. The Bolshevik leader did not respect or reverence peasants *qua* peasants but his Party was not the only one that saw in their discontent a major revolutionary factor.

It was precisely Lenin's strategy on the agrarian point which enabled his Party to secure power, although it was definitely Marxian and hence, like its Western European cousins, prone to regard urban factory development as the *sine qua non* of successful revolutionary activity. It happened that in Russia there was a regimented agrarian population possessing some of the characteristics that Marx had deemed indispensable for his desired proletarian aims. The increasing pauperisation of a large section of the peasantry, tied as it was to the *nadel* (allotment), the arable portion of which, until 1906, was not available for private ownership, produced an actual rural

[1] *Problems of Leninism*, 1926, pp. 15–16, Stalin.

proletariat. While technically non-proletarian in the sense of its holding of a land allotment, this group was finding it increasingly difficult to retain its grip upon the other physical agents of production such as ploughs and draught cattle.

Even before the outbreak of the revolutionary disturbances of 1905, Lenin had turned his eyes upon the agrarian problem, thereby revealing the fact that he remembered that the father of the Russian Marxian Party, Plekhanov, had himself been a *narodnik* or agrarian socialist. Lenin as an agitator recognised that, if the revolutionary Hercules were to succeed, he must endeavour to lift the autocracy, Antæus-like, from its earthen base, the peasantry. And it is exactly in the development of this principle that Lenin differentiated himself from most of his fellow Marxians. It was thus he was able to appropriate the extreme wing of the agrarian Socialist Revolutionary Party, the heirs of the old *narodnik* or peasant socialist doctrine. Their aims were similar as far as the transfer of land to peasants actually working it (*trudovoe polzovanie*) was concerned. Lenin did not mind walking arm in arm with the whole undistinguished peasant mass as he did in 1917, always provided that his ultimate aim—the socialisation of all the activities of the citizen with the elimination of individual profit—was not retarded. His aim was not a transfer of the attributes of private property from *dvoryanin* (squire) to *krestyanin* (peasant) but rather the extension of the principles of the old peasant *nadel* (allotment) to cover the whole landed property of Russia.

Lenin's evolution in his treatment of the agrarian question may be traced firstly in his analysis of the Social Democratic Party's programme in 1902.

How did he then approach Russia's cardinal political and economic problem?

In such a peasant country as Russia, an agrarian programme of socialists naturally appears mainly, if not exclusively, a "peasant programme," a programme determining the relationship towards "the peasant question." . . . Our party is quite young in Russia

—all the old Russian socialism being, in the last resort, "peasant" socialism.

The objectives disclosed in the programme of the Social Democratic Party (February 1902) which he was criticising contained, one may note, many of those requirements which Social Revolutionaries (1901) and the *Zemstvo* Group (1904) also advocated. This fact reminds the historian that it is wrong to ante-date the crystallisation of organised parties in Russia. It was largely the events of 1904–5–6 that definitely moulded the modern political trends of the country. The Social Democratic Party, before its split in 1903 into the so-called "Menshevik" and "Bolshevik" sections, desired: (1) The abolition of redemption and any other payments which fell upon the peasantry as a depressed class. (2) The return of money paid under the heading of redemption or rental dues; (3) to enable this restitution to be made the Party advocated the confiscation of monastic estates and Imperial Family lands and the imposition of a tax upon squires who had received redemption payments. (4) The establishment of peasant committees (*a*) in order to secure the restoration to village communities, by expropriation or, if in third party hands, by repurchase, of those lands which were "cut off" (*otrezany*) from peasant holdings at Emancipation (1861), and helped economically to reinserf them to the squires; (*b*) to abolish remnants of bondage conditions still existing in the Urals, the Altai, in the West and elsewhere. (5) The legal reduction of unduly high rents and the invalidation of agreements of a secretly-binding character.[1]

Lenin necessarily was interested not in the "peasantry" as a legal "estate" but in the development of an economic cleavage in the village which might ensure the overturn of the Autocracy. In fact, at this period—in common with, not only Social Revolutionaries, but also the more extreme *Zemstvo* Group (tending towards the Union of Unions, *Soyuz Soyuzov*), the destruction

---

[1] pp. 325–6, "Agrar. Prog. Russk., S.D.," *Leninsky Sbornik*, III, 1925.

of the historic Autocratic Power was put foremost. Accordingly Lenin agreed with the "minimal" programme for the urban industrial side but, conversely, was prepared to go as far as the furthest agrarian "maximalist" to destroy the political power of the squires.[1] He emphasised however that this policy did not correspond with his Party's final aim but only with immediate requirements.[2] The "maximum" at that date was represented by the demand for the return of *otrezki* (lands cut off in 1861)—such a policy being as far as it was possible to go at the moment.[3] The rural policy was directed against the *krepostniki-pomeshchiki* (serf-owning squires).[4] The urban industrial creed of the Party led towards the final aim of control over all production and distribution. In that cardinal respect the Party did not share Social-Revolutionary views. But the village must be "purified from all relics of bondage."[5] The Social Democrats must support fully a policy equivalent to that of the Social Revolutionaries—one that would effect a *bourgeois* revolution like that of France in the eighteenth century. In the countryside must be attained what the *krepostniki-pomeshchiki* (serf-owning squires) could not give and what could "only be attained by force through a revolutionary peasant movement."[6]

Thereafter the future Bolshevik leader dealt with the problem of the validity of the *narodnik cherny peredel* (peasant socialist general redivision) as contrasted with "nationalisation" of all (including peasant) *nadel* land. In this particular, Lenin's inevitable split with the future "Mensheviki" and even with the "Father of Russian Marxism," Plekhanov, became clear even in 1902. The coming schism—pregnant with great results not only for the Social Democrats but also for Russia and the world—did not depend simply upon Lenin's insistence upon the rigidity and unification of party

---

[1] Ibid., p. 331.   [2] Ibid., p. 331.   [3] Ibid., p. 331, footnote.

[4] N.B.—Lenin remarked that he did not use the term "feodaly" owing to its questionable application to the Russian *pomestnoe dvoryanstvo* (landed gentry), although he said he was inclined to do so.

[5] Ibid., p. 332.   [6] Ibid., p. 332.

activity. Beneath that lay the equally, if not more significant, attitude towards the land question. Lenin was in favour of assisting a general peasant rising, even if it seemed to imply a stabilisation of petty farming. He was not in favour of acknowledging the peasant's individual right of ownership even to the contemporary family or communal land. The *cherny peredel* was, he recognised, one of the most emphatic slogans of the *narodnichestvo* (peasant socialism). It contained (he asserted) both reactionary and revolutionary elements. On one side it embraced a "reactionary utopia" tending to universalise and perpetuate petty peasant ownership. To that idea Lenin was fundamentally opposed. On the other was the revolutionary desire to remove by a peasant rising all remnants of the old bondage relationship. That second aspect Lenin regarded as being capable of development for his ultimate proletarian aim.

"Nationalisation of all land," however, went further than the idea of the *cherny peredel* which was liable to be confused with *kustarnichestvo* (petty home industry). A call for "nationalisation" (itself not necessarily "socialist") would be incorrect either under the Autocracy or under a semi-constitutional régime. Such a policy would in the absence of democratic institutions serve to divert attention to "senseless experiments in State socialism rather than to give an impetus to the free development of the class-war in the village." Despite his desire (as shown in his original draft discussed with Plekhanov and the rest of the Social Democratic circle) to put forward a definite "nationalisation" scheme, Lenin agreed that the moment (1902) was inopportune. But the future Bolshevik leader emphasised that, as a "*bourgeois* measure," nationalisation could imply simply the transfer of land-rent to the State, so as to hasten capitalistic enterprise in agriculture.[1] But if private management were preserved while private ownership of land was abolished, then it would be reactionary to make an excep-

[1] "Agrar. Prog. Russk., S.D.," *Leninsky Sbornik*, III, 1925, p. 353.

tion of the peasant holder.¹ How much later history is embodied in this apparently simple statement! Even a *"bourgeois* nationalisation" should lead to a development of large farming enterprises in the same way as factory legislation tended to encourage large undertakings in industry.

To conclude Lenin's view of the agrarian problem on the eve of the impending peasant rising of March 20, 1902, in Little Russia, one may summarise it as follows: Firstly, there ought to be a clear path for the development of the class-war in the village, with no *narodnik* sentimentality. Secondly, all relics of bondage must be removed, the transfer from such economic bondage to capitalistic conditions being inevitable. Thirdly, while having no illusions as to the viability of petty production under capitalism, he emphasised the need for a revolutionary abolition of the old agrarian survivals. The *otrezki* should be restored, thus liberating the peasantry from *de facto* slavery (*rabstvo*).

> *We thus become—by way of exception and by force of special historic circumstances—defenders of petty ownership but we defend it only in its fight against the old régime . . . to attain complete freedom of movement, of the use of land, and the abolition of "estate" distinctions . . . against that most powerful and oppressive relic of bondage— the Tsar's Autocracy.*²

From the above one may gather Lenin's ideas upon the combination of a proletarian socialist future with a rustic and communal revolutionary present. Plekhanov, who had earlier been a *narodnik*, but had later despaired of the *narodnik* dream in the 'eighties, now saw a younger thinker searching for allies among the peasantry in whom he had himself lost faith as a revolutionary force. A temporary cleavage between the sections thereafter styled "Mensheviki" and "Bolsheviki" rent Social Democracy in twain. When the great struggle of 1905–6–7 was past, Lenin stood apart from his old colleagues. How

¹ Ibid., p. 354.   ² Ibid., p. 362, Kamenev, 1925.

did he reorient his revolutionary ideas to the Russia of Stolypin and the Third Duma?

What were Lenin's views as revealed in his critical essay of 1908?[1]

Firstly, Lenin quotes statistics relating to landed property in the year 1905 in the fifty European provinces of Russia. A "ruined peasantry crushed by bondage exploitation" held $10\frac{1}{2}$ million holdings over an area of 75 million *desyatines* (2·7 acres per *des.*), giving an average of 7 *desyatines*. The "middle" or "average peasantry" held 1 million holdings embracing 70 million *desyatines*, with an average of 46·7 *desyatines*. Finally, what Lenin regarded as *latifundia*, based upon peasant labour utilised under bondage conditions, included 30,000 estates, representing an area of 70 millions, giving an average of 2,333 *desyatines* per holding. Thus according to the table, there were in all 13,030,000 holdings covering 230 million *desyatines*, with an average of 17·6 *desyatines* per holding. An amount of 50 million *desyatines* was not distinguished according to ownership, which brought the total area of landed property to 280 millions, with the average thus increased to 21·4 *desyatines*.

The descriptive title of the first group in Lenin's table calls attention to his ideas upon types of economic relationship between employer and employed. The power of the employer with money resources contrasted with the weakness of the individual labourer with simply his labour to sell, produced a wage standard as fixed by the employer which, in Lenin's Marxian views, became the typical capitalistic labour contract. Hence arose the worst forms of exploitation. The Russian peasantry, however, particularly in the Central Agricultural and Middle Volga regions, occupied economically a peculiar semi-bondage, or pre-capitalistic, position. The employer, in this case usually the squire, possessed land but little ready money. The smaller peasantry, as in the first section of the table, possessed an allotment of land in 1905, but they had not sufficient for subsistence. If

---

[1] Lenin's Works, Russ. Edit., Vol. XX, Part I, pp. 273–303.

he were to continue cultivation in his native area, the peasant of this type had to obtain extra work locally, whether from the squire or from a richer neighbour. The conditions of this work would be determined by the employer who would be assisted by the competition between similarly situated peasants. A kind of "profit sharing" might arise instead of the capitalistic money wage. It was this arrangement that Lenin styled "bondage exploitation." The use of the term "bondage" in view of the specific conditions in the Russian countryside, inevitably possessed condemnatory colouring, even more than did the term "capitalistic." Peasants of course had ceased, since 1861, to be legally in bondage to their squires. Therefore Lenin's implication, as one might expect from a revolutionary, was, that in economic fact, if not in legal theory, large numbers of the peasantry —the overwhelming proportion—were actually living under the conditions of bondage.

But Lenin's chief point was the Marxian belief that it was only through the agency of the true proletarian or hired wage earner under a capitalistic system that a social revolution could be achieved. Then after a period of increasing capitalistic differentiation in the village between a new peasant *bourgeois* class and the increasing number of wage-labourers, a *borba v derevne*, or village class-struggle, would result in a socialist structure. An intermediate stage, leading to the elimination of the relics of the old serf-owning class as landowners, might cause a coalescence of the "bourgeois" and proletarian layers of the peasantry, thus impeding the village class struggle. Lenin did not regard such a coalescence as economically desirable. Yet he was prepared to accept it as a temporary measure—an emotional experience which would assist his ultimate ideal.

How does Lenin commence his analysis of the agrarian problem? He examines "the economic foundations and essence of the agrarian upheaval in Russia," as shown by the table already mentioned. He believed that the table vividly illustrated the cause of the revolutionary struggle in Russia. Thirty thousand owners of *latifundia* mainly belonging to the gentry and Imperial Appanage (Land Endowment) Department owned about 70 million *desyatines*. That was the "basic fact" contrasted with another of equal significance, that $10\frac{1}{2}$ million peasant households or other small owners held 75 million *desyatines*. The question of the degree of cultivation of the respective areas was not considered here by the writer.

The Agricultural Census of 1916 gave information regarding a total of 15,600,000 peasant household farms and 110,000 non-peasant farms employing hired labour. The peasantry owned 21,200,000 horses, while the remaining owners possessed 1,400,000. The peasant farms contained 25,800,000 head of cattle. The other non-peasant farms possessed 2,200,000. The population upon peasant farms equalled 82,300,000, while non-peasant farms represented 2,300,000. The area sown upon peasant farms was 64,020,000 *desyatines*, whereas that upon non-peasant farms was 7,600,000.

Lenin, viewing the situation purely in terms of area, maintained that the holdings of the small peasant cultivating class could be doubled if the *latifundia* owners were expropriated. That view was shared by many publicists and was expounded in the First Duma, 1906. The "essence of the agrarian crisis" was the fact that

millions of small, ruined, impoverished peasants, oppressed by need, ignorance and the relics of serfdom, could not live otherwise than in a semi-bondage dependence upon the owners of *latifundia*, working the owners' land with their own [peasant] implements and livestock.

This system was perpetuated by the peasants' need for pasture and meadow land to maintain their draught animals, or alternatively, simply as advances to tide them over the winter period. It resembled, one may note, the Roumanian semi-bondage system described by Mitrany.[1] It is interesting to remark that the peasant, while increasingly becoming pauperised before 1906, was

[1] *Land and Peasant in Roumania,* Carnegie.

still a landholder possessed in most cases of plough and plough-teams. Many of the larger estates depended upon leases to peasants and upon peasant means of production for their cultivation. It was this pre-capitalistic system which Lenin considered to be at the root of the agrarian trouble. The large owner was deprived of the need to indulge in high-farming, while the petty peasant household was deprived of the possibility of becoming a small independent farming entity in prosperous conditions. While in some cases the peasant used the extra-allotment lease from the large owners for profit, the peasant desire for land expropriation was conditioned by the fact that many households which required such extra land for subsistence were led by theories of *trudovoe polzovanie* (cultivator-ownership) to ignore the property rights which seemed needlessly to impede them. Lenin believed that the bulk of the leasing was for subsistence only.

The system of *otrabotki* or payment by personal work on the lessor's estate in return for a lease, seemed to Lenin to smack of the old *barshchina* (*corvée* or compulsory serf labour). It was a restoration of old pre-emancipation ways. The method of exploitation was not "the divorce of the cultivator from the land, but a forcible economic connection between the ruined cultivator and the land."

It was not the capital of the large owner but the simple fact of his possession of land that enabled him to exercise power over the peasant, even to the extent of utilising the primitive wooden plough (*sokha*) instead of modernised equipment. To Lenin, such relationship seemed not "free contract but liberty mortgaged at the hands of a usurer." As far as the peasant who was on the margin of poverty was concerned, such a statement was comprehensible. Yet so far as the peasant family was on a higher level of consumption it would be an exaggeration of the facts. Consideration will later be given to the proportion of peasants who could not be legitimately described as being in such conditions.

How did the mode of tenure affect the productive

efficiency of the cultivated area? According to Lenin's statistical material, crops on peasant *nadelnaya zemlya* (land allotted to the peasantry at the Emancipation of 1861 and liable to redemption payments) averaged 54 *puds* per *desyatine*. On non-peasant land cultivated capitalistically, or in other words, for the market, with the holder's own stock and hired labour, the average return was 66 *puds*. Under a system of share-tenancy, or extra-allotment lease, the average return was only 50 *puds*. The fact that large estates, cultivated under this quasi-bondage, or competitive lease, system, gave lower returns than even the most exhausted area represented by the peasant *nadel* or allotment, seemed to prove that it was not an economic advantage to the country.

The large estates were, in Lenin's view, the main obstacle in the development of Russia's productive forces. Increasing population led to congestion, particularly in the Agricultural Centre, where the struggle to secure leases caused the rents to rise, and enabled the large estate-owners to profit by the actual poverty of their neighbours, without being compelled to increase the efficiency of their farms by improved technique and modernised equipment. Since the peasants actually did utilise large portions of the so-called *latifundia*, the idea of *trudovoe polzovanie* (cultivator-ownership) was not a text-book theory, but an expression of an existing economic fact which undermined the property rights of the large landowners. It is the key to the agrarian movement in the Central Agricultural and Middle Volga Provinces. The supplementing of the peasant allotments would add about 12 per cent to such allotments, according to the figures of the 1916 Agricultural Census. Increase of population led in 1928 to the absorption of the addition. Hence additional land was but a palliative. Better technique and equipment were required.[1]

From the facts described above Lenin derived the conclusion that the capitalistic development of Russia

---
[1] Lenin, op. cit., p. 275.

might choose two paths. The *latifundia* might be maintained and gradually become the mainstay of capitalistic agriculture in the Prussian way, with the Junker or Squire as the master of the situation. This road meant economic subordination for the cultivator, while the productive forces were likely to be impeded as they had been in Russia between 1861 and 1905. Alternatively, a revolution might result in the destruction of the large estates of the squires, leading to the American type of the "free" farmer working on a "free" soil, that is, a state of affairs in which mediæval traces of feudal or communal subordination were banished. The American type of capitalism led to the quickest rate of development of the productive forces and was the most advantageous for the mass of the people of all forms under capitalistic conditions.[1]

The Russian Revolution was not a matter of "socialisation," the panacea of the *narodniki* or *populists*, which was a "petty *bourgeois*" concept, but a matter of the direction which the capitalistic development of Russia would follow —the Prussian or American. This economic basis of the revolution must be clearly understood.

Before proceeding further one must consider the question of the precise meaning of "socialisation." It might imply simply a transfer of ownership from squire to actual peasant cultivator (*trudovaya sobstvennost*)—a "social" but not "socialist" revolution—or further, the use or "user," by the actual cultivator, of the national land-fund (increased by expropriation of squire and church estates) which was termed *trudovoe zemlepolzovanie* (use of land by cultivator) and did not permit formal alienation of the soil which would lead to the rise of a new landowning class. Much of the discord between Right and Left Social Revolutionaries and between Bolsheviks and Mensheviks centred round the implications of the term "socialisation."

Lenin proceeded to discuss the "essence of the agrarian upheaval" which, he maintained, was obscured by the

[1] Lenin, op. cit., p. 275.

Constitutional Democrats.[1] Between 1899 and 1905 both types of capitalist agrarian evolution had already materialised—the "Prussian," or gradual development of the large farm under capitalistic conditions, and the "American," or differentiation among the peasantry, and the rapid development of the productive forces on the freer and more spacious south. Such development in the south was leading to the transition from sheep to wheat growing.

Lenin believed that the defeat of the *latifundia* owners would cause a great development of technique and cultivation and that the cultivable area would grow ten times as rapidly as it had been increasing since 1861. In further statistical elaboration, the writer declared that out of the total number of *desyatines* available in Russia,

	i.e. 1,965,000,000 *des.*,
nothing was known of	819,000,000 *des.* Hence there were
only	1,146,000,000 *des.* to consider
of which	469,000,000 were being utilised,
	300,000,000 being forest land.

In the Bolshevist's view, the immense area lying unused would rapidly become fit for cultivation if the *latifundia* were eliminated. Lenin, criticising the "liberal populist" economists, states that they believed in a policy of "supplementary allotments (*dopolnitelnoe nadelenie*) based upon the assumption that there existed a land shortage in the "Centre," while Siberia and Central Asia were not ready for migrants. The implication was, thought Lenin, that if there were no land-shortage, the *latifundia* could be left untouched. But the Marxian viewpoint must differ. Until there was a check to the process of consolidation of large holdings or *latifundia*, there would be no rapid development of the productive forces of the Centre or peripheries. Presumably Lenin here did not refer to large farming in the strict sense as such, but to the type

---

[1] This Party was predominant in the First Duma and strong in the Second, and was prepared to make radical changes to suit the peasantry, but upon a compensatory basis.

of large holdings dependent upon competition for leases in over-populated regions.

In his second chapter, the Bolshevik leader reviewed the agrarian programme of the Russian Social Democratic Labour Party in the light of the events occurring during the Revolution of 1905. The fundamental error of all preceding programmes of the Party consisted in the fact that there was a haziness of thought as to the type of the capitalistic agrarian evolution of Russia. The Mensheviks, at the Stockholm Conference (held shortly before Lenin's exposition of his views), had suggested "municipalisation" or a delegation of the land question to "local" committees as opposed to "national." That policy meant a neglect of the most important aspect of the question—the "economic." Instead of a true Marxist analysis, "political" considerations and demagogy had prevailed. This defect, in the writer's mind, was only partially conditioned by the fact that the Stockholm Conference was dazzled by the December days of 1905 and the First Duma's short and stormy career in the middle months of 1906. Plekhanov (formerly a *narodnik* [populist] and later the pioneer of Marxism in Russia) had supported the "municipalisation" policy propounded by the Menshevik Maslov, thereby in Lenin's eyes "completely misunderstanding the economic contents of the peasants' agrarian revolution in a capitalist country.[1] Lenin declared that it was either this that was the interpretation of Plekhanov's action or, alternatively, there was evident an attempt to secure peasant support by the use of demagogic policies or deceit, a method unworthy of a Marxian. If there existed an economic possibility of a rapid development of capitalism thanks to the victory of the peasantry, the significance of such a victory must be made quite clear. What was the road of agrarian capitalism and what was the system of relationships in land-holding which corresponded to this victory of the "peasants' agrarian revolution"?

The "municipalisers'" main argument was based upon

[1] Lenin, op. cit., pp. 276–7.

the view that the peasants were hostile to the nationalisation of land destined to be distributed. Maslov, the speaker representing the "municipalisers," exclaimed that there would not simply be one "Vendée," but a general rising of the peasantry against the attempt of the State to interfere with the peasants' *own* allotment lands, and against an attempt to nationalise them.[1] (Lenin showed his scepticism of the prospect of such a general peasant rising by inserting "How terrible!") N. Jordania (who later became President of independent Georgia and escaped when the Bolshevik forces reconquered it) at the Second Conference exclaimed,

> To go to peasants with the word "nationalisation" would be to drive them away from us. The peasant movement would pass us by, or would be against us, and we should find ourselves overboard after the revolution. Nationalisation weakens Social Democracy, cuts it off from the peasantry and thus weakens also the revolution.[2]

This statement was very apposite in view of the actual progress of events in 1917. Lenin's standpoint in 1908 with regard to it was characteristic. "If the peasants are hostile to nationalisation—the Menshevik view—is it not obvious that it is ridiculous to accomplish the peasants' agrarian revolution against the will of the peasants?"

The Bolshevik leader was much concerned over the question of the attitude of the Russian peasant to "nationalisation" of land. He noticed that P. Maslov, in 1905, had declared that "nationalisation" of the land, as a means for the solution of the agrarian problem, could not then be accepted in Russia because it was "hopelessly utopian." Would the peasants agree to "nationalisation"?[3] But Lenin was unconvinced, seeing that Maslov himself in the periodical *Obrazovanie* (1907, No. 3, p. 160) had stated that all the *narodnik* (populist) groups: the *trudoviki* (those who desired cultivator-ownership),

---

[1] *Protocols of Stockholm Conference*, p. 40.   [2] Ibid., p. 88.
[3] P. Maslov, *Critical Remarks on the Agrarian Programme*, Moscow, 1905, p. 20.

the *narodnye* (people's socialists) and the *sotsialisty-revolyutsionnerye* (social-revolutionaries), had declared in favour of nationalisation in one form or other.

To the Bolshevik leader's mind, Maslov's own words indicated the disappearance of any "new Vendée," or of any general rising of peasantry, against "nationalisation." The question was to become a very sore point in 1917. Even later it led to divergence among the victorious Bolshevist or Communist Party. The fact which emerged from the controversy was that the word *krestyanin*, or "peasant," had more than one signification. The more prosperous layer naturally had no desire for "nationalisation." But how strong economically was that layer? Could it replace the moribund squire-farming class? That was the problem Stolypin's legislation tried to solve. The habits springing from communal-tenure of the *nadelnaya zemlya* (allotment land) were in Lenin's favour, although he himself, as a Marxian, regarded the *mir* (commune) as a relic of *krepostnoe pravo* (bondage) to be eliminated along with the *pomeshchik* class itself.

Maslov, according to Lenin, alleged that the "Labour Group" (*trudoviki*) had assented to "nationalisation" from "petty *bourgeois*" considerations, "thanks to their desire for a central power." That the allegation was unfounded Lenin was at pains to prove. He quoted the Agrarian Bill introduced by the Labour Group (*trudoviki*) in the First and Second Dumas. Its 16th paragraph stated: "the control of the national land-fund shall be vested in the local government authorities, to be elected by universal equal, direct and secret suffrage, which, within the limits established by law, shall act independently." On the other hand, the Social Democratic Labour Party's agrarian programme as passed by the Mensheviks spoke as follows: "The confiscation of privately-owned lands, small holdings excepted, and their transfer at the disposal of democratically elected local authorities of the larger administrative areas" (covering urban and rural districts) (Cl. 3).

Lenin pointed out that, in his view, the difference

between the programmes did not consist in the words "control" (*zavedyvanie*) and "disposal" (*rasporyazhenie*). (He noted that an amendment substituting for the words "at the disposal," the words "into the ownership," had been rejected at Stockholm by the Mensheviks.) The fundamental difficulties consisted in the question of an indemnity (rejected at Stockholm by Bolshevist votes), and of peasant-held lands. The Mensheviks wished to treat peasant land upon a special basis but the Labour Group (*trudoviki*) did not. Therefore Lenin believed that the Labour Group had proved to the "municipalisers" that he was right, since he did not believe in giving peasant land exemplary treatment. There was no doubt, maintained Lenin, that the programme of the "Labour Group" as presented to the Second Duma represented the programme of the peasant masses.

In this attitude Lenin showed that he was ever ready to "put his ear to the ground" to discern any signs of approaching change in the peasant mind. It was his peculiar strength and the fact among others, which eventually enabled him to commandeer the Social Revolutionary Programme in November 1917. Both the writings of peasant delegates and the signatures appended to the programme, not to mention their provincial distribution, were, for Lenin, sufficient evidence of what the rural population had in mind.

Again he moved to the attack upon the Menshevik "municipaliser" Maslov, whom he quoted as saying in 1905 that "in general the *podvorniki* [heritable, family-tenure peasant landholders, mainly in Little Russia and the South-West Provinces] could not agree to 'nationalisation.'" Podolia (S.W. Russia), where the peasants were *podvorniki* or household owners, provided thirteen of the one hundred and four sponsors of the above-mentioned *trudovik* (Labour Group) Bill in the First Duma (1906), and ten in the Second (1907). The Bolshevik leader regarded it as significant that support of such character should come from a part of Russia where the *peredel*, or redivision system, did not exist, i.e. where the transition to individual tenure might be expected to be easier than in Great Russia where the *mir* (commune) was predominant.

Why, said Lenin, did the peasants declare for "nationalisation"? Because (he thought) they "instinctively understood the necessity of abolishing mediæval landownership much better than the short-sighted would-be Marxians." Mediæval landed property had to be destroyed to clear the way for capitalism in agriculture, as indeed, in various countries, and in varying degrees, capital had already destroyed old mediæval land tenure. That tenure had been subjected to market requirements and had been reformed in accordance with the conditions of commercial agriculture.

Marx had already, in the Third Volume of *Kapital* and also in his *Theory of Surplus Value*, shown how capitalistic modes of production, or the simple touchstone of market efficiency, had revolutionised land-holding. Clan, tribal, communal, feudal and patriarchal joint-family tenures had been subjected to supersession according to the requirements of profit. Lenin quoted the passage from Marx's essay on *Surplus Value*, where he stated that "nowhere had capitalism created for itself such adequate and ideally correlated conditions as in England." Estates were "cleared," villages were razed to the ground, and arable become pasture. The profitable application of capital required the change, and therefore the "farmer," as such, was no longer interested in the "ownership" of the land he cultivated. He was exclusively interested in money-profit (as were in 1919 the English mineowners in their readiness to eliminate landowners' royalties). For the rapid abolition of mediæval forms, and for the freest development of capitalism, it would be necessary to destroy the whole old-fashioned land system,[1] to abolish private property in land as an obstacle to the application of capital to agriculture.

To Lenin, such a revolutionary destruction of landownership in Russia was inevitable and "no force in the

[1] Lenin, op. cit., p. 280.

world would be able to stop it." His question was whether such a "nationalisation" (or might it not be termed "rationalisation"?) of land was to be effected exclusively by large landowners or by peasants. The squires had already, in the writer's view, commenced the process in 1861, when they had "robbed" the peasantry of land, seeing that the squires' peasants, in contrast with the State Peasants, received a smaller allotment than the one they had held prior to emancipation, and had to pay an indemnity for it. They were continuing the process by the Stolypin Reform of 1906 (which introduced as Government policy a destruction of the land commune, together with the establishment of an individualistic peasant land-owning class). Alternatively, the peasants might destroy mediæval forms and "clear the estates" for the advent of capitalism. That would be "nationalisation" of land in Lenin's conception. In fact the peasants would need "nationalisation," which was a *sine qua non* to capitalistic development.

It may be noted that Lenin does not imply that this "clearing" would lead immediately to "socialisation," which term was liable to misinterpretation as a glorification of the land commune, if viewed with *narodnik* or "populist" spectacles. The "economic essence of nationalisation in a *bourgeois* revolution carried out by workers and peasants" was not comprehended by Menshevik Social Democrats such as Maslov and Plekhanov. Lenin considered that this group of Marxian thinkers were simply trying to harmonise the old with the new, grafting on to the old trunk of the Emancipation *nadel* or allotment land, the new branches represented by the large estates confiscated in the coming revolution. Instead, it should be their task, as Marxians, to destroy the semi-bondage survivals of mediæval land tenure to clear the way for capitalism. In his attempt to show the "petty *bourgeois* reactionary spirit" of the "municipalisers" (who apparently were *narodniki* (peasant socialists) under a new name) the revolutionary leader produced figures relating to the Kamyshin district of the Saratov Province. He desired to make a comparison between the area of the *nadel*, or allotment, received by the peasants at Emancipation, and the area which they leased in addition. The "allotment" land the Menshevik Marxians would leave untouched as peasant property, whereas the extra-allotment leased land would be "municipalised" or placed in the hands of local authorities.

There were, between 1896 and 1900, 3·25 millions of homesteads (of a total of 11·1 millions) which did not possess that indispensable agricultural aid, a draught horse. In consequence it was necessary for them to let ten times more land than was held on lease by themselves. Their cultivated acreage was five times smaller than their allotments. The peasants owning one horse ($3\frac{1}{3}$ million homesteads in the whole of Russia) hired an area which hardly surpassed the acreage let by them, since the area cultivated by them was smaller than their "allotment" or *nadel*.[1] In the higher groups which represented a minority of the peasants, the area held on lease was several times larger than the area which they let. Consequently, the area cultivated by a peasant homestead exceeded the area let, and the cultivated area exceeded the area of the *nadel*, in proportion to the increased wellbeing of the particular homestead. Those then who secured the extra-allotment leases were those who had the best opportunity of cultivating them—the wealthier peasants. Therefore, in the revolutionary leader's eyes, a capitalistic differentiation, or stratification, was taking place in the land commune which was bound to lead to its dissolution.

Kachorovsky, however, a firm supporter of the levelling principle of the *obshchina* or land commune, regarded the situation as capable of readjustment. He thought that after the initial shock, received by it from the anti-communal legislation of Stolypin, had dislodged the less efficient members, that the commune showed signs of revival in the last years before the Great War.[2] The

[1] Lenin, op. cit., p. 281.
[2] Cf. Kachorovsky, *Slavonic Review*, July 1929.

stratification, or differentiation, causing an economic schism in the body politic of the *mir* or land commune, prevailed, according to Lenin, over the whole country. It became the basis of his reliance upon the *borba v derevne*, or village-struggle, between prosperous and poor peasants, which he afterwards claimed as the theoretical base for his proletarian Government in a peasant environment. At this time, however, he regarded the facts adduced as indicating a capitalistic development of the village and therefore the creation of an increasing proletarian peasant mass. Capitalism (or in other words, the market) was destroying the economic base of the commune, and was liberating the peasants from the power of the *nadel*, or Emancipation allotment. It was lessening the importance of the allotment for both poles of the villagers. Therefore, Lenin saw no need for the Mensheviks with their apparent regard for the existence of the commune, to fear a peasant rising against the nationalisation of the allotment itself.

Certainly Stolypin's initial success in shaking the basis of communal tenure—a process in force at the time of Lenin's work—gave ground for the belief that the *mir* as such was a colossus with feet of clay.[1] Yet, as Kachorovsky pointed out, there was a slackening of the dissolution even before the war and, as the events of the peasant movement of 1917 showed,[2] *otrubniki* (peasant owners of consolidated farms but with their homesteads still in the village) and *hutoryane* (peasant owners of consolidated farms with their dwellings actually upon them) were forcibly reabsorbed in the *mir*. The "habit" of communal action proved in 1917 stronger than the economic cleavage which both Lenin and Stolypin relied upon, although of course from opposite angles.

What Lenin as a Marxian, and what supporters of the Tsarist Government's policy inaugurated by Stolypin, asserted was that the equalising function of the *mir*, the levelling redistribution, did not touch the actual means

---
[1] Cf. Bilimovich, *Land Settlement in Russia*, Carnegie.
[2] Cf. *Krestyanskoe Dvizhenie v 1917g*.

of production. As long as some peasant homesteads had more draught cattle with which to cultivate their holdings, equality there might be *de jure*, but certainly not *de facto*. To Lenin, the "allotment" of the peasant was as out-of-date as the large estate of the squire. That was where he did not see eye to eye with Maslov, Plekhanov and their fellow-Mensheviks. It would be a retrogression to make allotment-holders private proprietors, while leaving the non-allotment land in the hands of public authorities as under "municipalisation." The land commune and the peasant holding of allotment land would "inevitably be destroyed by capitalism." In this view Lenin felt himself of the same opinion as Premier Stolypin who, however, was undertaking their destruction as a "reactionary representative" of the squires. The peasant also felt the necessity of the destruction of the land commune (according to the writer) and desired to destroy it in his own fashion "by a revolutionary democratic rising."

The fear of the Mensheviks that nationalisation would destroy the peasants' trust in Social Democracy, seeing that their land holdings and the very *mir* itself would be cast "in the melting pot," did not disturb Lenin in 1908. He remarked upon the fact that the "famous problem about the *mir*" was not even discussed in the St. Petersburg Conference of the All Russian Peasants' Union (November 6–10, 1905) during the very climax of the agrarian and industrial ferment, when the first "Soviet" was ruling the City and Witte was made Premier to save the State. It was "in silence answered in the negative."[1] The conference had required that the land should be in the hands of individuals or partnerships. The peasant delegates trusted that under nationalisation of allotments they would receive land by a new distribution. The peasant knew, said Lenin, that he would receive land from the revolutionary redistribution when the quasi-bondage *latifundia* or big estates of the squires were abolished.

[1] Lenin, op. cit., p. 282.

The *razverstka*, or redivision of land on a large scale, would have the significance of the nationalisation of all the land which the peasant proprietor needed in order to free himself from mediæval fetters, to "clear" the land to adjust its utilisation to the requirements of modern economic conditions.[1]

By the use of the expression "clear," Lenin seemed to imply that the new settlement in the eyes of the peasants would be compelled to remove the inconveniences of *chrezpolositsa* (intermingled strips) and common pasture, as being obstacles to modern farming. But when in October 1917 this redistribution of land was effected with the consent of Lenin as head of the new revolutionary Communist Government, the tremendous rural outburst of levelling and equalisation reached its climax and the individualistic peasant proprietors established under Stolypin's régime (the *otrubniki* and *hutoryane*, mentioned earlier) were drawn back into the communal "mediæval" *mir* which showed that the peasant habits of family and group tenure were not to be so easily suppressed. Even so, the dissidence revealed by Lenin's own statistical evidence of the cleavage in the *mir* as far as means of production—draught cattle and implements —were concerned, presented a prospective actual differentiation into so-called *kulak*, *serednyak*, and *bednyak* (the comparatively well-to-do, the medium-sized simple family peasant holder and the village proletarian), which helped in turn to split the Communist Party itself on the agrarian question in post-revolutionary years. But that —as far as the present study is concerned—is another story.

To prove that his own Marxian ideas as to the elimination of the old land-tenure were paralleled even by his "petty *bourgeois*," socialising and equalising, Social Revolutionary, *narodnik* opponents he quoted the words of Mushenko,[2] a member of the Second Duma (1907), to the effect that: "A rational settlement (of the agriculturist) will be possible only when the land is open for

---

[1] Lenin, op. cit., p. 282.   [2] Lenin, op. cit., p. 282.

distribution and when all enclosures which are imposed by the principle of private property are removed."[1]

To "municipalise" the land would, in the *bourgeois* revolution, be a *reactionary* measure impeding the economically necessary and inevitable process of destruction of mediæval landed property of both squire and peasant. It would prevent the establishment of *uniformity* in the economic conditions relating to land for all persons "irrespective of their position, their past, their allotment in 1861 and the rest." The future Head of the Communist Government desired a *tabula rasa* on which the people, under centralised control, should write afresh their "social contracts." The dreaded *tabulæ novæ* of Roman Catiline were to be introduced into twentieth-century Russia. After "nationalisation" had helped to reorganise land tenure, then it would be possible, with a new redivision, to inaugurate "modern free farming." The Marxist task was to help to support the "radical *bourgeoisie*" (i.e. the peasantry) to perform as completely as possible "the elimination or removal of the old rubbish, and to safeguard a rapid advance." But it was emphasised that there was no desire on Lenin's part to help the "petty *bourgeoisie*" (i.e. presumably the peasant mass as a whole) to settle quietly in accordance with the past.

In the summary provided by the revolutionary leader of his own Third Chapter, he crossed swords with Maslov, using the debating skill which was one of his chief assets. He impressed his Polish friends with the fact that "nationalisation of land in a capitalistic society meant abolition of absolute, not differential, rent." He was ironically sceptical of the "law of diminishing returns" (owing to decreasing fertility of soil) as explaining the increasing overseas competition in the world wheat-market, and undermining *narodnik* or populist ideas of equalised working land communities.

One who rejected the theory of absolute rent could not understand the meaning of the "nationalisation" of land in a *bourgeois* society, since "nationalisation" could

---
[1] Stenographicheskie Otchety Gos. Dumy, p. 1172

only suppress absolute, not differential, rent. Anyone who rejected absolute rent rejected also the economic significance of private property in land as an obstacle to the development of capitalism. That was the reason why Maslov and his fellow Menshevist Social Democrats viewed the question of "nationalisation" or "municipalisation" simply from the political aspect. They were apparently solely concerned with the problem "Who shall have the land?" and were ignoring its economic essence. To combine private ownership in allotment land (the worst in quality managed by the worst cultivators) with socialised property in the remainder of the land (better in quality), for a free, although not highly developed, capitalistic state was, in Bolshevist eyes, ridiculous. It was nothing else than "agrarian bimetallism." As a consequence the criticism of private landed property, as such, had been left to the Social Revolutionaries. Marx's teaching had been forgotten. The sole analysis of the defects of landed property which reached the ears of the masses was that of the *narodnik* or "populist" socialist, i.e. "a petty *bourgeois* perverted criticism of private property." (Lenin here presumably referred to the theories of the idealistic development of the commune on an equalising labour-family basis.)

Next the Bolshevist leader proceeded to deny that in reality "nationalisation" simply implied a money rent from individual peasant proprietors who might be established after the coming revolution. "Money-rent" was in fact, as shown in *Kapital*, Vol. III, a modern form of "interest." The contemporary peasant lease with the rental for the land was undoubtedly, to some extent, a money rent. By abolishing the semi-bondage *latifundia*, differentiation would be accelerated among the peasantry and would stimulate the peasant *bourgeoisie*, which was already capitalistically engaged in managing the land it hired.[1] That fact was proved by the evidence furnished previously concerning hiring of land by better-off groups of the peasantry. Lastly, was "nationalisation," as many

[1] Lenin, op. cit., p. 285.

Marxists thought, applicable only at a very high stage in the development of capitalism? Lenin answered in the negative. When that high degree of development was attained it would be met not by a *bourgeois* but by a "socialist" revolution. Land "nationalisation," on the other hand, was "the most consistent *bourgeois* measure."[1] It is interesting in view of Lenin's idea on this subject, to note that according to the Sankey Report, 1919, the British mine-owners by their readiness to assist in the abrogation of "royalties" acted on the lines of the revolutionary leader's description.

Developing his argument, he illustrated that Marx had asserted that "the radical *bourgeois* theoretically arrives at the negation of private ownership in land, but in practice has not the courage to do so, since the attack against one form of property and against existing conditions would be very dangerous for any other form of property." In addition, the *bourgeois* had "territorialised" himself, and thereby had lost his revolutionary force. In this passage is embraced a very cogent statement of the circumstances of any socio-political change such as the events of 1917 in Russia. The "deepening" of revolution, having a specific cause in the fear lest there should be a reaction, also results from the abandonment of successive legal landmarks. Once the old Government had been displaced, what was "legal" or "illegal" became a matter of "relativity." What "measure of value" was possible? It was little use one party proclaiming its infallibility when all stood upon the same basis of so-called revolutionary law.

In the following sentences are contained a very significant description of the chief factor in the imminent Russian Revolution. "In Russia, the *bourgeois* revolution is precisely involved in the conditions under which the *radical bourgeois (the peasant)* comes into being," possessing as he really does "the courage to insist upon a programme of 'nationalisation' in the name of millions of people, and *not yet having territorialised himself*." He,

---

[1] Lenin, op. cit., p. 285.

the radical *bourgeois*, the peasant, received more harm from the mediæval ownership in land than gain and profit from *bourgeois* ownership.

The Russian Revolution *cannot* win unless this radical *bourgeois* who wavers between the Kadet (Constitutional Democratic Party which played a dominating rôle in the First Duma (1906) and had an influential, though diminishing, influence in the Second (1907))) and the workman, is prepared to support, by a rising *en masse*, the proletariat's revolutionary fight.

Here is contained a very exact diagnosis of the mechanics of the Russian Revolution of 1917 by one who himself, aided by war conditions, forged the link between the rural peasant movement and the urban industrial, with the aid of the extreme sections of the revolutionary *intelligentsia*. The Russian revolution, declared Lenin in 1908, could not win "except in the form of a revolutionary democratic dictatorship of the proletariat and the peasantry."

In his Fourth Chapter, there were "political and tactical" considerations with reference to the agrarian programme. An important point he made at Plekhanov's expense was that in the case of "municipalisation" there would remain the distinction between allotment-land and former squire-land, at least *economically*. Therefore, "municipalisation" would facilitate the "restoration," i.e. the reassertion of the difference *de jure*. In the political sense "municipalisation" was a law about the transfer of possession of squires' land. The law being simply, in Marxian parlance, an expression of the will of the governing classes, were these classes likely to respect a revolutionary edict of Plekhanov, should a "restoration" occur? "Nationalisation" on the contrary had a tactical value. It would render a "restoration" in the *economic sense* more difficult since it would destroy all distinctions, all mediæval property and adapt the tenure to the new capitalistic conditions of production.[1] The only "*absolute*" safeguard against a "restora-

[1] Lenin, op. cit., p. 286.

tion" was, in Lenin's mind, "a social upheaval in Western Europe."[1] A *"relative"* safeguard would be the execution of the revolution at home with the utmost radical destruction of the old order, the highest possible degree of democracy (a republic) in politics, and the clearing of the way for capitalism in economics.[2]

It is evident that the leader had a very clear vision in his "inner eye" of the strategic requirements of a successful Russian Revolution. If he was an internationally-minded Marxian, he was certainly also a native-minded Russian reading his country's horoscope with the same air of detachment as revealed by Renascence Machiavelli; or, if the hyperbole is not too violent, a new Prometheus bringing down fire against the modern Zeus, to send over the wide expanse of the countryside a blaze of burning *usadbas* of the squires. Plekhanov's belief in the efficacy of local government as a bulwark of the future revolution, Lenin did not share. For him it was but lath and plaster. The peasants' revolution could not triumph in Russia if it did not defeat the central power.

The Third Duma (1907–12) (which was engaged, in collaboration with Stolypin, in breaking up old agrarian forms and with them the institution of the redistributory levelling commune) served as an illustration of the Bolshevist doctrine. A "relative" Menshevik democracy in the centre, as the Stolypin Administration was sarcastically termed, did not protect *local* democracy as far as the communal land holdings were concerned. "Municipalisation," as opposed to "nationalisation," led to a regional fragmentation of effort, a dispersion of energy over the vast expanse of the Russian borderlands, a fact which had already, in Lenin's opinion, caused the failure of the previous revolutionary campaign. Centralised effort was necessary and there must be a centralised solution of the agrarian problem, which would be settled by Central Russia. On the Borderlands it was but a matter of setting the example. That policy for a Bolshevist

[1] Lenin, op. cit., p. 286. [2] Lenin, op. cit., p. 286.

was not so much social, as pure, democracy. "The whole question was whether the proletariat should raise the peasantry to the highest aims or whether it should debase itself as low as the *bourgeois* level of the peasantry."[1]

To the argument that centralisation would strengthen the possibility of an arbitrary autocracy, Lenin replied that, even if "nationalised," the land would remain under the control of local bodies. General conditions only would be fixed by the Central Administration which would, for instance, forbid leasing. Even the Menshevik Social Democrats were prepared to place in the hands of "the Democratic State" both the land-reserve to be used for the internal redistribution of population, and forests and waters having national significance. And those functions of a centralised Government were quite as liable to abuse from unlimited arbitrary power. To Lenin, the only satisfactory protection against a possible reaction was a complete democracy at the centre—a republic would in fact be the only guarantee against a cleavage between centre and circumference. Mensheviks objected that the *bourgeois* State would be strengthened. But the Bolshevik leader's only response was to point out that there were but two alternatives of social development before Russia: the Prussian (Junker) or American (free yeoman farmer) type of agrarian revolution. Which did they prefer? The pseudo-constitutional squires' monarchy or a peasant farmers' republic? Any other diagnosis of the situation seemed to a Bolshevik Social Democrat to be shirking the issue of the revolutionary problem.

The Russian Revolution, continued Lenin, was a *bourgeois* revolution, because the struggle was not between "socialism" and "capitalism," but between two forms of capitalism, two lines of development, two forms of *bourgeois* democratic institutions. The monarchy of the Octobrists or of the Kadets was "relative" *bourgeois* democracy according to at least one Menshevik Social Democrat. In addition, the proletarian-peasant republic

[1] Lenin, op. cit., p. 288.

would also be a *bourgeois* democracy. The Social Democrats could not take a single step, and had not taken a single step, without in some way having supported some stratum of the *bourgeoisie* against the old order.[1]

"Nationalisation" did not mean the expenditure of land-rent for national defence, as opposed to the expenditure locally upon social services such as health, sanitation and education which "municipalisation" would, in Maslov's words, imply. That was a "petty *bourgeois*" socialist's argument and extremely parochial. The Mensheviks were trying "to conceal in the backwaters of local self-government the burning problem raised by history as to whether there should be in Russia a centralised republic of farmers or a centralised *bourgeois* monarchy of "Junkers." Municipal Socialism as a slogan of Fabian English, or any other, brand, was simply playing with the agrarian problem. The "petty *bourgeois*" could build his nest in the idyllic municipalities of the democratic Russia of the future. "The task of the proletariat consisted in the organisation of the masses not for that object, but for a revolutionary fight for democratisation to-day and for the social upheaval to-morrow."[2] "Nationalisation," said Lenin, was the least Utopian of any of the Bolshevik views. To call "nationalisation" a Utopia was "to forget the necessary correlation between the swing of political and agrarian changes." "Nationalisation" was no less Utopian from the point of view of the "petty *bourgeois*" than was a republic. Both of these in their turn were no less Utopian than the agrarian people's revolution, i.e. the victory of a peasant rising in a capitalistic country. All these changes, said Lenin,[3] were equally "difficult" in the sense of a humdrum quiet development.

Objection raised to "nationalisation" of land implied an incapacity to understand the necessary and indissoluble connection between economic and political upheaval. It was impossible to confiscate squire land and thus destroy the economic basis of the class, without previously des-

---
[1] Lenin, op. cit., p. 289.   [2] Lenin, op. cit., p. 290.   [3] Lenin, op. cit., p. 290.

troying the Autocracy—the political expression of squirearchy. To destroy Autocracy required a "revolutionary activity of conscious millions of people," a strong tide of mass heroism, a readiness and a capacity on their part to assail heaven.[1] For these prerequisites was required a radical suppression of all survivals of bondage hampering the peasants, and all mediæval ownership of land, all the fetters of the land commune (*obshchina*) and the land allotment system. It is evident that the Bolshevik leader had a completely realistic picture of what he anticipated to be the future revolution, which helped him to take advantage of an unparalleled climax of military and social disintegration at which Russians found themselves in the course of 1917.

Lenin's Fifth Chapter, dealing with "Classes and Parties in the discussion of the Land Problem in the Second Duma (1907)," tried to draw out the salient features of peasant opinion as expressed in the short space of the Second Duma's existence. To him, it seemed that they expressed

their passionate desire to overthrow the squire's yoke, their burning hatred for mediævalism and for the bureaucracy, and an elemental, immediate and often naïve, but perfectly distinct and, at the same time, revolutionary, disposition of the ordinary peasant which showed better than long discussions what a potentially destructive energy had accumulated in the peasant masses against the Gentry, the Squires and the Romanovs.[2]

With flashes of his *sæva indignatio* worthy of Roman Juvenal, Lenin proceeded to apply his solution.

The task of the conscious proletariat consisted in a pitiless rending of the veil and the removing of all those numerous "petty *bourgeois*" deceits, quasi-socialistic phrases, infantile, naïve expectations which the peasants connected with agrarian upheaval. *Their removal must take place not in order to placate and pacify the peasant* (the policy of the Constitutional Democrats in both Dumas), but in order to awaken in the masses a steel-tempered, unshakable and determined revolutionary spirit. Without this revolutionary spirit,

---

[1] Lenin, op. cit., p. 291.   [2] Lenin, op. cit., p. 291.

without an obstinate and merciless fight of the peasant masses, confiscation (of squire land), the republic, universal, direct, equal and secret suffrage, were "hopeless and Utopian."

It was here that Lenin revealed his recognition of the significance of the peasant movement of the revolutionary years without which there would have been no Russian Revolution as it emerged in 1917.

How did he formulate the contemporary Russian agrarian problem on Marxian lines? The two directions of the capitalistic development of Russia were those represented by hostile classes. The large landowners and the capitalists (Octobrists) had at last realised that they were forced to proceed along a capitalistic route. To this end they must destroy the land commune or *obshchina* which they were doing in a violent fashion, with little consideration for the peasants' feelings, employing police methods to achieve their aim. (Lenin obviously refers to the Stolypin Legislation approved with modification by the Third Duma.)

This operation was one by which it was easy to break one's neck (a very significant remark which in the outcome proved to have much truth in it); for masses of peasants during those three years had also very distinctly understood the hopelessness of their confidence in the Tsar, "the Father," and all expectations of a peaceful way, and the necessity of a revolutionary fight and the abolition of mediævalism in general and mediæval ownership in particular.[1]

Lenin here indicated his lack of faith in the *obshchina* or land commune as a mediæval relic of bondage. Yet he was prepared to rely in 1917 upon it as a socialising, levelling and equalising force tending to assist his communist ideals, while, economically, it retarded them by preventing a rapid development of the capitalist productive forces which he desired. The more one reads the theories of Social Democrat or Social Revolutionary— Marxian factory socialist or peasant communal socialist, the more one is convinced that the Communism of

[1] Lenin, op. cit., p. 292.

1917–18 as a Russian phenomenon, was based, in no small measure, upon the principles of *narodnichestvo* (peasant socialism). This peasant socialisation, it may be remembered, in the mid-nineteenth century, was a communal socialisation meant to apply to the towns as well as the country. Trotsky, an International Marxian with a contempt for peasant socialism as such, regarded Lenin as having utilised old *narodnik* ideas.[1]

But Lenin's contemplation of the "wormeaten" economic base of the *obshchina*, the primitive *sokha* (or wooden plough), did not embrace the old-world views of the happiness of a roseate past of manual or horse labour, to which increasing distance and the evils of modern factory production lent enchantment. Propaganda for a second campaign was (he thought) necessary, based upon a clarification of the results of Socialist investigations. Therefore Plekhanov, the pioneer of the Marxian theory of socialism in Russia, was, in Lenin's eyes, a reactionary, when he declared that the seizure of power by the proletariat and the peasantry meant a renascence of *narodnovolchestvo* (the People's Will Party).[2] It is interesting to find Plekhanov, an old *narodnik*, criticising Lenin's advocacy of a peasant-proletarian alliance—a criticism later in 1924 levelled by Trotsky, as we saw above. Yet it was to this policy of peasant-proletarian co-operation that the Leninist Communist Party owed its power. All its subsequent party heartburnings and schisms were indeed based upon the conflicting views of this very *smychka* (union) foreshadowed here.[3] Plekhanov, then opposed to Lenin on the point, had reached the stage, said Lenin, of agreeing to a peasant agrarian revolution without the seizure of power either by the proletariat or the peasantry. Even the Austrian Marxian Socialist,

---

[1] Cf. Trotsky, *Lenin*, "Populism in Lenin."
[2] The formation of this party, as the terrorist section of the old *narodnik* or populist socialist party, led to Plekhanov's retirement from it and directly caused the foundation by him of a Marxian Party, which in 1898 became the Russian Social Democratic Labour Party.
[3] The sense of innate dictatorship which Lenin possessed further widened such schisms.

Kautsky (with whom the Bolshevik leader was to have "wordy battles" in 1918 after the establishment of Soviet power), recognised in 1908 the necessity of a peasant proletarian union to achieve socialist aims.

If there were not a complete abolition of all mediæval landed property, i.e. "nationalisation," such a revolution as Russian Marxians contemplated was unthinkable. *It was the task of the proletariat to preach "the most consistent radical* bourgeois *agrarian upheaval,"* and, added Lenin significantly, *"when this has been done we will see what further perspectives will be opened."* [1] Was such an upheaval to be simply the basis for a rapid development of productive forces *à l'Américaine* under capitalism, or was it to be the prelude to a Socialist Revolution in Western Europe?

In his postscript Lenin summed up the cardinal points of his policy as at June 18, 1908. As there was an alternative between the two directions of the capitalistic agrarian revolution, the programme was necessarily conditional. At the time *they* (the Bolshevik and Menshevik Social Democrats) *were fighting against the modern trend.* They were supporting the revolutionary claim of the peasant in the interests of the development of productive forces, of a broad scope and freedom for the class struggle. In backing the revolutionary struggle of the peasants against mediævalism, the Social Democratic Party affirmed that the best form for the liquidation of quasi-bondage relations and for agrarian relationships in capitalistic society was "nationalisation" of the land. Only if connected with a radical political change and the abolition of Autocracy, together with the establishment of a democratic republic, was a radical agrarian upheaval possible—embodying the confiscation of the squires' landed property and "nationalisation." It is clear that Lenin understood the significance and approved of the technical principles of the Stolypin Reforms as far as the modernisation of farming methods was concerned. To that extent he admitted that he was, as he

[1] Lenin, op. cit., pp. 292-3.

said, "fighting against the modern trend." Where he disagreed with Stolypin, was in his aim, which was anti-squire. The methods adopted in pressing forward the Stolypin schemes he regarded as violent,[1] but the fact did not disconcert him as an advocate of class-war, seeing that it tended to increase the agrarian class schism, or *borba v derevne*, which assisted his plans.

The above illustrates Lenin's own analysis of Russia's agrarian problem during the period studied in the present work. It remains to show how Lenin's own personal efforts succeeded in securing the fruition of the desired agrarian upheaval in 1917. His speech at the Peasant Congress in Petrograd in May of that year further indicates his tactics, which led to the famous "Decree about Land" in October when the proletarian-peasant structure was built. His programme must now be tested by its practical possibilities.

In his *Rech po agrarnomu voprosu* (Speech on the Agrarian Question), delivered on May 22, 1917 (o.s.), before the All-Russian Council (Soviet) of Peasant Delegates, Lenin referred first to a motion of Smilga (Bolshevik representative upon the Central Land Committee), brought forward a few days before. This motion had proposed that the "Central Land Committee should express itself in favour of a speedy, organised seizure of squires' land by the peasantry." Furthermore, "the land must pass, as a whole, without exception, into the ownership of the whole people."

Using this motion as his text, the future Head of the Russian State explained that his ideas were based upon experience gained particularly from the peasant movement of 1905 and from the declarations of peasant deputies in the First and Second Dumas where a large number of peasant deputies from all parts of Russia had been able to express themselves. There should be no payment for the confiscated estates, but, on the other

---

[1] The "violence" of Stolypin is a matter of relativity. Witte and Kerensky both thought that administrative pressure was used unduly to effect what was perhaps a natural process of evolution.

hand, there should be no "ownership" as such, of lands distributed among the peasantry as a result of revolution. The land should be sown as a unit by the peasants of the given district acting according to a local majority. Land should belong to all the people and should be "the property of all the people." A central power, either a Constituent Assembly or a Soviet, must regulate the procedure of the transfer. Shingarev, the Provisional Government's Minister for Agriculture, had by telegram declared such a transfer of land illegal. There must be a "general law."[1] This "general law" must be (he asserted) the work of the Constituent Assembly. Lenin maintained that the Bolsheviks' advice was not illegal and that the State did not need an agreement between owners and agriculturists. Objections had been raised by critics that the Bolshevik policy would mean the "petrification of inequalities."[2] Inequalities would necessarily remain until the Central Government's rearrangement of affairs. If the squires kept the land, inequalities would also remain. The important announcement (amplified later in his *State and Revolution* [1917] where he asserted that the revolution did not imply anarchy) is made categorically that the "Bolsheviks are not anarchists."[3] Presumably this statement was meant to refute any suggestion of Bakunin and his policy of independent local communes uncontrolled by a central power.

To Lenin the agrarian problem was a "restoration of (peasant) rights."[4] To emphasise the fact he placed before the Peasant Congress a summarised version of his more elaborate analysis of 1908. There were 30,000 large landowners who held 70 million *desyatines*, i.e. 2,000 *desyatines* each. On the other hand there were 10 million peasant households with 70 to 75 million *desyatines*, i.e. $7\frac{1}{2}$ *desyatines* each. Was a "friendly agreement" possible between two such extremes? Leases could of course be had—at a price.[5]

The preceding words abundantly illustrate the ability

[1] Lenin, *Rech po agrarnomu voprosu*, p. 4.   [2] Lenin, op. cit., p. 5.
[3] Lenin, op. cit., p. 5.   [4] Lenin, op. cit., p. 5.   [5] Lenin, op. cit., p. 6.

with which Lenin utilised his economic background to drive home a point by which he could secure the alliance of the peasantry for his socialistic aims. A bald statement concerning a situation of obvious inequity was seen by him to have sufficient force to achieve an opening predisposition in his favour. Proceeding, he declared that an "organised seizure" of land was necessary even before the Assembly met. Local peasant committees should take the land. The "law," he announced, was not what pleased squires and officials but what pleased the majority of the peasantry. Until the All-Russian Soviet or the Constituent Assembly existed, the highest power locally was the district or provincial committee.[1] The peasants should seize the squires' land immediately. But there was an objection to that course. Would not the richer peasants gain under that policy? Lenin, ever mindful of the fact that the Bolsheviks were "the party of the hired workers and poorest peasants" and that "only through those classes could humanity emerge from the terrors caused by the capitalists' war," was always wary of possible misconceptions which his opponents might use against him. To parry this attack the Bolshevik leader asked whether an agreement with the squires would prevent the richer peasants from securing the advantage. It was the richer peasants who would gain most by an agreement with the squires, who, indeed, preferred the richer peasant as being more easily able to pay their price.[2] (In this remark might be seen a scarcely-veiled hit at one of the basic principles of the Stolypin legislation—the reliance upon the stronger peasant.) The "disorder" involved was slight—not so much as had occurred earlier. What would be the effect upon the soldiers at the front if the land seizure took place? They would have to remain there whatever happened "as long as the war lasted."[3] Such was Lenin's cryptic reply with visions probably in his mind of the inevitable disintegration of the Army. Why, continued he, should the soldiers fear the decision of a peasant majority against

[1] Lenin, op. cit., p. 7.   [2] Lenin, op. cit., p. 8.   [3] Lenin, op. cit., p. 9.

the squires? There ought to be no "privileges" for the squires, now the "greatest squire"—the Tsar—had gone.[1]

What promised to be the greatest difficulty was the degree in which cultivation would suffer. At a time when Food Committees were in power all over the country—when it was remembered that the disorganisation of food supplies had played no small part in the downfall of the Tsarist Government, it was little use presenting to a revolutionary people a prospect of further hardships due to declining agricultural power. The Party's advice must correspond with the experience of the people's own life. It was Lenin's aim to secure the power of peasants and workmen. Better cultivation and greater economy of human labour were required. Would the peasant sow worse if he knew it was for the people as a whole, and not for the squire, and if he paid, not the squire but the peasant treasury? The old "rule of the stick," long since disused in Western Europe, was now, Lenin alleged, being replaced by blandishment in Russia. The "organised seizure" of land implied, not separate ownership, but a "general use of the land by the whole people"—a further evidence of Lenin's already expressed opinion of 1908 and, even earlier, of 1902.[2] As in 1902 and in 1908, this was the rock on which the ship of Social Democracy split in 1917.[3]

While it has been stated that Lenin "stole the Social Revolutionaries' thunder" in October 1917, it is clear that he was never prepared to admit that the Social Revolutionaries alone wore the agrarian mantle of the *narodniki* (peasant socialists) upon their shoulders. It was the "peasant *narodnik*" sympathies of Lenin that enabled him (as Trotsky, the "Internationalist" pure and

---

[1] Lenin, op. cit., p. 9.   [2] *Agrarnaya Programma Russkoy S.D.P.*
[3] Cf. Kamenev's introd. (1925) to the *Agrarian Programme of the S.D. Party*, and also Maslov's municipalisation scheme in 1907, emphasising on both of the previous occasions the cardinal feature which differentiated Lenin from his erstwhile Social Democratic fellows—his uncompromising stand as a "maximalist" in any peasant policy of change, despite the fact that, as late as 1902, he was a "minimalist" in industrial policy.

simple, reiterates ¹) to secure his firm hold upon peasant and proletarian, linking the "hundreds of towns" with "the thousands of villages" ² and giving a crystallised philosophy to what might have become a meaningless outburst of anarchy.

So far the problem was fairly simple. Seize the squires' land. But what was to be done with the land when it was seized? ³ It was at this point that the Bolshevik leader revealed to the Peasant Congress his "higher aims" for the further development of the working forces of the country.

The arrangement of the land locally must always remain a matter for the peasantry. To declare that the land was for the people, implied the "working people." The land question would become one of State leaseholds. There would be free labour and free land.⁴ Each peasant would be able to lease land from the future workers' and peasants' State. Did that imply (Lenin continued) that land would be given to all those who cultivated it? It would imply the use of land by the "farmer" with intelligence. He had stated that there must be free land and free labour. But the future Head of the Government knew quite well that land without cattle, implements and capital was incapable of utilisation. It was for that reason that Lenin distrusted the Social Revolutionary successors of the agrarian *narodniki* (populist socialists) with their norms of labour-unit maxima and food-unit minima. Lenin had long realised (one may emphasise) that a "static" socialism envisaged by the levelling *"narodnik"* was inadequate to maintain the national productive forces.

As a Marxian, Lenin thought that a socialist, or rather more definitely, proletarian, revolution would lead to an increase of production, transcending that of contemporary capitalistic countries. A "dynamic" socialism was essential from his point of view—not a simple sharing-out or primitive communism, which could not solve the

---

¹ *Populism in Lenin*, Trotsky. ² Cf. Introd. *Krestyanskoe Dvizhenie*.
³ Lenin, op. cit., p. 10. ⁴ Cf. Lenin's views in 1907.

problems of a modern industrial State which it was obviously necessary for Russia to become. To the Bolshevik leader, such a plan as the *neo-narodniki* (as one might term them) had evolved, was but a "paper plan" while the old capitalistic methods lasted. The *narodnik* Social Revolutionaries "talked as if land and citizens were the only two things in the world." Absence of monetary relationships implied absence of a class of hired labourers—the corner-stone, one must insist, of Marxian industrial theory. One million richer peasants would exploit the poorer labourers.[1]

Attention must be carefully directed to the above remarks, because they represent the Marxian revolutionary's opinion of the policy that, after the Bolshevik *coup d'état*, was put into force to consolidate the peasant-workmen's alliance—the promulgation of the famous "Land Decree." Lenin's words envisage the defects of the Socialisation Decree of February 1918, which is outside the province of this work. Lenin knew what even the Social Revolutionaries of Chernov's type must also have realised, that the ability of the various layers of the peasantry to utilise any land they secured by revolution was ultimately conditioned by their possession of the physical means of production. This had been Lenin's criticism of the *narodniki* even in 1898 when, in his *Razvitie Kapitalisma v Rossii (Development of Capitalism in Russia)*, he had carefully analysed from *Zemstvo* statistics, the content of the contemporary *mir*. While many will regret the application and many will deny the applicability of Lenin's drastic economic surgery to a war-weary Russia, none will refuse him the credit of having "seen the peasant problem steadily and seen it whole."

It was necessary, emphasised the Marxian revolutionary, that people should remember that there were "horseless" peasants (who, one may add, if not "proletarians" from a technical point of view, were certainly "pauperised"). The "norms" (continued Lenin) which

---

[1] Lenin, op. cit., p. 13.

the *narodnik* philosophy regarded as essential for the solution of agrarian unrest were not in consonance with real life. The advice which he proffered to the Peasant Congress was to effect an organisation of agricultural labourers and the poorest peasants. There should be "committees for the poor" in every district. Otherwise land would pass simply into the hands of those peasants with stock. Lenin was still intent upon the maintenance of the *borba v derevne* (the struggle in the village) which he had deduced as an economic truth in 1898, had prepared for in 1902 as a counterbalance to a peasant "maximalist" programme, had welcomed in 1907 as a result of Stolypin's 1906 legislation, and later was to guard as the basic principle of post-revolutionary policy. This *borba v derevne* could necessarily only arise when the *pomestnoe dvoryanstvo* (landed gentry) had been evicted. Until that moment, the village was politically, as became clear in October, an undivided whole.

It was the speaker's antipathy to capitalism that led him to desire its defeat as a system. To secure that end, it was necessary for the large estates to be worked by the general labour of the poorer peasants. But Lenin fully realised the difficulty of perfecting such a plan. It involved, in his own words, "*a greater revolution than overthrowing Nicholas.*" Free land did not mean the end of capitalism as a system. Scientific socialist farming was accordingly his aim—an aim which must lead to a "general labour duty,"[1] necessitated by the exigencies of the prevailing state of warfare.

When the peasants' delegates returned to their villages they must dimly have been conscious that a new star had appeared upon the horizon of their practical sagacity.

And meanwhile throughout the countryside events moved onward with fatal persistence to the downfall of the old landed class.

After the preceding analysis of the Bolshevist leader's social-economic policy, the historian must return to the

[1] Lenin, op. cit., p. 15.

scene where such revolutionary remedies were to be applied. The actual emergence of a definite peasant movement will be described. The following section will show how the Provisional Government which succeeded Nicholas II tried to control and constitutionalise the outburst.

CHAPTER IV

THE ATTEMPT UNDER LVOV TO CONSTITUTIONALISE THE AGRARIAN MOVEMENT (Feb.–July, 1917)

Lenin's speech in May 1917 before the Peasant Congress in Petrograd, reminds the reader that affairs had moved nearer to the concluding events of the period studied.

A brief outline of the immediate causes of the February Revolution will now be given.

In July 1914, the country's manhood donned the Russian equivalent of khaki. The villages were denuded of their able-bodied inhabitants. Women perforce had to play a more prominent part in rural economy. The disloyal manifestations which many had feared [1] did not occur. The enthusiasm for war on behalf of orthodox Servia was almost too great to be believed. It seemed that Russia's impaired sense of national unity had been completely restored. No less did the alliance with Great Britain and France offer hopes to Russian Constitutional Liberals of new means of co-operation between official circles and the people at large.

It is idle to speculate what would have happened if the Central European Alliance had collapsed, leaving Russia as one of the victorious powers. Military success was certainly more vital to the Tsar's Government than to almost any of the combatants save Austria-Hungary or Turkey. It is not advisable for any Government to send its forces to overwhelming defeat twice in ten years. Less stolid troops than Russia's peasant soldiery would probably have endured less indomitably two such major reverses.

[1] e.g. Prince Volkonsky, *Reminiscences*.

RUSSIA
AGRARIAN DISTURBANCES IN 1917
No of cases occurring per 100000 of rural population in areas marked.
I.V. Igritsky. 1929 "1917g. v derevne"
Ed. Y Yakovlev.

Upon one person alone could the responsibility fall. That was Nicholas II. In a practical Autocracy (as Russia remained *de facto*, despite the diminution *de jure* of her Sovereign's powers in October 1905) the Fourth Duma was incapable of promoting an adequate alternative constitutional administration. Nicholas II was personally not a strong monarch. He did not possess what in the past has saved even weak monarchs—a strong minister who might bear the brunt of his own shortcomings. There was now no Stolypin.

The Tsaritsa, not herself Russian, had become identified in the public mind with one—Rasputin—who represented superstitious clairvoyant elements still surviving in Russia's countryside.

It is strange that a peasant *starets* (holy man) from the Siberian *tayga* (forest) should have assumed an influence in the Imperial Household out of all proportion to his own private morals or public capacity. It is strange that Nicholas II's Consort should have helped to throw the Imperial Crown in the dust through her feverish maternal desire to hand an undiminished heritage to the Tsarevich, her son.

The situation is vividly described by one who was an eye-witness of Russia's activities during the War.

> Russia was then confronted with a monstrous régime which would have seemed impossible in some small duchy in the Middle Ages. . . . In the midst of a world-wide struggle . . . the Russian Ministers were selected by an ignorant, blind and hysterical woman on the test of their subservience to an ignorant, fantastic and debauched adventurer . . . and the supreme commands of the adventurer permeated every detail of government in every branch of the administration.[1]

After the great débâcle of 1915, the Tsar formally assumed the active post of Commander-in-Chief at the Front. He thereby foolishly took an even more definite responsibility for the ensuing disasters of his country. The peasant Army suffered doggedly to the extent of

[1] Sir Bernard Pares, *Foreign Affairs*, Oct. 1927, p. 154.

Lvov and the Agrarian Movement

3,000,000 casualties. Of such casualties, their German opponents could replace 40 per cent more in the field. If a Russian soldier endured a head or stomach wound he was beyond the medical resources of his field hospitals.

The year 1916 witnessed the peculiar spectacle of a virtual Autocrat who reigned but did not govern. Almost frantically anxious lest "our son" (the Tsarevich) should not secure the reversion of an undiminished Empire, the Tsaritsa implicitly trusted Rasputin, whom she deemed indispensable. This individual who figured as "He" or "Our Friend" in the *Letters of the Tsaritsa* had gradually obtained overwhelming influence at Court. "Russia is to be made safe for Autocracy and Our Son" is the prevailing refrain of the Imperial Consort's correspondence. Hysterically she adjured Nicholas to "Be Peter the Great, John the Terrible, Emperor Paul." He was urged to act "against the small group of republicans who were (the Tsaritsa believed) waging a treasonous internal war." These "republicans," representing the progressive or constitutionalist element in the admittedly conservative Fourth Duma, must certainly have been surprised at such an appellation. The Empress even desired that Lvov should be exiled to Siberia. Samarin (she thought) ought to lose his rank.

In December (1916) the Tsaritsa went so far as to advocate the closure of the Duma and the execution of the recently appointed Premier Trepov. "I could hang Trepov," she said. . . . "Disperse the Duma at once," she continued. "Send Milyukov, Guchkov and Polivanov to Siberia. . . . My duty as wife and mother blessed by Our Friend." [1]

In her dementia the Tsaritsa simply antagonised those who were normally the Monarchy's firmest supporters.

The year 1916 ended with a conspiracy among the highest circles surrounding the throne. Rasputin was its object. Yet his murder by Prince Yusupov (a member of Russia's richest family) did not solve any

---

[1] Dec. 14, 1916. *Letters of Tsaritsa to Tsar, 1912–16.* Cf. *Foreign Affairs*, Oct. 1927, Article of Sir Bernard Pares, p. 153.

fundamental problems. Russian Society aimlessly moved on as if in a trance, until the catastrophe of February.

Breakdown in transport had already caused a food crisis which irritated the working population of the towns, including Petrograd. When the City Garrison threw off its allegiance and the Front failed to support the Tsar's authority, there was no alternative for Nicholas but abdication.

The Duma as an institution did not desire or attempt to assume sovereign power. It had, in fact, not resisted prorogation. Yet its members as private individuals did elect a Provisional Committee. But the immediate emergence of a popularly chosen "Soviet of Workers' and Soldiers' Deputies" created a dyarchy in the capital. This dyarchy was to persist until October.

Russia in February had entered upon a new phase. What part was the peasantry to play in it? Was 1905 to be re-enacted? Could the War be continued? Would moderate changes in the higher administrative personnel suffice to create a new spirit of national harmony? All that remained to be seen.

The almost unbelievable harmony displayed in the earlier moments of the great international struggle prevents the historian from imagining that there was an active "peasant movement" unifying the whole of the period (1906–17) treated in this work. Rather may it be said that the peasant movement resembled a volcanic phenomenon erupting partially in 1902, completely in 1905, and lessening in intensity in succeeding years until it seemed that a dormant stage had been reached giving prospect of total extinction. The description of Stolypin's changes and their effect upon the life of the village has shown that there were signs that all the latent forces were not however exhausted. The military and administrative failures of 1915–16 led in 1917 to the inevitable re-eruption which transformed the features of the Russian countryside and heralded a new régime.

The periodic telegraphic reports of Provincial and District Commissioners and local landowners to the

Department of Militia afford a detailed account of what actually occurred in the countryside from March to October (o.s.). They give too a clear conspectus of the social collapse that was preluded in February by Nicholas II's abdication, and resulted in the establishment of a Soviet system of government under Lenin's leadership which definitely registered and ratified the "Grand Redivision" (*"Cherny Peredel"*)—the aim of revolutionary *narodnichestvo* (peasant socialism) during the second half of the nineteenth century.

October 1917 thus witnessed the consummation of an alliance between a resurgent village *narodnik* communalism and an incipient Marxian factory communism, the fusion of an old native Russian rural socialism with one of a modern international industrial type familiar in Western Europe. It was the coalescence of these two streams of thought which caused such bitter strife among socialist thinkers abroad, and explained the apparent mystery of the relatively least industrialised Great Power being transformed upon Marxian-Leninist lines as if it were a highly urbanised political entity. Indeed, without the peasant movement of 1917 there would have been no Russian Revolution as the world has known it. There would have been social changes of course. But would or could Lenin have overturned Kerensky on October 25, 1917, had there been no village insurrection? Would the Kornilov episode in August (o.s.), representing an attempt to save the old Russia of the squires, have occurred at all with its subsequent undermining of the Kerensky régime? Kornilov represented an attempt to avert the remodelling of Russia upon Social Revolutionary (modernised and semi-*narodnik*) lines. Unwittingly it led directly to Leninism and a *narodnik*-Marxian liquidation of formal private property rights—a liquidation involving not only old squire but also new capitalist in a common ruin. In October 1917 Karl Marx's tomb lay neglected in a London cemetery "with none so poor to do it reverence." Lenin, the realistic follower of this same Marx, turned the gaze of his somewhat heterogeneous followers in the Russian capital to what was happening in the thousands of Russian villages in September and October. Without the peasant movement as a motive force in support, it is doubtful whether Lenin would have tried to effect his *coup d'état*. Without the peasant movement it is certain that his effort to emulate the Paris Commune of 1871 would have suffered the same fate as that of the socialists of Montmartre and it would have gone down in history as a similar event. Karl Marx's tomb would still perhaps have lingered in obscurity, for it is clear that his doctrines were in danger of fading into the ghostly outlines of a social myth. Like the myth of Plato's *Polity* they might have served to maintain belief among "the many-headed multitude" but for the *intelligentsia* they were being denuded of revolutionary substance by "revisionist" reformers such as German Bernstein or Russian Struve.

Does not this line of thought confer upon the peasant movement an outstanding significance in the sociopolitical evolution of Russia during the period under review?

The main "battle ground" of the agrarian struggle during 1917 included what are termed the Central Agricultural and Middle Volga regions (see map).[1] In these two regions occurred almost half of the total number of cases registered by the militia. To be exact, 23.7 per cent of the number of occasions of agrarian disturbance after February fall to the credit of the Central Agricultural and 20 per cent to that of the Middle Volga region.[2] It thus appears that almost half of the total disturbances are recorded from these two regions alone. A study of the characteristics of the movement in these areas therefore reveals most clearly the type and intensity of peasant

---

[1] In the regional division of the country as used in the *Krestyanskoe Dvizhenie*, that of Semenov-Tyanshansky, modified to some extent in 1917, was adopted. This classification embraced 14 distinct areas, the two regions above-mentioned including (1) Kursk, Orel, Tula, Ryazan, Tambov and Voronesh Provinces and (2) Simbirsk, Saratov, Penza, Kazan and Nizhegorod Provinces. Cf. *Predislovie, Krestyanskoe Dvizhenie,* p. xxi.

[2] Cf. *Krestyanskoe Dvizhenie,* p. xiii.

disorder. There is a continual expansion until June, a temporary decline after July and the final outburst on a wide scale in October. After July the organised nature of the disturbances died away. The "concealed" or semi-legal, "peaceful," manifestations of peasant community aggrandisement were replaced by the open "grabbing" or seizure movement leading to direct devastation and destruction of the property of the old possessing classes.

In May the so-called "peaceful," or pseudo-legal, forms of the movement reached 61·5 per cent of the total number: the open "grabbing" or seizures amounted to 28·8 per cent of the whole; cases of destruction and devastation represented 9·6 per cent. In October there were only 13·5 per cent of the pseudo-legal type, 29·5 per cent of the open seizure form, but, of the destructive or devastational class, including seizures of estates, one finds 57·5 per cent.

That these regions—Central Agricultural and Middle Volga—were the danger foci, the Tsar's Government had already had abundant evidence in 1905. Stolypin, whose Premiership had been devoted to a prevention of such a recurrence, had, as Governor of Saratov (Middle Volga), made this clear in his report to headquarters in 1904.[1] The evolution of the peasant mind, from the "peaceful," organised appropriation of squire or enclosed peasant proprietary estates to that of unorganised insurrection, needs no better illustration than that furnished in these parts of Russia.

But the most striking feature of the chronicle of the Peasant Revolt of 1917 was not provided by the events occurring in the above traditional "semi-bondage" areas of old Russia. White Russia (which, with adjacent Lithuanian Provinces, included Mogilev, Minsk, Vitebsk, Smolensk, Vilna, Kovno and Grodno) and the Ukraine (i.e. South-Western: Kiev, Podolia and Volynia; Little Russia: Harkov, Chernigov and Poltava) also furnished an important recruiting ground for peasant

[1] See Krasny Arhiv, Vol. XVII, 1926, pp. 81–90.

manifestations of discontent. Indeed, the South-Western Provinces of Ukraine (Kiev, Podolia and Volynia) were especially prominent. In these regions existed the most developed capitalistic farming known in the whole country—the South-Western Provinces having a distinctive reputation as highly cultivated sugar-producing areas.[1]

In May, the semi-legal forms of the movement represented one-third of the cases in the Southern Ukrainian steppe-country (i.e. New Russia), about half in the provinces on the right bank of the River Dnieper (i.e. Kiev, Podolia and Volynia), over half in the provinces upon the left bank (Harkov, Poltava, Chernigov), and about half in White Russia (i.e. Mogilev, Minsk, Vitebsk, Smolensk). But in October these "peaceful" forms comprised one-sixth of the cases in Ukraine upon the right bank of the River Dnieper, one-sixth in the provinces upon the left bank, almost one-quarter in the Ukrainian steppe-land and nearly one-fifth in White Russia. As in the Central Agricultural and Middle Volga regions, these "concealed" forms of the movement gave place to open seizures in October. Almost three-quarters of the total number were of that type in White Russia and in the Ukrainian Provinces of the left bank, two-thirds in Ukrainian steppe-country (i.e. New Russia), and slightly more than half in the Ukrainian area upon the right bank of the Dnieper.

It is clear that the relative technical progress of the White Russian and the Ukrainian regions did not prevent the peasant movement there from reaching the same goal of expropriation of estates. Even the regions most familiar with the advantages of enclosed farming, and having a minimum, or even an absence, of the "communal" redivisional characteristics, were not exempt

---

[1] Of course it should be remembered that the earliest occasions in the twentieth century of peasant disturbances had occurred precisely in Ukraine in the year 1902. The Ukraine was most prominent as an area of decadent communal, accompanied by *podvornoe* (heritable) land-tenure. It was a rich Black-Earth area with an exceptionally congested population.

from the general catastrophe. But in Ukraine and White Russia the "seizure" form gave ground less rapidly before that of "destructive" action than was the case in the Central Agricultural and Middle Volga regions. In the Ukraine and White Russia, the agrarian movement reached its most acute form more quickly in the guise of "open seizures" than in that of "destructive activity." (There is, however, to be noted the exceptional position of the South-West Ukraine which furnished in October one-quarter of the total number of cases of "destruction.")

The displacement in all the above-mentioned regions of the "concealed" forms by the methods of open seizure, corresponded with the general growth of the peasant movement in October. In South-Western Ukraine too, the elimination of the "seizure" movement was accompanied by the introduction of methods of violence and destruction.

In comparison with April the number of instances of the movement recorded in the steppe-country of the Ukraine (i.e. New Russia) and in White Russia was doubled. In Ukraine on the left bank of the Dnieper the October movement was four and a half times as intense as that of April. In South-Western Ukraine— the area of the highest cultural standards in the native Russian parts of the old Empire and devoid of communal tenure, such cases were even 27 times as numerous as in the earlier month of the year. Accordingly South-West Ukraine approximated to the type of the Central Agricultural region. Whereas April had seen the South-West Ukraine the least affected by the movement, in October it followed directly in the wake of the Central Agricultural and Middle Volga regions.[1] To this extent (the investigator must conclude) one of the basic features of the agrarian laws of Stolypin—the attack upon communal tenure *per se*—was based upon defective theory. The peasant movement in the Ukraine operated no less strongly against the separatist national

[1] Cf *Krestyanskoe Dvizhenie, Predislovie,* pp. xiii–xiv.

movement as typified by the "Rada" than did that in Great Russia during the months October (1917) to March (1918) against the Provisional Government (and the Constituent Assembly).¹

When one turns to the remaining regions of the country, what does one find? The Central Industrial (Vladimir, Moscow, Kaluga, Tver, Yaroslav and Kostroma Provinces) and the Lake region (Petrograd, Pskov, Olonetz and Novgorod Provinces) witnessed a much slower development of the peasant movement than that elsewhere. Here there were counter-forces which prevailed over a simple desire for more land. A very large number of the population found industrial employment in the towns where there was a concentrated factory industrialism. In these parts the customary peasant struggle to expel the local squire was obscured by urban industrial and even directly political ideas. And, of course, being within striking distance of the two capitals, Petrograd and Moscow, the Government's arm of authority merited more respect. The Provisional Government's attempt after July to control the increasing rural anarchy achieved its best results in these localities. Here the number of cases of "destructive activity" fell from 25·7 per cent of the total for August to 14·2 per cent of the total for October. Further, the month of October in these parts gave only a 42·8 per cent increase over the total number of cases of the peasant movement. Yet in the rest of the country, October averaged two and one-third times the number of instances in April.

It is evident then that the extent to which the economic "semi-bondage" relationship survived or had been supplemented, if not supplanted, by "capitalistic" farming did not affect the outcome. The old landowners were evicted in both cases.

But what was the course of events in the regions of more recent colonisation? Those regions were without large landed interests belonging to squires. There was

¹ Cf. *Krestyanskoe Dvizhenie, Predislovie*, p. xiv.

however present a powerful so-called *kulak*,[1] or more well-to-do peasant, layer to replace them. The dimensions of the movement here were not equal to those in areas of squire ownership. Still more significant was the fact that the agrarian movement in these parts was marked by extreme instability. The hostility to the "village *bourgeoisie*" was considerably higher than in the areas of predominantly squire landownership. But (Y. Yakovlev significantly remarks)[2] the link between the urban industrial workers' revolution and the peasant rising—the basis of the Soviet Worker-Peasant State— was missing in these regions in October. The instances of anti-*kulak* aggression covering the whole country for the period after the February Revolution revealed 11·4 per cent for the combined Lower Volga region (Orenburg, Samara, Astrakhan Provinces), Northern Caucasus region (Stavropol, Kuban, Terek, Black Sea Provinces) and Don Province (*Oblast*). For Siberia (Tobolsk, Tomsk, Yeniseisk and Irkutsk Provinces), they represented 11·7 per cent. While for the Central Agricultural region the ratio was only 3·7 per cent.

Therefore to sum up, it may be affirmed that it was in all the Great Russian regions of squire landownership that the combined industrial and agrarian movements were most firmly cemented together. They were the territorial foundation for the consolidation of Lenin's power and that of his party during the troubled years 1918 and 1919. Many historical characters (the investigator would emphasise) have effected *coups d'état*, but to consolidate them is a very different matter. While the Bolshevik Party had the agrarian support of the old Russian Centre and the two capitals it could trust in the peasant communities and keep its powder dry. The Ukraine had to face its separatist problem and also the

---

[1] *Kulak* originally denoted any hard-fisted peasant who had more money and influence than his neighbours. The *skhod* (peasant assembly) was liable to be controlled by such individuals. The term acquired a sinister connotation, indicating one who thrived on usury. Later it became a political term of abuse.   [2] Ibid., p. xvi.

German occupation and the counter-revolutionary blast before it made up its mind to side with Moscow. In the rest of the Russian dominions the absence of a squirearchy had led to a differentiation among the peasantry which prevented the whole-hearted support the older Great Russian peasant communities had afforded to the revolutionary administration.

A conclusion may also be drawn from the above analysis bearing upon the famous question of the *mir* or *obshchina*. Lenin in 1898, in his *Razvitie Kapitalisma v Rossii* (Development of Capitalism in Russia), had used *Zemstvo* statistics to attempt to prove the disintegration of the land commune owing to internal differentiation. Stolypin and his coadjutors had relied upon a similar idea in their anti-communal legislation. The *neo-narodniki*, such as Chernov, had been inclined to minimise and discount such differentiation. It is strange to see that both views were right! What was overlooked was the fact that Russia is a large country and that the conditions of the newer colonised areas were not the same as those of the old. Tyumenev (see earlier), himself a Marxian anti-communalist, has corrected Lenin's conclusions in this regard. The differentiation that Lenin relied upon for his anti-capitalistic revolution was taking place precisely in the outer fringes of settlement upon the less-congested steppe-lands where no squires had yet established themselves. The communal egalitarianism which Stolypin feared and was determined to destroy, persisted in the parts of the old Moscow Centre where it did not cease to menace the abodes of the squires. Stolypin's policy was most successful on the before-mentioned outer fringes of settlement where its political aim was least in evidence. What an irony of fate that Lenin profited by the very weakness of his own deductions of 1898 and was most nearly overturned by counter-revolutionary forces, largely representing Stolypin's views, that found most support in the more recently colonised areas towards the Black Sea (Crimea, Kuban, Don) together with Siberia, where differentiation was a definite factor but where squires were not! Then, too, it was the non-differentiation of the Centre, the predominance of a compact phalanx of so-called "middle-peasantry" which guaranteed and still guarantees the power of the Communist Government. Is it surprising that in post-revolutionary years the Communist Adminstration was able to continue a forceful differentiation policy in the outer fringes based as it was upon practical uniformity in the Centre?

One must next examine in more detail two regions of Russia already shown to have been the foci of the movement, i.e. the Central Agricultural and Middle Volga regions. The *Krestyanskoe Dvizhenie* and appropriate volumes of the "Krasny Arhiv" furnish such an abundance of material that the historian is in danger of not seeing clearly the Russian wood on account of the densely set trees.

Throughout the whole country cases of agrarian "lawlessness" or violence covered only 34 districts in March. Therefore the dimensions of the agrarian disorders were at that date comparatively limited—one-quarter of these involving destruction, of which one-third comprised fires.[1] When it is remarked that in April there were 174 districts subject to disturbances of this type, 236 in May, 280 in June and 325 in July, the modesty of the recorded area in the first post-revolutionary month is all the more remarkable. The significance of the break was not immediately expressed in official reports from the various districts. Possibly the very *vis inertiæ* maintained an uneasy *status quo* for the first few weeks.

Proceeding to the analysis of the movement in the chief areas of its expression, one naturally turns to the Central Agricultural region.

On March 11 the "Alexandrovka" Estate in the Sergiev Canton of the Fatezh District (Kursk Province) was attacked and partially pillaged by peasants at the instigation of two armed soldiers.[2] In the same district

---

[1] *Krestyanskoe Dvizhenie v. 1917g. Predislovie*, Y. A. Yakovlev.
[2] Ibid., Telegraphic Report to Militia Department, 16/111.

it had been reported on March 15 that a local priest, Evgeny Belayev, was urging the peasantry to disorder. The whole district of Fatezh was threatened, necessitating the summoning of military assistance.

In the Province of Tula on March 13 the peasantry in one place were reported as having prevented war prisoners and day-labourers from working on a landowner's estate. This phenomenon, it may be noted, was typical of a large number of similar occurrences in all parts of Russia during the earlier part of 1917.

Ryazan Province reported that in one village (Astapova) the peasants were pillaging and destroying granaries and farm stock belonging to neighbouring estates. From Ryazhsk District the Trubetskoy estate manager reported that he had been notified that the local peasantry proposed to assume control (March 22).

From Tambov Province[1] came a complaint that bands of unknown men were pillaging the inhabitants and also that an estate in the Shatsk District was menaced with devastation. Except for report of agrarian disorders in Voronesh the above exhausts the content of the March events.

Nor was the twin region, the Middle Volga, much more affected. Matters at one place (St. Inza), in the Province of Simbirsk, ended fatally for the local large landowner named Gelshert, who was killed by a crowd after he had been arrested by the militia. The report to the Government refers mysteriously to rumours concerning his estate. What the nature of these rumours was, it did not specify. It may not be out of place here to mention that the number of *pomeshchiki* attacked with violence in the period February–October 1917 was infinitesimal. Still less was the number of squires actually murdered. In the earlier months of the year, such

---

[1] An especially interesting account of the decline and fall of a *pomeshchik's* influence in the very centre of agrarian dissension is provided by the *Reminiscences* of Prince Serge Volkonsky, who lived on his "Pavlovka" Estate in the Borisoglebsk district. His recollections form a valuable picture of an interesting part of Russia at this particularly interesting period.

attempted or effected violence was most prominent in the Baltic Provinces. The case of Gelshert above-mentioned is accordingly not symptomatic of peasant action in general. During the period February–October there was no *pugachovschina*, no *jacquerie*. In this respect it certainly resembled the corresponding period of 1905. Of course, in both years *pomeshchiki* had not waited to face peasant aggression. It was the local manager who bore the brunt. Cases of murders of managers, however, were infrequent. The majority of the violent deaths during the period occurred either during robbery under arms or as a result of lynch-law applied by peasant communities against those deemed to have infringed the peasant code of ethics and property rights.

From another district (Syzran) was reported a case of the assertion of cantonal assembly authority in the form of the expulsion from the confines of the canton of three of the estate staff. That occurrence was believed by the sender of the despatch to be leading to the disorganisation of the estate's defence work.

Penza Province, in the same region, came into prominence (March 15) owing to an apparently false account of devastation having been committed upon an estate, the Provincial Commissioner announcing that it was a case of "provocation"—an attempt to secure repressive measures without any valid reason. Villages in the same district witnessed local peasant and Tartar destruction of farm buildings and cutting and removal of timber. There was also a threat of incendiarism (Saransk District: March 27).

The month of April, it will be remembered, revealed a sharp rise in the number of districts affected by peasant activity. Reverting to the Central Agricultural region, one finds in Kursk more interference with the hired day-labour of local estates, and also unimpeded flights of war-prisoners. These prisoners had, until recently, played a very substantial part in maintaining the economic strength of squires' estates—sadly bereft of their customary support from underemployed or landless peasants.¹ The Grand Duke Mihail Alexandrovich's estate at Derugin experienced interference from the local cantonal committee which also exerted its control over individual forest farms (April 18–19). In one district (Lgov) demands of the following type were presented to landowners: (1) Diminution of rent, (2) Prohibition of timber-cutting in privately-owned and Government forests, (3) Fixation of labourers' wages. The same district saw cases of illegal timber-cutting and expulsion of officials from estates. Agricultural labour was described as being deficient in another district (Novoskol).

The Belgorod landowners protested that cantonal and village executive committees were impairing all farm work in the district which supplied, among others, three of the largest sugar factories. In Karachevsk district a local estate-manager was expelled on demand of the local peasant committee. Orel district, according to a landowner, Baryshin, was subjected to the removal of labourers as a result of local peasant action. Cultivation was thereby stopped (April 16–17). "The Imperial Duma and the Soviet of Soldiers' and Workers' Delegates of the City of Petrograd" were asked to arrest and even execute A. N. Hvostov, a local landowner, "as a guardian of the old régime."² So indeed the Elets local executive was reported to have acted according to Hvostov's own account. The local Soviet deputies had to be invoked in some places, soldiers and officers being sent out to points of especial disorder. The "inadmissibility" of such actions was explained to the troublesome communities. Church land was seized in the Karachev district. In the Elets district the committee of security deprived Murinov—a member of the *Zemstvo* Board—of his authority. In the Bryansk district some squires' mansion houses were robbed. It was suggested that troops be sent to prevent violence. In the Livny dis-

---

¹ Of landless peasants, strictly so-called, there were approximately 2,000,000 in the whole of the country.

² A. N. Hvostov, Minister of the Interior (October 1915–March 1916), was dismissed for plotting against Rasputin.

trict, after church land had been seized, the priest was expelled (April 20).

According to a telegram of April 23, peasant disorders were occurring in the Malo-Arhangelsk district; cantonal committees were preventing the landowners from cutting timber, were seizing land and withdrawing labourers. Sowing of seed was held up. Illegalities and violence were being committed both in the above district and in Elets. Measures were being taken to tranquillise the population (Provincial Commissioner, April 25).

Some garrison troops of Mtsensk raided the estate of Sheremetev and also broke into the distillery in the same district. Drunken troops were threatening to destroy all estates and works. The Provincial Commissioner was described as taking measures to protect landlords and works. He sent his adjutant and also soldier and officer deputies. The district commandant was asked for assistance in pacification measures (April 28). Two villages in different districts (Sevsk and Karachev) illegally dismissed their church elders and elected new ones. In another district the priest was removed by the local population and the churches placed at the disposal of the People. A lady landowner named Vinogradska was subjected to confiscation of that part of her land which was leased to certain peasants.

The prestige now enjoyed by district and cantonal executive committees was indicated by the information of April 14 from a landowner, Lyubomirov, of Venev district. A resolution of the committee forbade field work upon squires' land. Sowing was consequently being prevented. Some individuals said they were prepared to work, but added that they were intimidated by their own district committee's decree (April 15). Inventories were even being taken of landowners' property (April 20). In Efremov district the local committee resolved to withdraw all war-prisoners from estates and to divide up the land. If opposition were manifested, it threatened arrest and punishment of estate-servants (April 17). In Krapivna district, the steward on Prince

Gagarin's estate, near the village of Tsarevo, was expelled by the peasants. The local executive committee of Kashira persuaded the inhabitants to seize, without compensation, church, monastery and squires' land for the use of cantonal committees (April 19).

Turning to Ryazan, one finds that the Ranenburg executive committee (destined to be prominent for its radicalism during later months) resolved that peasants should be allowed: to lease compulsorily squires' land at very low rates; to requisition seed, deadstock and draught horses. Violence and illegality were prevalent in the district. The situation menaced the complete destruction of farms, the ruin of cattle and the ruin of many individuals. Such at least was the burden of some landowners' complaints (April 2). On April 9, destructive activity occurred upon an estate in the district mentioned, while the above Ranenburg resolution was alleged to have caused peasant disorders in an adjoining district. Agitation by students for a state of calm pending the Constituent Assembly did not meet with success (April 7). On April 8, A. Shumakher, a local landowner and member of the Imperial Council from the *Zemstvo* of Ryazan, reported that peasants in the Ranenburg district had seized squires' land and live- and dead-stock. On his own estate horses and harness had been taken away by the local population. In another district (Sapozhok) of the same province, Prince Shuvalov's estate was claimed for almost complete expropriation by two cantons. Prices and allotments were to be decided by the cantonal authorities (April 11–13). The Provincial Congress sitting in Ryazan resolved to requisition grain reserves prepared for sowing operations and also timber and fuel. Land was to be compulsorily leased (April 15). A meeting of peasants in the Kudryava canton (Dankov district) under the presidency of the priest Nekrasov, resolved that:

All landowners must quickly proceed to sow their land. This operation must terminate in ten working days. The unsown area will be taken over by the local cantonal committee. The whole

1917 harvest is rated at 25 kopecks per *desyatine*, the rate increasing on every successive 5 *desyatines*, so that 100 *desyatines* will produce 500 roubles to assist the Government. If anyone does not pay the money to the committee, he shall be regarded as a traitor to his country.

The same committee "illegally transferred on lease" two-thirds of the land under spring-corn on the estate of the local landowner Shablykina at the rate of 5 roubles per *desyatine* (May 13).

The Mihailov district witnessed disorders, while, according to a lady landowner, Ermolova, the menacing attitude of peasants in the Ryazhsk district was spreading.

At a general assembly of representatives of all cantonal executive committees, of members of Ryazhsk *Zemstvo*, of representatives of co-operators and private landowners, there was presented the District Commissar's report upon measures for the preservation of peace and order in the district. An appeal to the local inhabitants was thereupon drawn up, asking for a speedy execution of all the points set out therein (April 18–19).

Succeeding reports only emphasise the virtual control now assumed by peasant communities over squires' and other landowners' estates. Towards the end of April (22) a general provincial meeting at Ryazan passed a resolution requisitioning land, sown areas, forest land, forest materials and wood saw-mills. Consequently agricultural work and forestry was at a standstill. On April 25 in Ryazhsk district was reported the arrest of a local landowner and President of the District Gentry, D. K. Sterligov. Similar evidence of local committees' power was provided by other localities in the Ryazan Province.

Tambov was another province which was prominent in the succeeding months. In Lipetsk district, a mob of peasants led by soldiers on leave pillaged the house on the manor belonging to a squire named Kozhin—an ominous conjuncture of military insubordination and peasant disorder that decided Russia's destiny in the following period. A telegram of April 6 announced that authority was unrespected. Violence and robbery were in progress. The district (Tambov) was in the throes of a rising peasant movement of serious proportions. This movement was directed against privately-owned land and threatened the prospective harvest-sowing. The arm of the law was obviously becoming weaker when an armed attack upon a local priest could take place, leading to the deaths of his daughter, a yard-man and a servant (village of Rasskasova, April 18). On the same day in the village of Othozhya (Borisoglebsk district) a parish deacon, his wife and two children were murdered. While the motive in the first case is not clear, in the second it was probably a matter of robbery—the village bank being kept in the priest's house.

In Voronesh Province, a *hutor* (separate or isolated farm) was plundered and burnt (April 4). Further cases of day-labourers being prevented from working, and also of disappearances of war-prisoners, showed the increasing hold the local communities were exerting over squires' land (April 15). A case of a village-committee's search for arms is recorded from the Zadonsk district (April 16). Voronesh district saw an instance of land seizure, even where part of the expropriated area had been already sown (April 20). The Countess Apraxin's estate, in the previously mentioned Zadonsk district, was seized by the peasantry, the servants being expelled and agricultural reserves stolen (April 25).

How did the Middle Volga region—the adjoining area of outstanding rural problems—fare in the same month? From the Province of Simbirsk a report was despatched by A. D. Pasukhin, a landowner of Kurmysh district, saying that the cantonal committee in Bortsumana had decreed as follows:

(1) To prohibit use of war-prisoners' labour.

(2) To utilise exclusively local peasant labour with wages fixed for men at 4 roubles and women at 2 roubles (i.e. slightly less than 8 shillings a week for men and 4 shillings for women).

(3) Servants working on estates for less were to be sent away.

(4) To introduce an eight-hour working day with special rates for overtime.

(5) At the first requisition to commandeer half of the estate cattle.

(6) At the first horse mobilisation, to take half of the estate horses.

(7) To forbid the sale of estate forests and to prohibit merchants from paying estates for timber sold in 1916.

(8) Money received for leasing of meadows must be returned; a new price was to be fixed according to the committee's resolution.

One can hardly obtain in a more succinct form an idea of the omnipotence that local (village and cantonal) committees had already acquired at this date (April 1–10). There was "an absence of executive authority in local areas" (April 10). The Provincial Commissioner of Simbirsk reported on April 10 a distinctly anarchic state of affairs—at least as far as old ideas were concerned. Throughout the whole province squires' stewards were being driven out or arrested according to the resolution of cantonal and village committees. Labourers were being removed from estates. Lands were being seized. Arbitrary leases were being fixed. A movement of *obshchinniki* (communal holders) against *otrubniki* (secessionists from the land commune, under the provisions of Stolypin's Legislation [1906–11] treated earlier) was commencing. Delegates sent by the executive committee supported the peasants. Benefits conferred as "doles" only evoked peasant demands from the squires. The situation in the province threatened the sowing of the harvest. The Provincial Commissioner pointed out the necessity of the speedy announcement that the land was national property—the decision as to methods of land-usage to be postponed until the Constituent Assembly.

Above is a sufficiently clear picture of the collapse of old property rights. The most significant feature for those who hoped that the Revolution could be stayed in its further course was the hostility between *otrubniki* and *obshchinniki*. The political objective of the Government's agrarian legislation after 1905 had been to secure a strong layer of conservative peasantry as a bulwark against further revolutionary events. That objective, already made clear in an earlier section and emphasised in an interview which the investigator had with N. Savich, one of its protagonists in the Third Duma, vitiated the more purely economic side of the attempted change. After the Tsar had fallen, the policy was seen to be bankrupt. "In the first few weeks after the February Revolution," declared A. Kerensky, the Head of the Provisional Government in the later months of 1917, to the writer, "all those who had left the communes were forced to return." While in some respects an exaggeration—the *Krestyanskoe Dvizhenie* provides a number of instances of still continued hostility during the year—A. Kerensky's statement is broadly true. The violence of Stolypin's policy, criticised both by Witte in his *Memoirs* and by Kerensky, probably defeated its own end, thereby depriving the purely economic virtues of land-settlement (*zemleustroistvo*) of an unbiassed verdict. *Zemlerasstroistvo* (unsettlement of the land) to use N. Oganovsky's term seemed to have been more marked than *zemleustroistvo*.

The reference to the desirability of declaring all land to be national property is interesting as showing that by the irony of fate the very class that had always opposed such a policy—the squires—were now by circumstances being compelled to assent to such a measure as a means, not of satisfying peasant needs, but as a way of saving something out of the wreckage of their property rights. That fact (the investigator would insist) requires to be correlated with the emergence of a Social Revolutionary Administration in July. Even an avowedly Socialist Administration with a programme of expropriation was preferable to the piecemeal and gradual extinction of the rights of the old possessing class in the village. Chernov's policy in this regard enabled Lenin to persuade his followers that the Social Revolutionaries were simply arranging "a bargain" with the representatives of the old order. Upon this question the Social Revolutionaries themselves became a disrupted party.

Returning to the Simbirsk Province, one finds a rather curious idea of peasant equity. In Karsun district the peasant assembly of Belogor deprived the local owners of land, leaving at their disposal 100 *desyatines*, with the proviso that, if any peasants were found to desire it, the squires must lease the aforesaid land at 6 roubles. Church land had been simultaneously seized (April 20). In Syzran district Count Orlov Davydov's estate manager and treasurer were expelled by the Usol cantonal committee. The same committee demanded the return of 25,000 roubles paid in rent (April 25).

The adjoining provinces of Saratov and Penza underwent much the same process. From Penza, there is an interesting despatch from the President of the Mokshan District Board (dated April 29). It gives a clear idea of the composition and desires of what were rapidly assuming the control in rural Russia—the peasant assemblies, or "agrarian soviets," as they may be termed.

The sowing of early spring wheat in the district is almost concluded. Almost all the seed to hand has been utilised and a good crop should be realised in consequence. At first the peasants co-operated with landowners and pursued their labours. But after the peasant congresses and the resolutions which were introduced there, they began to break their contracts with landowners, since they perceived the impossibility of punishment and the possibility of unfettered action. When cantonal and district executive committees were formed (in the month of March) they were largely composed of *intelligentsia*, but afterwards hostility arose against the "intellectuals" and already by the middle of April these bodies became everywhere exclusively of peasant membership. The tendency of these committees is clearly unrestrained by legal considerations and provokes seizures among the population.

This important evidence of the condition of Russia two months after Nicholas II's abdication, is reinforced by a report to the "Temporary Committee of the Imperial Duma."[1]

[1] Reproduced in Vol. XV of Krasny Arhiv, 1926.

In the majority of cases (it is therein affirmed) the impression derived from the relations of the peasantry at this most important moment of Russian political life, is regrettable (*pechalnoe*). There is no opinion among the rural population concerning the Constituent Assembly. The people do not understand pamphlets and cannot read. The peasant understands only when he himself speaks and asks questions. He does not understand when he hears what is said to Ivan, Peter or Sidor [i.e. Tom, Dick or Harry] without immediate address to himself. One can already hear a keen discussion: Shall we vote for a Tsar or for the students?" [1]

Further, after describing the universally emerging "soviet" committee system, and the clash and conflicts caused by competing authorities, it remarks[2] "local commissioners are not trusted unless elected by the people." On page 41, the compiler alludes to the difficulties of an overworked commissioner, who had, in the midst of organising cantonal committees, to go elsewhere to listen to a serious dispute between squire and peasant. The cantonal committees were, according to the *Obzor*, slower to organise than those of the towns. This was, it was suggested, due to the poor information of the population, the distance from the centre, the difficulties caused by spring floods and finally "the absence of intellectual forces." This last remark is contrasted with the experience of Penza Province above, where the *intelligentsia* was absent because it had not been invited to stay. Village and cantonal committees (as in Penza) had been universally formed in the first month. In some places the election had produced unsatisfactory results owing to such cases as that of a canton in Smolensk, where two monarchists had been elected—the local "psalm-singer" (*psalomschik*) who had been inciting to violence and grabbing, and a bankrupt *dvoryanin*, then an innkeeper. Other members included an owner of a steam-mill and a *kulak* trader.[3] All the "intellectual" forces of the village

---

[1] Cf. *Obzor Polozheniya Rossii za tri mesyatsa revolutsii po dannym otdela snosheniy s provintsey Okt. Rev. fond III, Dela Vrem. Pravitelst*, Kras. Arh. Vremennovo Komiteta Gosudarstvennoy Dumy, Vol. XV, pp. 33, 37, 1926.
[2] Ibid., p. 40.   [3] Ibid., p. 41.

left it during the first few days of the change. Teachers (especially female) had no influence over the peasants owing to their connection with the old régime. Even "intellectual" people earlier elected as presidents of cantons were then being turned out (i.e. May).¹ Penza was evidently in the van in that regard, since that had happened there already before the middle of April. The *otrubniki* (the *Obzor* continued) were as disliked as the *intelligentsia*. They, and the petty landowners of 30–50 *desyatines*, were absolutely not elected. Their interests remained unrepresented. Women had no part in peasant elections. They did not know their own powers. There were no cases of women's elections among the peasants.² Finally, said the compiler of the *Obzor*,³ "the link between canton (*volost*) and district (*uyezd*) was weak." This was one of the fatal factors which the First Provisional Government strove to remedy by the cantonal *Zemstvo*, which however met with little response locally.

Meanwhile, in Penza Province, a peasant congress, lasting from the 7th to the 10th April, resolved to direct cantonal committees to institute a definite redivision of various types of pasture land in the cantons. This was to take place without any compensation and with no consultation of the holders. Wood-cutting by the peasantry was a universal phenomenon at the same date. It was feared that the shearing of valuable merino herds of sheep would be prevented. As the peasants were still accustomed to obey the Government and especially the authorities in Petrograd it was deemed advisable to send delegates from the capital to guide and restrain such cantonal committees. (At least, so the local commissioner reported on May 12.)

From the Province of Kazan, the Provincial Commissioner telegraphed on April 23 that the most serious disturbances were in the Laishev, Spassk and Sviyazhsk districts where there had been illegal ploughing of land, seizure of reserve seed-corn, destruction of estates and

---
¹ Ibid., p. 42.   ² Ibid., p. 42.   ³ Ibid., p. 43.

confiscation of land of *hutoryane* (separate farmers) by fellow-villagers. Provincial and district organisations had sent out members to pacify those areas. The cause of the disturbances was described as being acute shortage of land, the incitement of the population by untrue statements and the "absence in villages of an educated element." It was reported by the commissioner that the disorders were being settled, and investigations were taking place. Measures were being taken to protect landowners' interests.[1]

K. V. Molostvov on behalf of certain landowners of one of the above districts (Spassk) complained to the Provisional Government that (1) It was impossible to carry on any farming, because the peasants were removing labourers, confiscating seed, in some places taking all property from manor-houses, threatening owners with violence and death, prohibiting wood-cutting for fuel and appropriating prepared timber. (2) Cantonal committees were prescribing very low rentals. (3) The Provisional Government's orders were unknown in the villages but on the other hand the Bolsheviks' proclamations were widespread. (4) The population did not know where to turn for instructions. There was no judiciary. Everyone was doing as he liked. The well-disposed section was in a state of terror. (5) Disturbances were increasing daily and simultaneously with them, dissatisfaction. (6) Kazan and other towns were likely to run short of food and fuel. (7) The district commissioners were giving no help. On the contrary some of them were adopting measures clearly contradicting the Provisional Government's instructions (April 30).[2]

Before this particular evidence of agrarian disorder in the Middle Volga region is passed, some points should be noted. In the first place, as a landowner K. V. Molostvov would not be likely to paint a less vivid picture than the events warranted. It might be subject to exaggeration, but other reports from different centres give no ground for such belief, although the fact that his wife

[1] *Krestyanskoe Dvizhenie*, p. 19.   [2] Ibid., p. 20.

had to run from his estate might have tended in that direction. Secondly, Bolshevik propaganda is mentioned. Lenin had returned from Switzerland via Germany on April 3 (o.s.). He was to deliver his policy speech to the All-Russian Soviet of Peasants on May 22. Meanwhile his so-called April Theses were helping to create a Bolshevik Party—which, contrary to what many people might assume, was at that date but a nucleus rather than a party. Despite Lenin's outspoken agrarian policy of "Seize the Land!" there are not many references in *Krestyanskoe Dvizhenie* to Bolshevik activity and only rare mentions of Lenin by name. Marxians, of whichever wing of the Social Democratic Party, had been primarily urban industrial in outlook, in accordance with Marx's own attitude in Western Europe. However, Lenin's peculiarity as a revolutionary was his dualism. He was an orthodox industrial proletarian leader as far as Western Europe was concerned, but, for Russia, he also descended from the mid-nineteenth century Chernyshevsky and the old *narodniki*. This dualism as has been shown elsewhere was his paradox and yet his power. The Bolshevik Party could claim little formal credit (or discredit) for "capitalising" the agrarian disintegration. That was the Social Revolutionaries' business. When the Social Revolutionary general staff lost touch with their rank and file Lenin simply instructed his general staff to take charge.

The significance of the preceding months, March and April, with its impact upon the international fortunes of Russia as a Great Power was clearly indicated in Victor Chernov's speech at the commencement of his fateful Ministry in the Agricultural Department in succession to the Constitutional Democrat, Shingarev.[1] The great theoretic protagonist of land socialisation and the perfected land commune (*obshchina*), later President of Russia's short-lived Constituent Assembly in January 1918, spoke *inter alia* as follows:

[1] "Agrarny vopros i sovremenny moment." Lecture at the Shanyavsky University, Moscow, April 30, 1917. *Zemlya i Volya*, No. 44, Moscow.

Our Army is a peasant—a village Army.... The War is an industrial one.[1] The village principally bears the dreadful obligation of shedding its blood in this colossal War.... But bearing the principal rôle in the War the Army is especially interested in the land question. We noticed this particularly at the time of the occasional seizures of land by peasants.[2] Rumours of such seizures reached the Army. Soldiers from many parts of the front began to desert to their homes. There appeared a possibility of mass desertions. This shows the vital significance of the agrarian question for the Army.

Continuing on page 13 he said:

The land question naturally stands in the centre of all the organised tasks of the moment.... It is clear that in the future Constituent Assembly labour democracy will be present in unusual strength. This has made us anticipate perhaps the glorious history of the First and Second Dumas.

(What irony when one thinks of the later dissolution of the Constituent Assembly—that body thereby disappearing like those Dumas, where also labour democracy had been present in unusual strength!)

Naturally [he proceeded [3]] in the Constituent Assembly, the land question will occupy first place.... The Socialist Revolutionaries (the party of Kerensky and Chernov) have attacked any kind of extra-legal seizures and outrages and have therefore instructed the peasantry consciously to prepare for the Constituent Assembly. ... The most systematic slogan seems to be "Land through the Constituent Assembly...."

Then on page 15 he uttered a warning:

One of the obstacles to a complete determination of the land question appears to be the squires' consciousness that the old land arrangements have ended. Hence there is a feverish rush to sell land to foreigners. There are fictitious sales. A law is about to be published preventing such sales.[4]

---

[1] "Agrarny vopros i sovremenny moment." Lecture at the Shanyavsky University, Moscow, April 30, 1917. *Zemlya i Volya*, No. 44, Moscow, p. 7.

[2] Probably Chernov knew that such seizures were certainly, as has been shown, much more than "occasional" at this date. [3] Ibid., p. 14.

[4] N.B.—A cognate phenomenon is mentioned in the *Obzor Polozheniya*, March–May, 1917, Krasny Arhiv, Vol. XV, p. 48, where certain owners "hastened to cut down their forests" but were prevented by village community action.

Until the present [continued Chernov], there has been only "land anarchy." Until now there has not been perfected any differentiation among the peasantry.[1] In the path of the development of this natural process private property has always stood in the way, at the head of it being the private property of the dynasty (as large in area as Germany) now gloriously reconquered by the Russian people. The policy of the (Social Revolutionary) Party is that of a general land fund. . . . There will be a new land structure. . . . All the land will be united in the hands of the whole People. Belonging to the People, the land will be ruled by special organs of State power in direct contact locally with the land itself, embracing all its peculiarities, requirements and needs.[2] . . . There will be higher organs also.[3] There will be equal rights of all citizens to land. . . . Objections have been raised. . . . Firstly, is there enough land? . . . There is [maintained V. Chernov]. . . . Secondly, will redivision empty the towns? . . . No, because the average townsman is not sufficiently enthusiastic about farm-labour to exchange his present situation on that account.[4] . . . The Social Revolutionary Party does not think by one stroke of the pen to change the old order of land usage and land ownership. . . . It realises the differences of usage and tenure in different parts. . . . There will be a free Provincial Committee system which will be elastic. . . . Mode of usage will be left to local conditions.[5] . . . There will be three "norms" of distribution, the "labour," the "consumption" and the "average norm." . . . The "labour norm" [V. Chernov explained] is an allotment to be worked by a given family. The "consumption norm" is an addition to an inadequate allotment or the creation of a new allotment where a family is landless. . . . Lastly, there will be an "average," the best possible for the given area. . . . The Agrarian Project of the Social Revolutionary Party in the Second Duma (1907) gained much support [said the speaker] among the peasants. It appealed to the great majority of peasant members. It is now [i.e. April 30, 1917] being considered. . . . It will be an insurance against reaction. . . . That is why the Social Revolutionaries regard it as being the chief point of their programme. . . . The Soviet of Peasants is now entering the Soviet of Workers and Soldiers [an allusion to the approaching All-Russian Peasant Congress in Petrograd in May 1917].

---

[1] N.B.—*Narodnik* view contrasted with the Russian Marxist view.
[2] *Zemlya i Volya*, No. 44, p. 16.
[3] Ibid., p. 17.   [4] Ibid., p. 18.   [5] Ibid. p. 19.

In conclusion V. Chernov declared:

> Sam narod etot istinny Samoderzhertz Rossii (The Peasantry is the real Autocrat of Russia). . . . The Constituent Assembly Elections are fixed for September 17.[1]

The above speech of the Minister directly responsible for the treatment of the Land Problem gains force when the chronicle of the previous two months (March and April) is remembered. It also bears comparison with that of Lenin at the Peasant Congress in Petrograd in the ensuing month (May 22), already treated elsewhere.

The occurrences in Kursk (Central Agricultural region) in May reveal the steady progressive *de facto* control of estates—whether agricultural or forest—that has previously been described. The prevalence of deserted troopers and the danger which stores of spirit presented in the hands of unruly individuals caused much anxiety to local officials, e.g. in the Orel Province of the same region.[2] From Orel Province too, came information regarding the sequel to the disturbances of the preceding month in the Mtsensk district. Troops that had been expressly sent from the towns of Orel and Mtsensk had been stopped on the road. The Mtsensk district commissioner had stated that their arrival would only promote further excesses. It would be preferable to send soldier and worker deputies who would produce a better effect. One can see that even a local district commissioner was sufficiently overawed by local cantonal influence not to risk the unpopularity of using military force from the centre. Further particulars on occurrences at Mtsensk[3] indicated that it was due to regimental insubordination. On the alleged pretext of searching an estate for arms a regiment had, under soldier delegates, and without its commander's permission, searched the manor house, found no arms, but had broken into the spirit cellars and consumed too much for good discipline. It had then started destroy-

---

[1] *Zemlya i Volya*, No. 44, p. 20.
[2] *Krestvanskoe Dvizhenie*, p. 37.   [3] Ibid., p. 38.

ing the house. The local Mtsensk garrison, hearing the news, had rushed up 5,000 strong to share the liquor, and the consequences might well be imagined. The damage was "colossal." The attacks upon spirit stores in other parts of the district had followed. Eventually 2 officers and 400 troopers had been arrested after officer and soldier deputies had been sent from Orel to enquire. Stores of spirit from other distilleries were sent for safety to the railway line. To such a state was the military organisation of the rear degenerating.[1] At a village in the Sevsk district, the lack of reverence for religious observance, now increasingly evident generally, was shown by parishioners and soldiers stopping the progress of a synod, interrupting a church service and insulting the priest.[2] The old veneration for his church, which Russia's Orthodox peasant was supposed to possess to a marked degree, did not seem to be a restraining factor in the general social anarchy that the great defeat of 1915 and its sequel, the fall of Nicholas, had initiated.

The complete disrespect for the old order was revealed when, in Bolkhovsk district, a priest was expelled by a village assembly and, in Livny district, Yaskovich, a former *Zemsky Nachalnik*—the old arbiter of village life—was arrested in his own house!

From Tula on May 5 came particulars of a particularly flamboyant cantonal committee (Kurkina, Efremov district) which assumed the style and appellation of "Committee of the Imperial Duma" and proceeded to "infringe property and personal rights and introduce disorder among the peasantry of the district, which was, generally, moderately and sensibly disposed."[3] After exercising control of the land and possessions of two local squires, Staff-Captain G. Ignatyev and V. Meller, it first determined to expel Ignatyev, then kept him under arrest, ultimately ordering him to go immediately to the Front. The Provincial Commissioner's authority was ignored and only that of the Minister of the Interior

[1] Ibid., p. 39.   [2] Ibid., p. 39.   [3] Ibid., p. 42.

was considered. The aforesaid Committee struck a levy of 20 kopecks per *desyatine* to enable a peasant-landowners' union to be formed.¹

From Ryazan Province came information on May 31 of occurrences in the Ranenburg district (one of the hotbeds of peasant community activity during the whole year). Prince Volkonsky reported illegal activities of the local committee with regard to his estate. The committee had compulsorily leased all the land which was under spring wheat, specifying 10 roubles per *desyatine* as the rate. In addition, 10 draught horses were taken for 330 roubles and 15 *pud* of rye at 1 rouble 60 kopecks. All this interference was to be applied to the advantage of the local population. The squire was not permitted to send his produce away. He was also forbidden to sell his livestock.

A namesake of the above—Prince Serge Volkonsky —lived in the neighbouring province of Tambov. A member of the old ruling class, pre-eminently distinguished for his cultural attainments, a descendant of the aristocratic Decembrists who had tried to prevent the accession of Nicholas I in 1825, he has written his *Vospominaniya* (Reminiscences). These *Vospominaniya* are valuable for a student of these years, as the reflex upon a well-read mind, bound up with the old régime, of the events of the whole revolutionary period 1917–21. Even if one marvels that the cultured *obshchestvo* (society) of the old order did not sooner share its attainments with the lowly and ignorant *narod* (peasantry), nevertheless there is a certain "pathos" in his description of these times—a "pathos" that exudes, not only from a consideration of the downfall of old pillars of the past, but from the *oblomovshchina* (dilettantism) apparent in his autobiography.

"The spirit that reigned in March did not last long." ² It is true that the people behaved so well that during the first three weeks there was not a single arrest in

¹ *Krestyanskoe Dvizhenie*, p. 42.
² Volkonsky, *Reminiscences*, Vol. II, p. 163.

Borisoglebsk (the town adjoining the Volkonsky estate "Pavlovka"). But already in the second month the trouble began and gradually all restraints were broken. It seemed as if a wind of irresponsibility had blown over the free abundance of our steppes. All the applications I made to the president of our *Zemstvo* to draw his attention to the felling of the trees and the damage done to the fields by the peasants' cattle, remained without effect, and when I saw him he said there were no means of counteracting these acts.

Later,[1] speaking of the cantonal control exercised over his property, of which the instance quoted from *Krestyanskoe Dvizhenie* is an example, he illustrated what must have been the prevailing sentiment in the squire class during the spring and even more emphatically in the summer ensuing. "I prefer a man who comes to you and tells you: 'I shall take from you this plough, because it is mine,' to him who says: 'I warn you that you have no right to sell this plough because it is not yours.'" That aptly describes the "pseudo-legal" or "concealed" expropriation of private property which, in the spring and summer of 1917, was the prevailing feature in Russian rural life.

Proceeding with the review and analysis of events in the Central Agricultural region, one finds a communication from the provincial commissioner of Tambov, which described the need for an instruction from the Provisional Government, explaining that "the forthcoming transfer of land to the working population does not signify the confiscation of the whole moveable property of the landowners." Thus, by implication, it may be assumed that such a drastic view did prevail locally.

Among the real forest of telegrams of protest to headquarters regarding the agrarian movement, many have the same tone of monotonous reiteration. The ubiquitous and omnipotent cantonal assembly—the old *obshchina-obshchestvo* with its inevitable "committee"—allowed no obstacle in its triumphant path. The final

[1] Volkonsky, op. cit., p. 165.

report for May from Voronesh Province (Central Agricultural region) gives, with a real *Baedeker Guide-Book* perfection, a catalogue of its activities in that province.[1]

Cases of varied breaches of the law, and of irregular activities, grow more frequent each day in the province, particularly in the agrarian question. The peasants are everywhere hindering the further conduct of private farming: they are seizing estates either fully or partially: they are pasturing stock upon private land: they are trespassing on corn, hayfields and young forest plantations: they are driving away servants and labourers, removing war-prisoners, preventing the sale of live- and dead-stock, fixing very low rents for leases, which frequently do not cover bank charges. These rents they make payable not to the landowner but to the cantonal committee. They are fixing abnormally high wages, forbidding the employment of labour from other cantons. They are levying communal dues, preventing the legal cutting of timber even for the interests of defence; they are appropriating monastic and church lands and Treasury timber-estates. All these actions are carried out, frequently in accordance with cantonal resolutions, or with the approval of cantonal committees. Sometimes even the district committees ratify them. The Provincial committees are doing their best to prevent these activities. The provincial commissioner draws attention to the fact that there is noticeable among the peasantry an increasing tendency to redivide expropriated land among themselves. Complications and excesses may be anticipated at the corn and hay harvest. Searches and arrests according to resolutions of communal organisations, or on private initiative, are a frequent event. There have been a few cases of the violent expulsion from their locality of officials of the former Government, of priests and private citizens. The public prosecutor is enquiring into such arrests and banishments. The executive committees regard themselves as possessed of the highest executive power in the given region. They issue resolutions and, having no definite instructions from the Government of the exact limit of their rights and duties, they hasten to make searches, arrests, to impose fines and to close trading and industrial enterprises [June 2].[2]

One hardly needs further particulars of what cantonal committees could or did do in the first three months after the February Revolution!

[1] *Krestyanskoe Dvizhenie*, p. 47.   [2] Ibid., pp. 47–8.

Among the reports concerning Simbirsk Province (Middle Volga region) appears one about a general meeting held on May 26, 1917 [1] (but for some reason the information itself did not reach the Government until August 28, the facts having been reported by the Provincial Commissioner on August 17).

Representatives of the combined peasantry of the villages of Deyanov, Romanovka, Belovka, Timofeevka, Maltsev and Balabanov of the Kurmysh district and of the villages of Ulyanovka, Bolshoy Rtishchev, Maloy Rtishchev, Vashutin and Pletnika of the Vasilsursk district, Nizhegorod Province, met to consider the following measures: to prohibit the use of war-prisoners as agricultural labour by squires and *kulaks*; to propose to squires that they should hand over all land to the cantonal committees; to take over and transfer to the peasants land in cases where squires and *kulaks* declined to cultivate it with their own hands; to lease land from squires and *kulaks* at prices fixed by the above peasant union, the money to be deposited with the Treasury and not in the hands of the squires; to endeavour by organised means to compel squires to leave their estates; to forbid the sale and disposal by squires of live and dead stock of estates unless the cantonal committees had previously permitted it.

It is clear that aggrandisement on the part of the fully revived cantonal *obshchina-obshchestvo* had already reached its limit, even the richer peasant (so-called *kulak*) elements now being reduced to the same impotence as the squire.

Further afield in the same region, there had taken place a peasant congress in Penza on May 14.[2] This congress assumed the attributes and functions of a provincial constituent assembly. It carried a series of resolutions directed against private ownership and especially against the right of disposing of plough-land, hayfields, woods, live- and dead-stock. The work done by servants and labourers was placed under the control of cantonal and village committees. These resolutions were put into force by the committees and, according to local landowners, were causing class dissension and creating a situation threatening the market. Moreover,

[1] Ibid., p. 49.   [2] Ibid., p. 51.

according to a telegram of May 18, there were violent seizures of land, stock and even domestić property in the Penza district. They were becoming "endemic." Social organisations received no support from the centre and were affording none themselves. In Kerensk district, the local executive committee was putting into force the above-mentioned resolutions of the Penza Congress and the peasants were expropriating private property (May 20).[1]

The Province of Kazan presented a picture of rural disorders which had commenced on April 22, affecting land of considerable value. These occurrences were particularly noticeable in districts such as Spassk, Laishev and Chistopol, where there were large private estates. In some districts there was noticed a tendency of communal holders to interfere with *hutoryane* (owners of separate farms)—another evidence of the local attacks upon the principles of Stolypin's pre-revolutionary legislation. The provincial commissioner had to emphasise that it was "impossible to decide land questions before the Constituent Assembly met, unless by mutual consent."[2] The food problem was becoming apparent. In one district, the head of militia was replaced by a man possessing local influence. Landownership was under a cloud in view of the tendency exhibited by peasants to rush to divide up the land.[3] There had been arrests of prominent officials as, for instance, a district commissioner and a town mayor. In one place a member of the Imperial Duma had been placed under guard. All these people were eventually released. But (added the official despatch from the province [May 18]) "the frequent re-election of those responsible for administration serves to hinder the establishment of firm order and legality."[4] The weakness of the Central Authority in its dealings with the peasant communities was evident of course during the whole period from February to October (o.s.).

The cantons of Spassk district met in congress and

[1] *Krestyanskoe Dvizhenie*, p. 51. [2] Ibid., p. 52. [3] Ibid., p. 53. [4] Ibid., p. 53.

demanded that, even before convocation of the Constituent Assembly, squire-landowners' property should be transferred to the peasants. The squires were to be allowed to retain as much land as an individual peasant (May 20). On May 24 from the same province of Kazan came news that the agrarian movement was continuing. Communal-holders were taking land from *hutoryane* (private peasant-holders). To leaseholders notices were being given that the harvest must belong to the village community. The idea was well established that woods and land generally were common property (May 24).[1]

As three months had elapsed since the Tsar's abdication, and already the First Provisional Government was showing a steady change in personnel, in some ways Russia had reached a point where it was becoming obvious that a nominal change of leadership had not been as efficacious as many hoped. Milyukov, the guiding hand in February, had departed. Guchkov too had gone. The Ministry of Agriculture had passed from Shingarev to Chernov. Kerensky was becoming ever more prominent. The Octobrist and Constitutional Democratic elements were losing, or had lost, weight. Socialism in its varied forms was gradually gaining ground. Prince G. Lvov was to be nominal Head of the Government until July 8, but he possessed little popular appeal and his influence waned before his resignation.

Reverting to the previously quoted *Obzor Polozheniya*, one finds abundant proof that the administrative circles in the capital were living even in May upon a volcano no longer dormant. The cantonal committee, ubiquitous and omnipotent, as was remarked earlier, was the real factor in Russian rural and by extension, in Russian political life. And how are these committees described? On page 44 it is said:

The working capacity of the cantonal committees is interfered with by a flood of all kinds of orators in the village who have re-

---

[1] Ibid., p. 53.

placed former officials. . . . These are mostly soldiers from the Front and from Petrograd. They largely excite sympathy because they express the most extreme opinions—the desires of the landless or of the people hungry for more land. . . . They have no limitations, no restrictions. . . . They speak much, long and frequently using words which are not understood.

Earlier in the same report, it was remarked that there was an absence of "intellectual" forces. In fact, such forces, even where they existed, were ignored by the local population. There was, in addition, an absence of ordinarily educated people.[1]

As regards law, any resolutions from newspapers were allegedly taken as binding.[2] What was adopted one day would be contradicted on the next. Even where the "Administrative Messenger" was taken as guide, the peasant committees did not apparently distinguish projected from definitive laws—though, one might well ask, what authority was there in Russia at this date to promulgate definitive laws? Party resolutions were being adopted without any consideration for other classes' interests. The cantonal and village committees preserved their "estate" (i.e. purely "peasant") composition.[3] The committees were more like *skhody* (the peasant assemblies of the *Svod Zakonov*) than like established institutions. (Surely, one might remark, the reporter overlooked the fact that *skhody* were actually "established institutions.") The peasant assemblies frequently became playthings in the hands of the political agitator. Yet (continued the compiler of *Obzor*) on the other hand, there must be remembered the state of mind of a person who had only yesterday left the framework of a centralised State.

Thence it was that resulted the increased *palomnichestvo* (pilgrimage) to Petrograd. But, as it was previously difficult for a *muzhik* (peasant) to approach the

---

[1] Krasny Arhiv, Vol. XV, p. 43.   [2] op. cit., p. 43.
[3] Of course when it is remembered that, in the earliest orders issued by the Central Post-Revolutionary Government, there are indications that the peasantry was still legally regarded as a civil estate, such a local view is not so surprising.

Tsar, so it was difficult (even after three months of revolution) for him to approach the Law.[1]

There were cases where a peasant delegate had been despatched to Petrograd with its confused noise of parties. When asked on his return what he had heard: "I have forgotten," said he, "I have completely forgotten what I heard. I heard so much that eventually I could recollect nothing." His fellow-villagers then gave him the cold shoulder because he spent communal money and found out—nothing.[2]

If such were the controlling forces of village political life, what were the peasants themselves doing? To avoid grain requisitions under the Central Government's food policy, they were establishing illegal distilleries to utilise the grain they were not prepared to sell at the fixed prices. They were declining to pay taxes. . . . As for the village or cantonal militia it was badly organised, was poor in resources and had no arms. It had no pay. The committees had no money and did not know where to obtain any.[3] The courts were in disorder. "For the whole three months of the Revolution in the Village there has not been one case of the adoption of armed force to suppress the criminal acts of the peasants."[4] Frequently the squire had fled, leaving his land to fate. The peasants were puzzled as to what to do in such cases. They came to town to ask for explanations, came to the committee, to the commissioner, to the Workers' and Soldiers' Soviet, to the Social Revolutionary Party, and everywhere they received different instructions. Yet (the *Obzor* continues) "one circumstance is worthy of attention."[5] "With the rise of cantonal committees any excesses were stopped."

There was "a general and firm conviction of the peasantry that land must pass, and will pass, into the hands of the people (*narod*). Hence, "owing to this belief, there have been comparatively few excesses. The majority of the excesses usually occur where the

[1] Krasny Arhiv, Vol. XV, p. 43.   [2] op. cit., p. 43.
[3] op. cit., p. 44.   [4] op. cit., p. 44.   [5] op. cit., p. 45.

people are not sufficiently acquainted with the substance and dimensions of the change." But, on the other hand, instead of excesses, there existed and continually increased "cases of 'peaceful' expulsion and banishment from the land of all owners, large and small." There was a tax upon labour, sometimes amounting to 20 roubles a day. The war against private ownership was conducted, not by individual peasants, but by cantonal committees which regarded it as their principal work.[1] The petty *hutoryanin*, the average landowner and the great squire together experienced the burdensome, and sometimes inequitable, imposts of the cantonal committees. When it was pointed out that all land should, if possible, be occupied, the peasants, leaving their own land, took the squires'. As regards the *otrubniki* of the Stolypin period there were cases where squires' land was left untouched while that of *otrubniki* or of incoming settlers was taken. "Everywhere," said the compiler of *Obzor*, "where the (Stolypin) law of November 9 is in operation, hostility to *otrubniki* (independent farmers) is encountered." Not even the fact that the *otrubnik* was serving at the Front prevented active hostility. Generally the *otrubniki* voluntarily returned to the village-community.[2]

The *Obzor* found the land question especially acute in the Province of Penza.[3]

In some places at the very beginning of the changes peasants had asked for the suppression of commercial transactions in land and forests. Owners in some parts had hastened to cut down forests. The peasant communities stopped them and controlled the estates.[4] Companies were forbidden to remove timber. (This fact is clear also from the copious information in *Krestyanskoe Dvizhenie v 1917g.*, for March, April, May and, later, became a widespread phenomenon.) There were diverse reactions locally to attempts to cut timber by private individuals. In Smolensk, peasants simply took

[1] Krasny Arhiv., Vol. XV, p. 45.   [2] op. cit., p. 46.   [3] op. cit., p. 47.
[4] op. cit., p. 48.

over estates, whereas in Minsk those of one district burnt the woodland portion.¹ A characteristic feature of peasant farming economy—hayfields—was in great demand in the more northern areas. Whereas the inhabitants used to purchase extra hay from outside, they now prevented any such purchases.²

The chief features of the land question as at the end of May were in the *Obzor's* opinion, (1) Insufficient land in the Central Provinces. (2) The demand for all land to be transferred to the working peasantry without compensation. (3) Local excesses and seizures as a result of lack of information or pressing need of land. (4) The struggle with private ownership and its displacement. (5) The absence of any instruction among the peasantry concerning the difficulty and complexity of the land question, and the inadequacy of land for their allotment in the bounds of their canton.³

But the question which agitated the minds of both village and town (and more urgently the town) was the food question, which overshadowed the land question. Indeed, the present writer would assert from his examination of the abundance of documentation upon the whole peasant question in 1917 that it was largely the food question which brought the year to its catastrophic close. If there was an "elemental" movement in September and October it was "elemental" because it was based upon the satisfaction of "elementary" needs of life—food supply in particular. The lofty schemes of constitutionalists, politicians and even economists are liable to collapse over such a homely, yet vital problem. It is evident from the *Obzor* that the food question was prominent even in May —a fact that need not surprise the student when he remembers that the very abdication of Nicholas II himself had resulted from disorganisation of supplies in the capital in February. What was this food problem? On one side there was inadequacy of goods. Secondly, the reorganisation of town administration had led to "democracy" taking over affairs, and "neglecting the experienced

[1] op. cit., p. 48.   [2] op. cit., p. 49.   [3] op. cit., p. 49.

advice of former officers." There ensued higher prices and higher wages. The food problem had become the general and chief object of dissatisfaction. In the provinces there was no sugar, no white flour, no butter. The influx of corn from the villages had greatly increased in the first days of the changes but it had diminished on the announcement of the Government Grain Monopoly.[1]

Yet while boycotting the towns, the peasants were bringing in a large amount of grain for the Army. But owing to disorganisation at the railway receiving depots, even this supply was slackening in volume. In one case the peasants (e.g. Voronesh) had given free grain for the Army. Transport arrangements were defective however. Grain was rotting at the stations.[2]

The local cantonal organisation of food supplies had usually resulted in the entry of the food committee into the main cantonal committee. Where the food committee decided to be independent, there were continual disputes. The difficulty caused in the villages was allegedly due to the previously-mentioned absence of "intellectual" and educated people on the food boards, members of the village *intelligentsia* and even of the co-operative society's board being usually boycotted. There was at this date (May) sufficient grain in the villages (a comparatively small amount of spring-corn, but an adequate amount of winter-corn), if the Western Provinces in the War Zone were excepted. In that part of Russia, frequent requisitions, combined with the flood of deserters and troops generally, had depleted local stocks. The non-producing (i.e. Northern non-black earth) provinces, such as Vladimir, were experiencing the greatest privations.[3]

The chief feature of the Grain Monopoly was necessarily its fixation of prices—a subject in which economic historians of the War of 1914–18 have unlimited scope. What were some of the attributes of fixed prices which peasant communities disliked in May 1917? When fixed prices were established in the grain market, the

[1] Krasny Arhiv, Vol. XV, p. 49.   [2] op. cit., p. 50.   [3] op. cit., p. 50.

amount which the consuming townsman paid was admittedly below the value of the product. Of course one may, to parody Pilate, say "What is value?" and similarly stay not for an answer. Certainly the townsman probably believed that the peasants were profiteers. No doubt some of them were. But, keeping in mind the low standards of peasant rural life, one might say they might well be profiteers to make up ground lost in the "hungry 'nineties." In any event when requisitions were made on the basis of corn brought to *bazary* (the markets) and when some peasants who "asked for more" than the stipulated price were flogged, a necessary consequence followed—one that was to haunt Russian political economy for many years afterwards—the peasants ceased to bring grain to market in the district towns and villages. A strange position emerged. There was money to buy grain but there was the prohibition of sale above fixed prices. The peasants felt themselves in an awkward situation. Once more the old Russian question arose, "*Shto delat?*" ("What is to be done?") Inadequate sowings would create future trouble. On the other hand there were at the moment (May) preparations for a "hunger insurrection."[1] Peasants of moderate opinions who had lived hard-working lives told delegates that they would willy-nilly soon be reduced to seizing one another's goods if they did not receive speedy help.

What was the real "fly in the peasant's ointment"? It was the fact that the whole scheme of fixed prices was one-sided. It was a "proto-communism" in which one side —the peasant—"gave" and the other—the townsman— "took." It lacked that mutual "give and take" which human nature requires. There were no fixed prices for the objects of prime necessity which the peasants wanted from the town. In many cases the town had ceased, for reasons arising out of the state of virtual blockade in which the country found itself in 1914, to be able to supply adequate manufactured goods. Keen dissatisfaction was now expressed in May 1917. In some

[1] Presumably in the "consuming" provinces.

provinces the village was fighting the town, and, in reply to the dearness of objects of prime necessity, was replying by a determination to leave the town foodless. Already, it may be noted before the February Revolution, in the year 1916 Russia had ceased to be a unified market or trading entity. Provinces had become a law unto themselves. This feature of Russia's economic life was simply extending and, instead of the province, the market was contracting into the narrow confines of the canton—economic disintegration as usual, preceding the political. That intensely local psychology which, as often, made the peasant community ignore the calamities that culminated in Brest-Litovsk, was already past the embryonic stage.

At the end of April one could buy grain in desired amount, but in the middle of May it was impossible to obtain it anywhere. Rye bread reached in some places 20 kopecks per *funt* (0·90 lb.). Despite searches and requisitions the need of grain was so great that district and cantonal committees began to attempt to raise fixed prices by their own authority. Simultaneously they tried to fix prices of other goods, as, for instance, calico and nails.[1] The population was beginning to fix its own prices—economic anarchy was evidently developing fast. Delegates wrote that they witnessed "broken noses and bloodstained mouths" (*"razbitie nosy i okrovavlennye rty"*). Frequently there could be seen members of food committees going to requisition grain while the owner stood on guard near his barn with a gun.[2] The peasants were described as not understanding the Grain Monopoly. They regarded it as plunder, and hid their grain. Where however its meaning was explained, they viewed it sympathetically despite the fact that it hit their pockets. The only proviso they made, was that they were ready to give grain to the Army, but not to the town. They also remarked that they had given all to their country and were giving their own sons too, and their grain. They were compelled by force to do this, if they refused to accede. "But (they said) why are none of these measures taken

[1] Krasny Arhiv, Vol. XV, p. 51.   [2] op. cit., p. 51.

against the rich to make them contribute their capital for their country's needs?" What was later called "Bolshevism," i.e. the phenomenon, not the specific Party creed, was thus developing fast even where "Bolsheviks" were not. As N. Savich (a *pomeshchik* of Chernigov and A. Guchkov's right-hand man in the Third Duma) said to the present writer: "The peasants believed the richer classes were having all the good things of life." One must remember too Prince Volkonsky's remark in his *Vospominaniya* already mentioned: "There would have been Bolshevism even if there had been no Bolsheviks."[1]

That Russia was developing into a series of small economic units—the provinces—was stated earlier. This fact was of vital importance for the so-called "non-producing" areas in the northern half of the country—including Petrograd and Moscow. The stoppage of the export of grain from one province to another thus caused great alarm and actual privation in the consuming centres. In one case, Pavlovo, in the Nizhegorod Province, with its 20,000 workers for defence, there was no bread at the end of May. If anyone desired to buy at prohibitive rates he had to go into the neighbouring provinces.[2] But he was not allowed to remove what he had purchased. As was to be expected, rioting ensued.[3] Often grain was bought at a certain price in one province and requisitioned and sold in another at a higher price. "The prohibition of transfer of grain from one province to another makes people locally think that the present Government is proceeding on the same paths as the old."[4]

Meanwhile as one might expect, the grain that was not coming to market was being utilised in other ways. The old régime at the outbreak of the War had instituted prohibition of the sale of liquor, thereby increasing savings-bank deposits but at the same time wrecking the old budget-balance which had depended considerably upon this source of indirect taxation. Illicit distilleries were

---

[1] Volkonsky, op. cit., p. 166.
[2] Cf. post-revolutionary "bagmen" of 1919, 1920 and 1921.
[3] Krasny Arhiv, Vol. XV, p. 52.   [4] op. cit., p. 52.

a concomitant of prohibition in Russia no less than in other countries. The requisitioning of grain, at prices below current market value, necessarily caused the illicit distiller to thrive when he could get 40–60 roubles per *chetvert* (5·77 bushels) i.e. per *pud* (0·32 cwt.) of grain when turned into liquor.[1]

Food questions were endemic during the year and the problem of the preservation of existing stocks of spirit, combined with the ever-increasing private supplies, also presented the Provisional Government with unlimited trouble.

Before an examination of the further progress of peasant grievances and activities is pursued, there are still a few interesting remarks included in the *Obzor* which are worthy of note.

One significant statement recalled a fact well-known in the country—the division between the illiterate peasantry (*narod*) and the cultured *obshchestvo* (society). "Nothing so divides man from man as difference of language" is the sapient conclusion of the *Obzor*. That difference which Disraeli had observed in his fictional achievement *Sybil* or *A Tale of Two Nations*, when depicting the gloomy social schism revealed during England's industrialisation, was present in Russia in 1917 as a disruptive phenomenon. The average peasant understood the language of official decrees even less perhaps than a simple Roman soldier would have understood the literary language of Cicero himself. That again is a factor that played into Lenin's hands in October. He used concrete and homely phrases while keeping his big artillery barrage for rarer academic controversy.

Throughout Russia prevailed a fevered quest for books. Despite illiteracy, or perhaps because of its consciousness of its defects in this direction, the *narod* desired to learn. The "dark people" wanted light. "The prestige of the Imperial Duma" (reported the *Obzor*) is everywhere very high, but it is being asked, "Are they taking measures to spread enlightenment? Are they doing their best to give

[1] e.g. Smolensk Province, op. cit., p. 53.

wider information upon such questions as that of a republic, or of the Constituent Assembly?" And further, "Now Russia has returned to the Age of the Apostles when through the whole land from end to end people are moving and propounding new principles."[1] Yet paradoxically enough, it was said that "teachers were too dear." Instead was heard the frequent remark, "Wait until the soldiers come back from the front. They will teach us for nothing!"

Such were the conclusions drawn in May from enquiries covering the Provinces of Arhangelsk and Vologda (North), Pskov, Novgorod, Petrograd, Olonets (Lake), Kazan, Simbirsk, Samara (Middle and Lower Volga), Vladimir, Kostroma, Yaroslav, Nizhegorod, Tver (Central Industrial), Perm, Vyatka (Ural), Penza, Orel, Voronesh, Kursk (Central Agricultural Black Earth), Kiev, Poltava, Chernigov (Little Russia), Tauris, Don (New Russia), Minsk, Mogilev, Smolensk (Western War Zone).[2]

The entrance is now open to the period when the Social Revolutionary Party, owing to its real or supposed influence over the peasant masses, increasingly occupied the seat of Government to the exclusion of other parties. That is, save for that of the so-called Menshevik wing of the Social Democratic Party whose agrarian programme was almost a replica of that of their new colleagues.

The records in *Krestyanskoe Dvizhenie* render still more clear the picture already presented in the preceding pages. A general meeting of the Ryazan Section of the All-Russian Union of landowners complained of

the impossibility of supplying the country in the existing conditions with fuel, food and forage. It asked the Provisional Government to take measures for the undeviating execution of the Circular of the Provisional Government of May 17. [June 8.][3]

On the same date (June 8) the same body complained

[1] op. cit., p. 56.
[2] P. Romanov, *Obzor Polozheniya*, March, April, May 1917
[3] *Krestyanskoe Dvizhenie v 1917g.*, p. 88.

that illegal activities of local committees were increasing in volume. The provincial commissioner, they alleged, was not taking energetic measures to terminate disorders.[1] On June 24 landowners assembled in Ryazan "to discuss questions concerning agricultural disruption." To the meeting, representatives of the Soviet of Workers', Soldiers' and Peasants' Deputies were invited. The relations between this group and the landowners were so strained "that the meeting broke up to avoid violence at the hands of the Soviet" (June 26).[2]

Tambov Province reported (June 5) that the council of united landowners stated that seizures of land were universal in the Tambov district. Lease agreements were being cancelled. Workers and prisoners were being removed from work. An amount of 150 *desyatines* of sown land was left for each individual. Peasants were being given the services of war-prisoners without any fixed rates of pay. The food and executive committees and the district militia were largely assisting such actions.[3] Prince Volkonsky complained (June 24) that resolutions of cantonal committees were hindering the harvesting on his estate (Pavlovka, Borisoglebsk district). As he says in his *Vospominaniya* in his chapter styled "Disorganisation":

> The summer of 1917 was unpleasant. Afterwards we had to endure all sorts of privations, insults and mockery but, with all their frank insolence, these later contacts with the Revolution were less repugnant than that malicious crawling penetration into our private life. When you have been entirely thrown out of your usual conditions, nothing surprises you; but when you are still living in your own house surrounded by your own things, your own farmstead, the intermeddling of foreign control has not as yet received that character of lawlessness before which it is necessary to humble yourself as before a brigand. . . . We lived at home, but were not the masters—you felt that there was another man's hand in your pocket. It could not continue thus; this state of things grew up on an inclined plane and on an incline it is impossible for things not to go farther.

---

[1] *Krestyanskoe Dvizhenie v 1917g.*, p. 88.   [2] Ibid., p. 89.   [3] Ibid., p. 89.

Such is the description of events as it appeared to a squire of Tambov Province in the midst of the Central Agricultural Region—the zone of greatest disturbance. S. Volkonsky criticised the Social Revolutionaries for what he thought to be their lack of comprehension of the fact.

They thought [he said] that they were establishing a certain order on certain foundations, but they lost sight of the fact that by this order they were educating the people towards destruction, they were arousing their greed and pushing them towards seizure. This they did not foresee, but it was quite natural. When does connivance stop half-way?[1]

The shaking of the instinct of property [he continued] went on with astonishing rapidity. "This will all be ours," some of the peasants said to me. They were the village talkers. I met some small boys in the garden with bunches of currant branches. "Why did you break them off?"

"It's all the same, they'll be ours."

"I know they are yours; but why do you break what is yours?"

I was always surprised as to why they said "They will be ours." Why did they not say "are ours"? It took some little time for them to realise that it was easier than they thought formerly, than the Social Revolutionary had told them it would be. The Social Revolutionary said to them "Wait, we will give it to you, it will be yours." The Bolsheviks came and they said, "Why are you fools waiting—take it."

As has been quoted earlier, it was Volkonsky's opinion that "there might not have been the Bolsheviks but there would have been Bolshevism all the same.[2] One must be careful to distinguish, therefore, between Bolshevism as a special form of Marxian Social Democratic creed and the phenomenon the world knows as such, arising out of the widespread peasant movement of September–October which Lenin crowned by leading his Party to seize power in Petrograd.

So much for the general state of mind. The records of *Krestyanskoe Dvizhenie* regarding Voronesh Province (Central Agricultural) reveal a revolutionary cantonal committee introducing a resolution concerning trust in

[1] Volkonsky, op. cit., p. 165.   [2] op. cit., p. 166.

the Provisional Government, pending the transfer of treasury, appanage and monastic land to the labouring class for cultivation by its own hands. It also asked for the speediest possible summons of the Constituent Assembly (June 13).[1]

The Middle Volga region, in particular Simbirsk Province, provides further proof of the effect of the organised nature of the movement which was to culminate in July.

The peasants of Simbirsk district, hearing of the resolution of the peasant congress of the Simbirsk district regarding the transfer of private land to the tenancy of the labouring people, are presenting landowners with illegal demands. Thanks to this situation, a certain calm which has set in, is giving place to a new tendency to seize other people's property [June 20].[2]

The hostility which was becoming general towards *otrubniki* was shown by a complaint from these private peasant landholders (June 23) that the communal peasantry of the villages of Kuranino and Ardatov had confiscated their separate landholdings and were inflicting all kinds of violence and indignity upon them.[3] Further, separate farms (*hutornye uchastki*) belonging to three soldiers were divided up among the Andreevsky village-community, Kirzhemanskaya canton, the soldiers having been flogged and under duress compelled to give their written consent (June 27).[4]

The agrarian movement has received a very wide extension and seriously affects the interests of landowners. The provincial executive committee and commissioner are taking every possible measure to divert this movement into legal channels. In this direction there is complete support, both on the part of the Soviet of Workers' and Soldiers' Delegates and district executive committees and on that of the Peasant Delegates of the All-Russian Union and generally of the intelligent peasantry.

Such was an optimistic report of June 28 from Simbirsk Province (Middle Volga). That was the path that the

[1] *Krestyanskoe Dvizhenie v 1917g.*, p. 91. [2] Ibid., p. 93.
[3] Ibid., p. 93. [4] Ibid., p. 93.

Social Revolutionary "general staff," with Chernov in control, was increasingly endeavouring to follow.

Saratov Province was once more distinguishing itself as it had done in 1905, until curbed by its Governor, Stolypin (later Premier), who won his spurs particularly for his personal initiative in checking disorder in the Balashov district.[1] Now, in common with the remainder of the Saratov Province, Balashov once more appeared in the list of mutinous areas. Indeed, it became once more pre-eminent and there was now no Stolypin to exert a restraining influence. The local union of landowners begged for the district commissioner to be compelled to act against "violent seizures of meadows and the removal of hay, with the assistance even of the cantonal committees and—the militia!" Those participating in the seizure threatened to do the same with the corn. The hay had all been taken. There was none left even for stud farms or for valuable horned cattle. Forage supplies for the Army had also been seized (June 20).[2] On June 28, in the same district, agrarian disorders were in process of development. Already earlier in the month (June 13) Gaydygurov, a landowner of Ivanov canton in that district, reported that the local peasantry were illegally cutting timber, seizing ploughland and cutting grass for hay. They had burnt his residence and were generally infringing personal and property rights.[3]

Therefore if it may be concluded that before September–October, the peasants proceeded on the lines of "peaceful appropriation" by semi-legal methods, nevertheless all over the country there was a "running fire" of actual violent seizure also.

The resurgence of the land commune was once more indicated by news from Kerensk district that the communalists had confiscated forest land belonging to the separate farm holders (*otrubniki*) (Penza Province, June 3).[4] In Saransk district "agrarian disorders had

[1] Cf. Krasny Arhiv, *K istorii agrarnoy reformy Stolypina*, Vol. XVII, 1926, pp. 81–90.
[2] *Krestyanskoe Dvizhenie v 1917g.*, p. 95.   [3] Ibid., p. 94.   [4] Ibid., p. 96.

attained exceptionally large dimensions". Peasants were burning outer buildings on estates, seizing property, confiscating land and meadows, thus preventing maintenance of stud-farms providing army remounts. Landowners were being insulted (Penza Province, June 12).[1] "The position grows worse each day," complained the chief manager of the Balashov estate, Gorodische district, Penza (June 18).[2] An interesting telegram of June 18 (Penza) spoke of an agreed arrangement between the provincial commissioner's office and the executive committee by which the land committees' functions were to be extended so that "all preceding seizures were to be considered as if upon a contractual-lease basis." [3]

It should be here noted that Shingarev, the first Minister of Agriculture of the Provisional Government, issued, on May 3, 1917, a decree establishing land committees in every canton, district and province as well as a Central Committee for the whole of Russia. The objects of the committees were to be as follows:

> The Central and local land committees under the supervision of the Ministry of Agriculture, are established in order to prepare the way for land reform and to draft provisional measures to be adopted pending the settlement of the land question by the Constituent Assembly.[4]

The Central Committee included the Minister of Agriculture and his official assistants, the Committee Chairman, business manager and twenty-five members appointed by the Government; representatives of the All-Russian Peasants' Union and the Soviet of Peasants' Delegates; three representatives respectively, from the Provisional Committee of the Duma, the Soviet of Workers' and Soldiers' Delegates and the All-Russian

[1] *Krestyanskoe Dvizhenie v 1917g.*, p. 97.   [2] Ibid., pp. 96–7.
[3] Ibid., p. 97.
[4] *Sobranie uzakoneniy i rasporyazheniy pravitelstva*, No. 98. Sect. I, Parag. 543. There were supplementary enactments on Sept. 5, 1917, No. 222, Sect. I, Parag. 1631. *Russian Agriculture during the War*, Antsiferov and Bilimovich (Carnegie).

Co-operative Union; representatives of societies for the study of economics and also persons of competence invited by the chairman simply to give advice. The Central Committee contained 161 members and together with its advisory members exceeded 200. Later in the year a decree of August 25 (published September 15) gave the Ministry of Finance and the State Nobility and Peasant Banks official representation. The local committees, to which the telegram above-mentioned in the *Krestyanskoe Dvizhenie* referred, were similarly constituted. The committees, it is essential to remark, had administrative, judicial and executive powers.

The Central Committee could make representations to the Minister of Agriculture and to the Provisional Government on the following lines: (1) The restriction or cancellation of existing laws, if they were likely to impede the satisfactory solution of the agrarian problem in the Constituent Assembly, or cause perplexity among the population through being out of keeping with the new régime, or to interfere with the regular course of agricultural life. (2) The abolition of existing offices and institutions concerned with land if their activity were found to be superfluous in the new conditions, and the distribution of their work, property and personnel among other offices and institutions. (3) The co-ordination of the land policy of the Provisional Government. (4) Other measures for the purpose of regulating economic relations arising out of ownership of land (Art. 3).

By the above-mentioned provision (2) the administrative machinery created for the purpose of executing the policy known generally under Premier Stolypin's name (1906–11) was finally abolished. Thus May 3, 1917, liquidated the policy definitely put into force by the decree (*ukaz*) of November 9, 1906. It is interesting to note that the Party, that of the Constitutional Democrats (Cadets), which had been in process of creating a "bloc" with the peasant *trudoviki* (equivalent to Social Revolutionaries in policy) during the First Duma (April–

July 1906) was destined to provide the sponsor of the Act which destroyed a decade's work of old régime's *zemleustroistvo* (land-settlement). The original elaborator of the "Cadet" Agrarian Bill in the First Duma, Professor Hertsenstein, shortly after the dissolution of that body met a violent death at the hands of its reactionary opponents, while Shingarev, the promoter of the decree of May 3, 1917, also later met a violent death at the hands, this time, of more extreme left-wing partisans. These two facts amply illustrate the strong party feeling exhibited at the beginning and the end of the Reforms of Stolypin.

Besides the *Glavny Zemelny Komitet* (Central Land Committee) described above, there were the local land committees of which the cantonal showed the most vitality and eventually took complete control in September–October. These local committees had wide administrative and judicial powers—the provincial, and even district committees, having the right to issue compulsory regulations concerning agricultural and agrarian relations—a power in excess of that possessed by the old district *Zemstvo* boards. The local committees could settle questions, disputes and misunderstandings in connection with agrarian and agricultural affairs and, when necessary, appoint arbitrational tribunals. They could stop the proceedings of private persons likely to decrease the value of landed property. They could ask the Central Committee to withdraw such property from the persons in question—a power of virtual sequestration. They could make agreements with the local food committees and other state institutions regarding the best possible use to be made of those properties. All or some of these rights could be conferred upon the cantonal committees. It was simply necessary for a district committee to pass a resolution to that effect.

The history of the agrarian movement consisted (as the *Krestyanskoe Dvizhenie* abundantly testifies) in the progressive annexation of complete control by the cantonal committees until, in October, the superstructure was left entirely devoid of material or political significance.¹ The progressive realisation of the self-determination exhibited by both land and food committees, led the Provisional Government in its last stage of dying paralysis to ordain that "land and food committees are subordinate to the Courts of Law" (published Sept. 29, 1917). Seeing that the majesty of the law at that date was a minus quantity, such a decree was destined to remain a pious wish. The peasant committees were in full process of declaring their complete independence of other social orders.

The Land Committees were gradually formed during May and June all over Russia—perhaps it might be said that the peasant committees already existing simply received them as a further means of "legally" securing the estates in the vicinity.

Returning once more to the records contained in the *Krestyanskoe Dvizhenie* one finds a further instance, among many, of local peasant aggression. The Chistopol congress of peasant delegates supported the resolution on the agrarian question adopted by the May Congress of the All-Russian Peasant Soviet. It declared that in view of the necessity of proceeding with farm work, it desired an immediate decree from the Government providing for the transfer of all arable land whether squire, treasury, appanage, monastic or ecclesiastical, to be placed at the complete disposal of cantonal food and land committees (June 4).² Further, the Kazan Soviet President reported on June 5, that, in accordance with a resolution of the provincial congress of peasants and also of the Spassk district food committee, peasants had begun to confiscate and divide up squires' land, to cut timber, remove all stock, horses, horned cattle and to cause labourers to leave.³ It is evident that, whether peaceful or otherwise,

---

¹ Cf. Sir Bernard Pares, *Russian Memoirs*, p. 462. "You see, now every village committee dictates to the district committee and every district committee dictates to the provincial committee. . . ." (Provincial Commissar of Voronesh).
² *Krestyanskoe Dvizhenie v 1917g.*, p. 98 (Kazan Province).
³ Ibid., p. 98.

the land-seizure movement was now prevalent in the Middle Volga and Central Agricultural regions. In some localities in the Province of Kazan "Bolshevik agitation" was noticed on the part of persons coming from Kronstadt (the naval fortress near Petrograd) (June 4).

On May 3 (13?) a Kazan provincial peasant congress had resolved "without waiting for the Constituent Assembly" to confiscate all land from landowners. Consequently, it was announced by the Kazan president on June 6, that circulars of that tenor were being broadcast over the whole province. The peasants were putting the resolutions into force, thus causing "complete disorganisation in agricultural life." A resolution of a conference of delegates and representatives of cantons and villages, large and small, of Spassk district decided immediately, throughout the whole district, to conduct a requisition (without compensation) of all agricultural machinery and of almost all cattle belonging to landowners. All land should be taken over before the Constituent Assembly met and transferred free into the people's use. "In the district there is complete anarchy." Such was a landowner's telegram of June 9.[1]

The position in the province is growing more strained because the resolution of the general Soviet of Peasant Delegates of May 13, concerning the taking over of land, stock and cattle from owners, and the withdrawal of labourers, is being actually put into force. The local administrative authorities are not able to restrain cantonal organisations from irregular measures.[2]

The agrarian movement appears with especial force in Spassk and Laishev districts, somewhat weaker in Chistopol, Kazan and elsewhere. The cause of it has reference to the resolution drawn up on May 13, by peasant delegates concerning the immediate transfer of land to peasants and committees (June 15).[3] On the same date was reported a "chronic and complete sub-

[1] Kazan Province, ibid., p. 99.   [2] ibid., p. 99.   [3] ibid., p. 99.

version by the cantonal committees of all the rights of private landowners."

The provincial commissioner of Kazan reported on June 21 that he had summoned a conference of district commissioners and cantonal committee secretaries. The following resolutions had been passed.[1] (1) The immediate formation of cantonal and land committees under whose control the farming operations of the land of the canton will pass: before the formation of such committees, their duties will be borne by cantonal committees of security. No irregular seizure or expropriation shall be allowed. (2) The formation, at the provincial *Zemstvo* board, of an official body to co-ordinate activity in the preparation of elections for the cantonal *Zemstvo*: in the composition of this body the conference find it necessary to introduce representatives of the Soviet of Workers', Soldiers' and Peasants' Delegates. (3) To form simultaneously with the land committee, a forest committee from representatives of the Treasury and of *Zemstvo* and town self-governing institutions, of the Soviet of Workers, Soldiers and Peasants and of the provincial commissioner. This forest committee shall review requests for the cutting and removal of timber and give suitable decisions. But the Soviet of Workers', Soldiers' and Peasants' Delegates must be assured of a majority. The conference agree that it is impossible to hinder the transference of fuel. (4) As far as the food question is concerned the conference recommends all the food organisations of Kazan Province to support the fixed prices set up by the Provisional Government and also the consumption and forage ration: to put determinedly into force the Grain Monopoly and to support the existing system of state regulation of consumption, since only by such means can there be secured to each person his fair share of products, and the army and rear preserved from the consequences of famine: in addition the conference finds it necessary that the Provisional Government should proclaim fixed prices for all products of prime necessity.

[1] Ibid., p. 100.

(5) To execute army orders for hay, it is necessary to place the required area of privately-owned meadows under the provincial food committee's control. (6) To acknowledge that seizures of *otrub* (private) holdings are not to be allowed. (7) The conference acknowledge the necessity of transferring blood-stock (including racehorses) through the provincial food committee where such was left without appropriate attention; the blood-stock to be used for agriculture, the racehorses to be sent to the State studfarms. On no account shall such stock be plundered or requisitioned and there shall be no obstacle to its free sale. (8) Unused farming implements shall pass into the disposition of food committees for distribution among the rural population actually in need of them. (9) The conference finds that, to lead the country to the goal of the Constituent Assembly, unity and solidarity are necessary among all the organs of the Provisional Government and no individual criminal act must be allowed (June 21).[1]

The whole telegraphic announcement gives a very clear picture of the difficulties current during June, besides the optimism with which the Central Government hoped to control the already extremely independent cantonal village communities.

No better comment upon the whole programme of orderly activity can be afforded than the series of messages from the same province during the rest of the month.

One cantonal committee took an inventory of property, expropriated a mill, divided up land and meadows, took away timber and dismissed an estate manager (Ivanov estate, Sviyazh district, June 28).[2] In Spassk district the agrarian movement continued. "The congress of delegates of villages and cantons supported the Peasant Soviet with all its energies." Peasants on Aristova's estate "occupied pasture-land, took stock and cut down trees." Another canton determined "to forbid removal of timber and intended to divide up squires' land among peasants."

[1] Kazan Province, ibid., p. 100.   [2] ibid., p. 100.

In a whole series of estates agrarian disorders continued. There were occasions of the burning of a number of manor houses. In one village ecclesiastical land was seized and the priest expelled. Seven Volga villages in Kazan district resolved to divide up meadows belonging to Kazan and to a nunnery. The Urakchin committee, Laishev district, arrested Princess Gruzinskaya on June 24. In another district, "the local authorities were inactive"—a phrase that appears to become a regular refrain right through the mass of reports in *Krestyanskoe Dvizhenie.*

July is now at hand—that month when Kerensky's Government, having attained power on the strength of Social Revolutionary organisation of the upper strata of the peasant movement, tried to control it. The inauspicious offensive of June 18 (o.s.) had shown Hindenburg that he need not anticipate a new Battle of the Heights of Valmy. A Dumouriez had not appeared. The Russian Peasant Army had seen too much of unsuccessful strategy on the part of its old leaders in the past to show much enthusiasm over new ones. Army committees were predominant. The death penalty was in abeyance. The old process of peasant cantonal aggrandisement proceeded apace and there was no possibility of any counter-force to check it.

Kursk (Central Agricultural region) gave further evidence [1] of the omnipotence of peasant committees and of the division of privately-owned land and stock among the villagers. War-prisoners continued to be removed from estates.[2] Landowners were protesting against the executive and land committees as impeding farming and harvesting. There were complaints concerning destructive activity and trespassing upon meadows. Stock and dairy-farming were becoming impossible. Fallow land was being leased at uneconomic prices. There were threats of the removal of crops from fields. Illegal arrests were occurring. Labourers and war-prisoners were being also expelled. No day labour was allowed.

[1] Ibid., pp. 141–2.   [2] Ibid., p. 144.

Former lease-agreements were being annulled. Farming was in an impossible position.[1]

A definitely violent attitude is revealed in a telegram of July 5,[2] E. Myasvedova, a lady owning land in Epifan district (Tula), being thrown from a balcony, if the lady's own report is correct. She thought the local militia were unreliable.

It has been said previously that the peasant actions against private property during the early months of 1917 revealed a certain sense of legality, which was not entirely a sham, as it has been represented. They did utilise the powers conferred upon food and land committees to further their own ends no doubt; but those powers were such as the Great War in progress appeared to justify. The possibility of the use of the forces of the law to enable them to occupy the squires' estates was assisted by the great decline in productivity of those estates shown by the statistics of the war period. That decline cannot, it seems to the writer, be explained, as it has been, entirely on the assumption that the agricultural labourers in the whole country were now conscripts. The number of permanent agricultural labourers in the whole country was not more than 2 millions. The place of a large number of recruits was taken by the war-prisoners frequently mentioned in *Krestyanskoe Dvizhenie*. A fact which explains more plausibly the decline in squire-estate productivity and which rendered it peculiarly vulnerable on social grounds was that of the short-term lease which had been an almost dominant feature of Russian Agriculture. The bulk of the peasantry was now in the Army. The old competition for leases thus largely ceased. Squire-farming was rarely capitalistic, i.e. based upon permanent hired labour. Thus the cantonal committees were simply taking control of what they, either as individuals or communities, regarded as peculiarly their own. Hence their antipathy to labour from outside the canton

---

[1] Complaint of Prince Kurakin, President of Conference of Orel Landowners (July 10).
[2] Ibid., p. 145.

whether it was Russian or foreign (prisoner). It was precisely this attitude of semi-legality that explains much in 1917.

The village communities allowed no breaches of the ordinary code of property among their own members. For instance, in Krapivna district, in the village of Sergiev (Tula) a crowd of people attempted to arrest two well-known thieves (July 5). The thieves began to fire at the crowd, which seized them and killed them.[1] In another case on July 8, a deserter was arrested. A crowd of local peasants applied lynch-law to him and he was flogged to death.[2] In the one case, theft, in the other, even repudiation of war-service obligations, caused local irritation. That is why one must agree that the peasant movement against squires and "otrubniki" (private holders) generally was "sui generis" as far as an ethical code was concerned.

On July 12 local landowners of Tula protested as follows:—The executive committee of the Soviet of Peasant Delegates decided immediately to enforce the temporary agrarian law project of the Central Land Committee. All land was to pass into the control of local land committees. Existing rental agreements could be reviewed and changed. The cantonal committee was to determine the amount of the rent and the person who was to receive it. It was proposed that the All-Russian Soviet of Peasant Delegates should immediately protest against the suggestion of Prince Lvov (the Minister for the Interior and Premier, who resigned on July 7) for the immediate adoption of measures to terminate agrarian law-breaking. It was decided to take away immediately all war-prisoners from squires, and to utilise without exception all agricultural implements. Such a resolution, the local landowners considered, threatened unavoidable excesses in the villages and the illegal destruction of agriculture in the province (of Tula) (July 12).

The above-mentioned decree emanating from Tula was significant of much. It indicated the influence of the newly projected land legislation of the Central Land

[1] Ibid., p. 145. [2] Ibid., p. 145.

Committee. It revealed the power of the local, i.e. cantonal committees. The resignation of Prince Lvov from his post of President of the Provisional Government and that of Minister for the Interior, was eloquent in itself. It was of evil omen for the squires, as a class, and for those who thought that February had meant simply a superficial change of personnel in administrative circles and not a fundamental, all-embracing social revolution. What did Prince Lvov say in his letter of resignation—the swan-song, one might say, of the squire class?

Although I believe [said he (July 7) in his letter published (July 9) in the *Novoe Vremya*] that land ought to be handed over to the peasants, I cannot agree either with the content or the spirit of the land laws submitted by the Minister of Agriculture to the Provisional Government for ratification. The Provisional Government has declared that the occupation of land should be organised in the interests of the working classes and of national welfare, but the Minister of Agriculture seems to me to depart from this principle and introduce laws which undermine the people's conception of justice. Far from combatting aggressive tendencies or bringing order into agrarian relations, he appears to justify the disastrous seizures of property that are taking place throughout Russia and aims at confronting the Constituent Assembly with a *fait accompli*. To my mind, the laws proposed by him are part of a party programme, and not measures necessary for the good of the country. I foresee that eventually they will disappoint the people and make it impossible to carry out a national land reform. I consider the Minister for Agriculture's land programme disastrous for the country, for it will ruin and undermine it both morally and materially and I very much fear that it will create throughout Russia the state of things against which the Provisional Government has been, during the last few days, so energetically struggling in Petrograd.[1]

It is an historic document, yet who could have supposed that the popular forces which caused Prince Lvov's resignation in July and gave the Social Revolutionary Party a temporary supremacy, were to cause the downfall of

[1] A reference to the Bolshevist rising in Petrograd in July—one of the sequels to the breakdown of Kerensky's Offensive of June 18 (o.s.).

Kerensky, his successor, in October? Even more dramatically did they cause that of Chernov against whom Lvov inveighed—destined as he was to see the Constituent Assembly commence the discussion of his land socialisation project but to be rudely interrupted by the physical force of his even more extreme opponents (January 5, 1918).

CHAPTER V

THE FAILURE OF KERENSKY TO CHECK THE RURAL REVOLUTION (July–Oct., 1917)

CHERNOV, the Social-Revolutionary Minister of Agriculture, was now free, in Kerensky's purely socialist administration, to try to put his ideas into effect. The new Provisional Government's Proclamation of July 8 referred to land reform as follows:

The measures of the Provisional Government with regard to land will, as before, be based upon the conviction that, inaccordance with the vital needs of the nation, the often-expressed desires of the peasants and the programmes of all democratic parties, the future land reform must be determined by the idea that the land is to pass into the hands of those working it. This is the principle underlying the project to be submitted to the Constituent Assembly.

In the immediate future the Government intends:—(1) to abandon completely the old land policy which ruined and demoralised the peasantry; (2) to secure complete freedom for the Constituent Assembly in the matter of the disposal of the nation's land; (3) to regulate agrarian relations in the interests of national defence and welfare by extending and strengthening the network of land committees; these will be endowed with carefully defined rights of dealing with the current problems of agrarian policy, but the fundamental question of the ownership of land, which is to be settled by the Constituent Assembly, will not be pre-judged. (4) By thus introducing order into agrarian relations, to obviate the serious danger to the country and to the future land-reform, arising from seizures of land and other arbitrary methods of dealing with the matter locally, in contravention of the principle that the future land-reform is to include the whole of Russia in its scope. Announcing its aims, the Provisional Government believes that it has a right to reckon in its hard and responsible task upon the whole-hearted support of all the living forces of the country. It demands from every citizen a self-sacrificing readiness to give all he has—his strength, his possessions, his very life for the great cause of saving the country, which has ceased to be a stern stepmother to the peoples that inhabit it, but seeks to unite them all in complete freedom and equality of rights.[1]

Such was the result of the increasing pressure of the village revolution upon the Central Government.

Meanwhile, in the countryside further disintegration was evident. Tula Province afforded several cases of activity which resulted in manorial houses being plundered, destroyed or burned. The residence of the Marshal of Nobility for Tver was burned in Efremov district (Tula). The dividing up of land, produce and implements, under cantonal control, was a frequent occurrence.[2]

Ryazan Province reported in one district (Sapozhok) that a squire had been illegally arrested by a cantonal committee. Land was being divided up in accordance with cantonal decrees.[3] Prince Trubetskoy's stock was taken over and sold by the local committee (July 7).[4] The seizure movement in Ryazan was rapidly extending.

Zimarov cantonal land committee (Ranenburg district, Ryazan) after meetings on July 1 and 5, resolved to take under control all land regardless of its ownership and, also, stock and rental payments (July 22). The well-known Ranenburg committee obliterated all land-lease agreements.

The Zimarov cantonal peasantry in spite of the orders of the Ryazan food committee continued, in accordance with the Ranenburg Committee's resolutions, to remove sheaves of corn from private land seized by them. The local authorities were described as being sympathetic (July 28). The Ranenburg district landowners asked for measures to be taken against seizures of squires' grain by local peasants and desired legal proceedings against the local commissioner for his inactivity (July 28).

[1] *Novoe Vremya*, July 9, 1917. Reproduced in *Russian Agriculture during the War* (Carnegie).   [2] *Krestyanskoe Dvizhenie v 1917g.*, p. 145.
[3] Ibid., p. 147.   [4] Ibid., p. 147.

The aforesaid district commissioner's defence is interesting. The use of the squires' farm stock was due to the peasants' needs and the necessity of sowing and harvesting all the fields. Generally in all their resolutions the local committees, in the commissioner's eyes, were "guided by considerations of social advantage." The resolution of the district committee concerning the transfer of all squire-land and stock into peasant hands, was introduced under the menace of the ruin of 2 million *puds* (0·32 cwt.) of grain in various estates and also the degeneration of the cattle. As a result the committee compromised and excepted the small landowners and also highly-cultivated properties. In addition, in all the large estates, the conduct of agriculture was secured by no less than 30 *desyatines* of arable land. The Provisional Government's demand for the abrogation of the aforesaid order and the return of what had been seized was carried out. Any kind of unorganised or provoked criminality by committees was being punished. In this way, any attempts at redivision of land were prevented. At the moment there was being put into force the resolution of the united session of July 24, of the Ryazan district and provincial executive committees, with representatives of the provincial commissioner and of the Minister of Agriculture. The squires' complaints did not give a true picture of the situation in the district. (The Ranenburg Commissioner's Report (August 3).[1]

Proceeding to Tambov Province, one finds that in Elatma district a landowner was arrested, but liberated by the authorities. The peasants threatened him with death and also the destruction of his estate, of which eventually the meadows were seized, the woodland interfered with, the blood-stock and studfarm exposed to ruin (July 5).[2] Prohibition of the use of outside labour occurred in three cantons.[3] On the Duke of Leykhtenberg's estate (Tambov district) the manager was expelled by force, with the assistance of the local food board and

[1] *Krestyanskoe Dvizhenie v 1917g.*, p. 149.
[2] The said owner Michurin's telegram, ibid., p. 149. [3] Ibid., p. 149.

the militia. The estate was seized by a mob led by an unknown person in military uniform who exhibited a card of the Soviet of Soldiers' and Workers' Delegates (July 8). Among several similar happenings, was the seizure of Princess Shcherbatova's estate Marievka (Ostrogozhsk district of Voronesh) by the cantonal committee which had previously demanded the return of rents paid for the preceding year. The harvest was confiscated; also the cattle which had been sold to the Treasury. The lady landowner asked for military protection in view of the helplessness of the local authorities (July 20).[1]

Voronesh was exhibiting all the characteristic signs of the agrarian movement. The cantonal authorities (July 22) led the villagers in attacks upon small owners of property—probably including such as had left the communal bond under the Stolypin Acts. On July 24 a village commissioner conducted a raid upon crops in another district. On July 27 a convent was raided by a crowd of peasants from two villages, led by an ex-*Zemstvo* schoolmaster. The superior was arrested and sent under guard to the Voronesh Soviet of Soldiers' and Workers' Delegates, whence she was banished to the Pokrovsky Convent. The peasants of the villages concerned formed a committee from the sisters of the convent and the local priest. As the event was reported on July 22 there is an apparent discrepancy in the date. However, the facts are clear and indicate that the educational and ecclesiastical forces of the district were acting in collaboration, although the telegram simply leaves such a construction to be implied. On July 29 another case of interference with a convent was announced, the land belonging to it being divided up among the local peasants with the approval of the Nizhnedevitsk district executive committee.[2] Seizures of land, civil or ecclesiastical, and also of the crops thereon, were thus prevalent in Voronesh Province during July.

In the neighbouring region (Middle Volga) within the

[1] Ibid., p. 151. [2] Ibid., p. 152.

confines of Simbirsk Province, it was revealed that in Kurmysh district

seizures of arable land and meadows were widespread, as a result of the proposal of the President of the Kurmysh *Zemstvo* board not to obey the resolution of the Simbirsk executive committee of July 14, which asked peasants to refrain from illegal seizures of other people's land (July 8).[1]

The same province (Karsun district) provided an interesting case of alleged leadership by the district commissioner himself, of the agrarian movement. There had been "a whole series of excesses and occasions of lawbreaking in agrarian matters" both from unorganised peasant groups and under incitement from cantonal committees. The chief agent of such arbitrary action and of violence was stated to be the district commissioner himself, one Druzhitsky. He it was who was the "intellectual culprit" responsible for the murder at Inza of the *Zemstvo* worker Gelshert, the killing (*izbieniya*) of the landowner Ryutchi and the seizure of the lady landowner Rodionova's estate, among other occurrences. The authority in the district was in undesirable hands. Druzhitsky was stated to be introducing trouble and disaffection in the village masses. An agent of the Central Government, it was suggested, should make an enquiry locally as to the above happenings—one preferably not associated with the local party conditions and class struggle (July 29).[2]

The Saratov Province, with the previously-mentioned Balashov district to the fore, was feeling the full force of the peasant movement. Seizure of meadows was general. Harvesting was proceeding on arbitrary lines. The soldiers of the local garrison (Balashov) were seizing farm machinery for their own use. The *otrubniki* and those who had separated from the commune were suffering from the violence of their fellow villagers. The Gagarins' estate (Petrovsk district) was taken over by the cantonal authorities (July 11) as was also that of Countess

[1] Ibid., p. 153.   [2] Ibid., p. 153.

Shuvalova (July 21). A most significant feature was the participation of a priest in one place and, in another, the benevolent neutrality of the militia, of the president of the food board and of the district executive committee.[1]

How pathetic seems the provincial commissioner's announcement (July 25) that members of the provincial council had been sent to the villagers, as had also the commissioner's assistants, to "regulate land relationships." The resolutions and orders of the Provisional Government about the land question had been scattered abroad in the form of pamphlets. In some "exceptional cases" troops had been despatched to arrest law-breakers, and culprits had been summoned to court. These measures had "induced tranquillity" but, added the commissioner, "with the formation of land committees agricultural law-breaking has grown more common."[2]

Saransk district (Penza) provided a further instance of the local liquidation of the work of the Stolypin régime. The differences between communalists and *otrubniki* had arisen "owing to a misunderstanding of the resolution of the Penza Peasant Congress, which had given occasion to a few village communities to require from owners of small holdings the cession of land for general redivision." The movement in the Inza district was not general. It was, so it was stated, more frequently directed against *otrubniki* and other small peasant-owners. There was a continuance of illegal timber-cutting. Chembar district revealed a tendency to "liquidate private ownership of fellow-villagers and particularly *otrubniki*, on the part of certain communities and individuals." The executive and food committees were dividing up, among peasants in need, the surplus implements and unused cattle. There was to be provision for payment for their temporary use. Compensation was to be paid at the market price to the various owners (July 19).[3] From Saransk district came telegraphic particulars of the seizure of the best land on an estate and a notice of expulsion within 30 days, served upon the possessor (July 20). The provincial

[1] Ibid., p. 154. [2] Ibid., p. 154. [3] Ibid., p. 156.

commissioner of Penza gave details, on July 31, of the local harvesting then being executed. In accordance with the provincial land board's decree, portion of the crop which was grown under conditions of share-farming (*métayage*) was to be allotted to the share-farmers. Preparations for the elections for the cantonal *Zemstvo* were then proceeding (July 31). As is known from other sources, it was hoped that these new cantonal institutions, intended to provide the link between canton and *uyezd* which was missing under the old régime, would politically "sublimate" the prevailing factitive control by cantonal committees and soviets. That hope grew less as October drew nearer.

Kazan reported (July 9) hostility to the introduction of the Grain Monopoly and interference by soldiers with the attempt to commence the new Agricultural and Land Census. This Census, it is interesting to note, was to be the basis of the new labour and consumption units whereby the land was to be redistributed, if and when it was socialised legislatively by the future Constituent Assembly. At least, so the present writer gathers from the Minister of Agriculture V. Chernov's speech to the All-Russian Congress of Soviets which met in Petrograd in May.[1]

That the instructions of Tsereteli (now Minister for the Interior in succession to Prince Lvov) and of Peshekhonov (the Social Revolutionary Minister of Food Supply) were being ignored was telegraphed from Sviyazh district. The said committee was, on its own authority, settling the agrarian question in its district, dividing up all the land and declaring forest-land to be district property (July 20). The same area witnessed the confiscation of purchased land belonging to 24 heads of households. An anti-*otrubnik* movement was in evidence. Corn mills were expropriated and *hutors* attacked in various parts of the same province (Kazan). In ten cantons food committees could not even be formed owing

[1] *Zemelny vopros*, Doklady Ministra Zemledeliya V. M. Chernova Vseross. Sov. Krest. Dep., p. 41.

to peasant hostility to the Grain Monopoly. It was likely that troops would be required to assist the district authorities.

An account received from Kazan by the Minister for the Interior, on July 31, boded ill for Russia's economic life and preluded the swift collapse of the remaining social bonds. "In view of the weakness and disorganisation of provincial and district food committees, the hostility of peasants to the Grain Monopoly and the absence almost everywhere of cantonal (food?) committees," the representatives of the food committees of the northern consuming provinces who "required 655,000 *puds* of seed rye, were losing hope of obtaining it in time." The provinces mentioned here included Petrograd, Moscow, Vladimir, Nizhegorod, Kostroma, Novgorod, Tver, Pskov, Lifland (Latvia) and Esthonia.

The regions which contained the above provinces were what were termed "consuming," i.e. for climatic reasons, or from density of industrial population, they could not meet their own requirements. Therefore one of the bases of Russia's internal trade—the main basis geographically, was the interchange of manufactured articles (besides certain agricultural) for the grain of the southern producing provinces of which the Central Agricultural and even more the Middle Volga (not to mention the regions further south and east which used to be the granaries of the export trade) were the suppliers. Defective transport and also the reduction of the supply of manufactured articles from Poland, the Baltic Provinces, Petrograd and Moscow had already been potent causes of Nicholas II's fall. Russia was in a state of virtual blockade and, in addition, part of her own manufacturing areas had been captured by Germany and Austria-Hungary. These facts, clear in 1915 and 1916, were self-evident in 1917. The harvest of this last year was not a good one owing to the exceptionally dry summer. There was a shortage of supply in consequence.

It may be noted that the fact that the peasants had plenty of money has been continually insisted upon by certain writers. Money however is the unique measure of value only if it still remains the medium of exchange. Russian roubles had lost, since 1914, much of their utility as measures of value because the goods, of whose exchange they were supposed to be the medium, were no longer bought and sold to the same extent. Manufactured articles could not be obtained by peasants in the southern "producing regions." Hence trade slackened. The line of cleavage between north-west and central "consuming" areas, and south-east and southern "producing" areas, became extremely sharp.

This fact furnishes the key to much of Russia's subsequent history—indeed, its influence was at that date fundamental. It explains much in the post-revolutionary epoch and, partly, the dethronement of Petrograd as the Russian Capital. The influence of food committees *per se* in the north would naturally be greater than in the south. "The almost complete absence of (food) committees" recorded here as a feature of the Kazan and, by implication, of the other producing provinces, contrasted with their activity in the northern consuming areas and the two capitals has, it is evident, deep economic and social significance. Russia had become sharply divided between the northern (and north-western) "consumers" and the southern (and south-eastern) "producers." Hence the great social tension which contributed, the writer would insist, to the inevitable fall of Kerensky and the signing of a disruptive Brest-Litovsk Treaty.[1]

The provincial commissioner's account of events in the Nizhegorod Province (July 26) has much that is eloquent of the ceaseless turmoil in agrarian social relationships.

The acts of violence, and land and forest seizures, beginning already in March (he states), have grown more frequent. All the

---

[1] When the present writer interviewed N. Avksentyev (Social Revolutionary Minister for the Interior and President of the All-Russian Peasant Soviet in October 1917) he found him inclined to discount the food supply question as the chief economic factor in Kerensky's fall. Yet surely there is much to be said in favour of it.

law-breaking and illegality is connected with the appearance in the provinces of deserters, soldiers on leave or delegates of regimental committees, and also sometimes of delegates of the Soviet of Peasant Deputies. Under the influence of the agitation of the aforesaid delegates and soldiers, the conviction has been strengthened among the local peasantry that all civil laws have lost their force and that all legal relationships must be regulated by peasant organisations. In one district (Sergach) a demand was expressed in the *Zemstvo* assembly for the arrest of a representative who affirmed that the laws still preserved their force.

The attempts of certain cantonal committees to combat illegal activities of the peasants almost always result in failure and lead to the changing of the whole membership of the committee. Elections of new committees frequently bear a fortuitous character and therefore the committees do not always enjoy the confidence of the population. . . .

The provincial executive committee does not possess any authority either over the population or in the Soviets and at present is near to self-abolition.

District commissioners do not adopt any measures to suppress agrarian disorders, because they are afraid of evoking criticism and unpopularity from the people, on the grounds of their defence of the interests of large landowners. The village militia, except for its upper ranks, represents in itself an untrustworthy element. There have been cases where the militiamen have actually joined the mob in committing violence. The military guard sent to the various districts to protect distilleries from destruction does not fulfil its intended mission either. For instance, in Ardatov district the owner of a distillery has asked for the military guard to be withdrawn, owing to the troops' indiscipline. The majority of occasions of law-breaking have taken place in Lukoyanov, Sergach and Vasilchursk districts.[1]

The above complaints of the weakness of any authority, outside the canton or in the "Soviets," aptly describe not only Nizhegorod Province but the whole of Russia at this time.

During the month of August the Provisional Government, now, as mentioned previously, largely socialist in composition, had the unenviable task of trying to keep the country on a war basis, but its "feet of clay" in the

[1] *Krestyanskoe Dvizhenie*, p. 161.

countryside increasingly failed to support it adequately. Prince Volkonsky has described his personal experience of the Social Revolutionaries whom he met. They fell between the stools of the overt or covert hostility of the old governing class and the militant activity of the cantonal assemblies. They secured no gratitude from either. To the first they were little better than Bolsheviks. To the second they were compromisers with the old order. Such was the pathetic position of Chernov in particular. To the squires who helplessly watched the inevitable loss of social prestige and property rights, he was simply a *zimmerwaldian* (internationalist), hardly to be differentiated from Lenin or Trotsky. To the peasants, angered by the delay in settling the land question and embittered by the inequities of the food requisition system, he was no different from Lvov. Kerensky and Peshekhonov, his colleagues, shared his fate. As one of their supplanters put it, "The 'devout seminarists' of the Capital gazed in adoration at the new dispenser of agrarian justice and were inclined to murmur, 'Stay, O moment; thou art so beautiful!' But time ruthlessly passed on, and supporters of what Trotsky termed the 'Kerenskiad' and the 'Chernoviad' soon came to see that their days were numbered."[1]

The influence of executive and land committees grew steadily. That of provincial commissioners faded away. Searches for arms caused invasions of estates and irruptions into manor houses. Rent payments were becoming rarer. Even priests were not respected. The militia sporadically intervened but lacked "morale." From Kursk Province it was reported on September 8 that, in August, a case regarding peasant seizure of land had been tried. But a mob of peasants had broken into the courthouse and acted violently towards judge and prosecutor.[2]

The Province of Orel gave evidence of incessant agrarian troubles—seizures of ploughland and meadows, besides the harvests upon private and *hutor* estates. Rents continued to be arbitrarily fixed. Agreements

[1] Cf. Trotsky, *Lenin*, pp. 154–7. [2] *Krestyanskoe Dvizhenie*, p. 207.

were broken. Labourers and war-prisoners were being removed as usual. Trust in the gathering of the harvest was regarded as having disappeared. To struggle against the seizures then in vogue, the provincial food-board had been invoked. This body was utilising troops withdrawn from the Front (August 2).[1] A landowner in Kamyshev was reported as having been wounded (August 10). Committees were described as controlling estates. Armed robberies had taken place accompanied by deaths (August 23).[2]

Tula reported sporadic attacks upon local property and gardens.

Ryazan announced that soldiers on leave were interfering with judicial work and that there were many deserters in the villages (August 14). Soldiers were robbing apple-orchards. A watchman had been killed. Raids were occurring upon private estates and on monastic farms. One village, incited by its "elders," seized and divided up peasant owners' land, leaving the fields unsown and grain and hay uncut (August 23).[3]

Tambov reports described local landowners as running away from their estates. A valuable apple-orchard was raided and the watchmen were violently treated (August 5). (Such action would indicate disobedience towards the Minister for Agriculture, Chernov's Instruction of July 16, which stated that experimental farms, gardens, vineyards, sugar-beet plantations and undertakings of high standard generally, were to be preserved intact. It was only insufficiently cultivated estates that were to be "socialised" under that Order.) A manor house was devastated and its staff subjected to violence. On August 9 it was announced that raids upon squires' residences and estates were frequent.

From Prince Gagarin, one of the chief sufferers from the peasant disorders, one may gather a picture of conditions in the province. The Prince was Marshal of the Elatma District Gentry. He expressed his views to the Premier (Kerensky) on August 16.

[1] Ibid., p. 207.   [2] Ibid., p. 208.   [3] Ibid., p. 210.

Different Committees [he stated] are usurping power and, by their arrangements, are introducing confusion and strife in the life of the people. Disorderly understanding of freedom breeds illegalities and seizures among the population. The provincial and district commissioners are not supported by any authority and are thus deprived of any possibility of putting into force the direct orders of the Government. The militia has been enrolled too hastily and does not answer the aim of its formation. All this not only undermines the authority of the Provisional Government locally, but places the inhabitants in a defenceless position. Thus, during the last few months, round my house there have been hiding deserters, who commit daring burglaries, principally on the railway. Everyone knows about it, but fears to speak. The militia has so far failed to catch one thief. No measures are being taken against secret distilling. The absence of firm authority in the villages causes irregular justice and illegal arrests. Fixed prices for grain, in view of the high wages, keep the grain in the villages, thus imperilling the general food situation of the country. The Grain Monopoly also meets opposition everywhere, and in the future will stop production of grain. To cure the food crisis, it is necessary to allow free trade in grain, to establish order everywhere and to introduce immediately armed force with the aim of supporting executive authority locally. (Letter of Prince Gagarin. August 16.[1])

Whether Prince Gagarin's advice was entirely disinterested or not, the state of affairs in Tambov is clear. But in what a dilemma were now placed the Socialist ministers of the Provisional Government! To take Gagarin's advice involved reliance upon Kornilov's approaching attempt to destroy the Petrograd Soviet (August 26). To fail to do so, meant the inevitable omnipotence of a combined Soviet-Cantonal Assembly Sovereignty. Truly Kerensky, Chernov, and Peshekhonov were in an awkward situation.

The Ranenburg District Committees exerted, it was said, an "evil influence" upon the surrounding areas of Tambov (August 16). The *Vospominaniya* (Reminiscences) of Prince Volkonsky give a "snapshot" of conditions in that province and in the southern provinces of Russia during the late summer.

[1] *Krestyanskoe Dvizhenie*, p. 210.

Kerensky and the Rural Revolution

During the summer [he states] it was still possible to sell—private property had not been definitely seized. The corn was sold, certain stocks of material were sold, including bulls and motors. The sums I realised by these sales I decided to take to Novocherkask, in order to pay them into the branch of the Volga Kama Bank there. It was then that, for the first time, I made a journey in a goods' waggon: for the first time, I say.

What changes had befallen our railway stations: everywhere there was a surging sea of khaki overcoats and sacks.

I was standing waiting for the train to arrive and was looking at the great arch. Suddenly a huge monster appeared and gently rolled into the station: it was a train that appeared to have been captured by the soldiers. They were standing on the platforms, on the buffers, on the roofs—there were soldiers everywhere. On the engine, at each side there were two soldiers who looked like allegorical figures in a picture representing military capture. That was the time when the khaki overcoats and sunflower seeds reigned supreme.[1]

During this period, Prince Vyazemsky's model farm near Lotarevo Village, Usman district, was raided and devastated by a mob of 5,000 peasants who arrested the Prince himself and put him under the control of three militiamen and delegates from the crowd. Going to the railway station (Gryazi) the whole party was killed by soldiers of an approaching column. The mob passed over to the neighbouring model farm of the Velyaminovs, which they also devastated. Both estates had been commandeered by food and land committees in the spring of the year. It was reported that the local garrison was unreliable. It was announced that the reinforcement of dragoons from Tambov was insufficient. Disorders were spreading (August 25).[2]

The fate of the Stolypin *hutoryane* was revealed by a communication from one district of Tambov that 80 of these enclosed farmholders had been completely ruined by a "general redivision" of 12,000 *desyatines* of land. This redivision had been effected by the illegal resolutions of two village assemblies. The resolutions had been confirmed by the district land committee on August 14.

[1] Volkonsky, op. cit., p. 172.   [2] *Krestyanskoe Dvizhenie*, p. 212.

All complaints were described as useless, since the president of the land committee was simultaneously district commissioner (September 2).[1]

On July 12 preceding, the Provisional Government had issued a decree "restricting transactions in landed property" with the aim of preventing speculation in land, fictitious sales, mortgages, sales of land to foreign subjects and other transactions that might make it difficult for the Constituent Assembly to dispose of the nation's land. This decree was announced by telegraph, instead of through the Senate, as was usual. Thus the Russian landowners saw the virtual expropriation of their land. For them, short- or long-term credit was dead. Upon tacit confiscation of the large landowners' estates by the Decree of July 12, there ensued the Decree of August 23, already telegraphed, which discontinued the land settlement of the Stolypin epoch—that land settlement which had seemed so fundamental in Nicholas II's eyes and had been the outstanding act of collaboration between the Imperial Bureaucracy and the Third Duma. Its primary political aim, the hegemony of the old squire class, had, through the events of 1917, missed its mark. *Pomeshchik*, *hutoryanin* and *otrubnik* simultaneously experienced the new sovereignty of the *mir* and the dominance of the cantonal assembly. The Decrees of July 12 and August 23 simply registered *de jure*, what had already occurred *de facto* in the cantons and districts of Russia.

Meanwhile, in Voronesh Province, committees were either conniving at, or acknowledging, land seizures. A peasant congress held at Voronesh had passed resolutions empowering committees to take over all the land on the estate and divide it among the peasants on lease at fixed rents, in one case 3 roubles per *desyatine*. The rent was payable to the committees which, on the estate of Baroness Pritvits (Ostrogozhk district), left only 122 *desyatines* of wheat-land and 200 *desyatines* of hay.[2]

A district Soviet of workers and soldiers interfered with an estate and struck a levy (August 17). A

[1] *Krestyanskoe Dvizhenie*, p. 212. [2] Ibid., p. 213.

president of a local committee was alleged to be terrorising the inhabitants (August 19). Zvegintsev, a well-known owner, had his estate interfered with by a committee. A local speculator was alleged to have "bought" a committee and to be inciting peasants (August 28).

Food committees were stated to be lacking in the fulfilment of their duties owing to bad arrangement of work and unsuccessful personnel. Famine was described as threatening the People and the Army. By arrangements of a committee, a mill-owner in the Bobrov district of Moscow had been compelled to stop milling flour for the Army and had begun to work for local needs (August 30). This phenomenon was not an isolated occurrence at this date.

Turning to the information supplied to the Central Government by the Middle Volga region, one finds that in Simbirsk Province (August 7) villagers attacked the property of *otrubniki*. Houses and buildings were destroyed. The district commissioner arrested the cantonal executive committee (August 11), troops having to be employed.[1]

The Kurmysh district land board assented to a resolution of the All-Russian Soviet of Peasant Delegates which expressed itself in favour of the transfer of land, and of all questions respecting land usage, to the Department of Land Committees (August 17).[2]

Food committees were unpopular. There was difficulty in enforcing decrees. Countess Tolstoy's estate was devastated by peasants of neighbouring villages. Land was seized. *Hutors* were being broken up. One such enclosed farm was burned. Forest rangers were removed and also some servants. Irregular timber-cutting was in vogue. Grain was being removed from estate granaries. Gardens and orchards were being destroyed despite the Instruction of the Minister of Agriculture of July 16. On the above-mentioned estate of Countess Tolstoy lived 300 persons (mainly family servants). There were three studfarms and there was

[1] Ibid., p. 215.   [2] Ibid., p. 215.

a registered horned-cattle herd. But as a result of the pillaging of fodder reserves, the studfarm and cattle-rearing must be ruined. So at least it was reported on August 21.[1]

The unpopularity of food committees could not be better illustrated than by the fact that one of the members of such a committee was killed in the execution of his duties (August 28). The peasants were opposed to the Grain Monopoly with its fixed prices, and were hindering requisitions. Military forces were sent, at the request of the provincial executive committee, to villages in the Simbirsk district to carry out the Grain Monopoly. They did not fulfil their duties in this respect but, on the other hand, supported the peasants, saying that they would not allow grain to be removed from granaries (August 28). A president of a cantonal committee, Absalyamov, and one Baymashov, agitated against cantonal and regional food committees; as a result of which members of food committees ceased work and peasants took home the requisitioned grain (August 30).[2]

Saratov Province gave evidence of equal instability. Tsarytsin district was "a centre of anarchy supported by local committees" (August 5). On an estate of the Duke of Leykhtenberg near Danilovsk, Petrovsk district, the staff tried to organise a managing committee to control estates. They were dismissed and were announced as inciting peasants against the owner (August 19).[3] Forest land was being divided up according to inhabitants' needs (August 28). Monastic land was being claimed by village peasants (August 31). Penza Province asked, as far as one district was concerned, for the appointment locally of "persons who would re-establish order and legality and would not be partisans of class and party warfare" (August 2). Seizures of stock and land, clashes induced by land committees between communalists and private owners, inactivity of militia and paralysis of food committees form some of the features of the August record. The seriousness of the food question was clear

[1] *Krestyanskoe Dvizhenie*, p. 215.   [2] Ibid., p. 216.   [3] Ibid., p. 217.

from one telegram, which reported a cantonal committee as having prohibited transport of grain outside the boundaries of its locality (August 30). To enforce the Grain Monopoly Decree and to execute orders, one food committee was compelled to adopt force. It was reported that elections were proceeding for the new cantonal *Zemstvo*, while preparations had begun for elections to the district *Zemstvo*. Illegalities had occurred and elections had been cancelled (August 30).[1] Such belated attempts to canalise the activities of omnipotent cantonal committees and soviets were soon to reveal their fatuity.

Kazan Province witnessed a similar conjuncture of events. There was an appeal to Kerensky against a cantonal commissioner's "anarchist actions." The agrarian movement continued. Seizures of meadows, grain and stock proceeded, sometimes on the part of cantonal committees, and sometimes on the part even of the militia. The census taken for the Grain Monopoly was steadily culminating towards that final October insurrection which overturned Kerensky. It seems clear from *Krestyanskoe Dvizhenie* that it played a large part in the fall of the Provisional Government on October 25 ensuing. General seizures, whether by individual peasants or by cantonal committees, proceeded with unfailing persistence (August 12).[2] It was complained that the priesthood were not adequately supporting the introduction of the Grain Monopoly. One is not surprised when the contemporary insecurity of the very parish churches showed a decline in old religious observance. Agitation was proceeding against the Provisional Government; prices were rising; supply of food was poor. Riots leading to bloodshed among villagers were reported. The anti-*hutor* (enclosed farm) movement was in full progress. Peasants and soldiers were attacking estates and enforcing favourable leases. A landowner's manager on Novosiltsev's estate was thrashed and arrested while superintending the transfer of grain to the railway station. A president of an electoral commission for the cantonal

[1] Ibid., p. 219.   [2] Ibid., p. 220.

Zemstvo was flogged. Those who assisted were arrested by militia but afterwards freed by the crowd (August 31).

Nizhegorod Province announced that the "absence of food supplies was causing a threatening disposition among the population." Peasants were hindering the harvesting of grain for Army supplies (August 14).[1]

The stage was being set for the scenes of October. An uncontrollable movement (according to the present writer's conversation with A. Markov, Provincial Commissioner for Kursk, May–September) was now rapidly displacing the compromising and moderate Social Revolutionaries. It was leaving their upper ranks unsupported.

Prince Volkonsky in his *Vospominaniya*[2] has described his personal experiences of the Tambov Province as autumn approached.

> Life in the country became less and less pleasant. By the autumn it became difficult to bear it and we began to think of removing (from the Pavlovka Country House) to town (Borisoglebsk). We were sorry to leave: the autumn seemed to know it was the last. Such splendour I had never seen before; such a conflagration of leaves before their demise I cannot remember. The whole time Tyuchev's lines rang in my ears:
>
>> Injury and weariness rest on all
>> Like a meek smile when tired nature wanes;
>> Such as in reasoning creatures we would call
>> A noble modesty in bearing pains.

For Volkonsky, representative of a dying class: "In nature there was all that was no more to be found in the life around us, where there was neither meekness nor reasonableness nor nobleness nor modesty, and therefore the nature we were leaving was all the more dear to us." At that moment, the world being locked in one of its grimmest warlike struggles, it was not surprising that such should be its reflex in one of the most unfortunate of the belligerent countries.

How did September find the Central Agricultural and

---

[1] *Krestyanskoe Dvizhenie*, p. 223.   [2] Volkonsky, op. cit., pp. 171–2.

Middle Volga regions, whose fortunes have been discussed in the preceding pages?

A. Markov, Provincial Commissioner for Kursk, a Don Cossack who, as previously mentioned, had been elected in May, has described to the writer the September change in the peasant attitude to the Central Government. That Government, now bankrupt in popular estimation after the Kornilov fiasco (August 26), failed to maintain prestige against that of the Congress of Soviets by the various expedients of the "Democratic Conference" and the "Provisional Parliament." A. Markov's report from Kursk (September 15)[1] stated that there was a noticeable tendency in the province, in particular among committees of peasant origin, for the displacement of district committees which were firm in their enforcement of the Provisional Government's orders. The district committees, in view of the increasing quantity of business, were asking for the establishment of an assistant commissioner's office. "The Provincial executive committee does not enjoy the people's confidence and therefore is gradually being, in effect, abolished." This fact was explained as being due to that body's unsatisfactory composition. The number of crimes was increasing. The absence of a good militia rendered control difficult. The local court was unpopular. To struggle against the land committees' policy was not easy in the absence of exact data as to the position of those committees. Energetic food measures were being taken but increase of prices threatened to produce disorders. A member of the Provincial executive committee had been arrested, though on what grounds it was not reported. There was dissatisfaction in consequence among local peasants and Social-Revolutionaries. Complications on this account were possible in one district. One may therefore assume that the arrest was an attempt to support the Provisional Government's authority and check the rising tide of unrest.

From the usual budget of reports concerning divisions

[1] *Krestyanskoe Dvizhenie*, p. 261.

of land and raids upon estates, emerges one in particular, the burning of a manor-house, reported by Count Orlov —Davydov's manager.

The elections to the new cantonal *Zemstvo* caused much misgiving among those who thought the peasant discontent might be diverted from abnormal channels. An electoral commission's president was arrested. The Party that had secured all the seats was that of the Social Revolutionaries who had stood on "tickets" composed by Shchigry Soviet of Peasant Deputies. It was noticed that one programme (*spisok*) only was effective and any attempt to issue any others was greeted with noisy protests. In the Party's ranks was allegedly present a criminal long sought by the public prosecutor. The attitude of the Shchigry district was awkward and menacing. The district commissioner desired the despatch of an inspector of militia to investigate matters (October 4).

In Orel Province, besides the usual cantonal committee interference with estates, and the steady weakening of central control, the most important case of law-breaking *en masse* was the removal of grain from the province by peasants of the neighbouring Kaluga Province. This was effected by road and railway. An amount of eight or nine thousand *puds* (0·32 cwt.) was daily removed at very high prices and without receipts being furnished. Armed forces eventually stopped transport of grain by rail from the province, but it was still proceeding by road. The local authorities were powerless. The peasants were very reluctant to bring in grain to the collecting stations. This phenomenon was explained by the fact that they did not receive any manufactures from the towns in return for their exported products. Iron tools and agricultural implements were not to be obtained.

This circumstance once more emphasises the cardinal economic factor in the rural revolution and explains much of the psychology exhibited by the peasant during the period. It was reported further that it was impossible to expect a sufficient supply of grain from private estates because squires had neither horses nor labourers in sufficient quantity for the timely harvesting of fields or the milling of a new crop. According to the Food Board's accounts, there was an imminent provincial shortage on the year's transactions of eight million *puds*.

Robberies, murders and secret distilling were frequent. Two districts could not obtain a suitable man for the post of head of militia (September 14).

The disintegration of the Army, already evident from Kornilov's unsuccessful *coup d'état*, was obvious from the increasing leadership of uniformed men in the agrarian disturbances. Even the cantonal *Zemstvo* elections were hindered by sailors and troops. The assistance which Lenin secured from the Baltic Fleet is well known. It is however interesting to see sailors described as participating in a land movement in the centre of Russia. As a result of the local elections now almost concluded, the representatives sometimes exhibited *malokulturnost* (lack of education).

Later in the month, it was announced that the food crisis was keener. In many districts peasants supported by the cantonal food boards refused to bring grain to the towns where there were now no reserves. An attempt had been made to wreck a Food Board depôt. Woodcutting *en masse* was proceeding. Prepared timber was being stolen. Landowners and industrialists were prohibited from obtaining timber. Stakhovich's and Novosiltsev's estates were affected. Armed burglaries were common.

On September 23, a combined conference of representatives of public prosecutors, of *Zemstva*, towns, and the military department, passed a resolution requesting the sending of small cavalry brigades to support district commissioners in maintaining order. Criminality was increasing (October 7).[1]

In view of the slowness in bringing culprits to trial, belief in security from punishment had developed in Tula. The militia of that province too was inefficient. The majority of militiamen hardly knew in writing what

[1] *Krestyanskoe Dvizhenie*, p. 264.

their instructions were. They were badly armed. They possessed revolvers, but no cartridges. There was need for exact and detailed guidance and courses for the preparation of militiamen.

The manor-house of the great L. N. Tolstoy (*Yasnaya Polyana*) was, it was stated, not free from devastation. The Russian Academy of Science asked for measures to be taken to protect the residence and grave of the great novelist (September 27).

An agitation against food and land committees was in vogue. Hand-written proclamations signed by a committee "for the happiness of Russia" and meant to incite the people, were being distributed. Whole villages were timber-cutting. Troops were reported to be necessary (September 29).[1]

Ryazan's prospective food shortage was causing unrest. The revolutionary movement in Tambov was affecting Ryazan, Dankov, Ryazhsk and Ranenburg districts (September 16). On September 20 a postmaster, a schoolmaster and a psalmsinger united to form a committee to control an estate. Squires' and enclosed property throughout the province was being plundered. Buildings were being burned. There was even personal violence. Authority was helpless (September 21). Troops were sent on the 22nd to prevent armed peasants raiding estates in Ranenburg and Ryazhsk districts. The provincial commissioner with a delegate of the Soviet of Soldiers' Deputies and the assistant public prosecutor went to Ranenburg. Cavalry was needed, it was said, in the three districts of Ranenburg, Ryazan and Ryazhsk.

Semenov-Tyanshansky, a landowner, was arrested by local peasants but later released by the Provisional Government's order (September 22). On September 27 a mob raided the estate of Petrovo-Solovovo and killed the manager. On the 30th of the same month, a Duma member, Shumakher's estate was plundered and burned at night (Ranenburg district). In Dankov district peasants were dividing up land and burning squires' houses.

[1] *Krestyanskoe Dvizhenie*, p. 265.

In Ranenburg area Semenov's estate was plundered and divided up (September 30).

From Tambov, the announcement that Prince Vyazemsky's model estate was to be transferred to the local committee was regarded with misgivings by the All-Russian Union of Landowners who believed that the violent death suffered by the Prince might lead peasants in other localities to attempt similar action. They desired a cavalry section to be sent to the local railway station (September 1). Village committees were driving out clerks and also estate managers. They were arresting or flogging them (September 9). Everywhere there was complete disorganisation and ruin (i.e. as far as the old property relationships were concerned (September 11)). In three days in Kozlov 24 estates had been burnt. Great agrarian disorders were in progress in Kozlov district.[1] Twelve estates were burned. Squires were forcibly expelled from mansions, live- and dead-stock being pillaged. A rumour was spreading among the peasantry that "if before September 20 the land is not divided up, it will be too late afterwards" (September 13).[2] It would be interesting to know the precise significance of this rumour.

The attempt of a Captain Mironovich's punitive force (September 15) to restore order resulted in the declaration of martial law and the forbidding of assemblies. Before the arrival of the force, it was announced that 170 robbers had been jailed by cantonal authorities and the Soviet of Workers' and Soldiers' Deputies, and much pillage recovered. In Kozlov district four cavalry squadrons were acting energetically on September 15. Mironovich had come from Moscow and was restoring order by disarming the mutinous regiments of the Tambov garrison. The Tambov provincial nobility's special assembly complained of the difficult position of the agricultural industry in the province, owing to the locally established organs of government. The cantonal and district land and food committees were "frequently formed haphazard from

[1] Ibid., p. 269.   [2] Ibid., p. 269.

irregularly-elected people."[1] Their activity was introducing ruin in agricultural life, fundamentally uprooting the idea of law and justice in the popular masses. Rents paid, even in 1916, had been arbitrarily lowered by 50 per cent and 75 per cent. Such revenues were not reaching the lessors. Acting on the resolutions of these committees, peasants were seizing the best squire-land, "leaving their own uncultivated and unsown." The Government's orders, as a result of the weakness and the inaction of commissioners, remained unexecuted (September 18).[2]

The final sentence amply illustrated what N. Avksentyev, the contemporary Minister for the Interior, said to the writer. When asked to express his opinion on the effect of Kornilov's venture of August 26 in causing Kerensky's Administration to collapse, he said "All revolutionary governments are naturally weak. Kornilov's attempt necessarily further weakened the Provisional Government." The peasant communities, already confident that the land was really theirs, mistrusted, or were persuaded to mistrust, the existing Ministry. The Constituent Assembly promised for September 17 was not convoked. The politics of the Capital were mainly engaged in finding substitutes, such as the Democratic Conference or the Provisional Parliament, which might replace it. It seemed as if a democratic government was frightened of peasant radicalism. The cry of "All power to the Soviets" in the peasant mind signified "All power to the Cantonal Assemblies." Lenin's adjuration, "The Bolsheviks must seize power," implied seizure of central power. In the villages the cantonal assemblies had already secured virtual control before September. The months of September and October represent their proclamation of effective control aided by the armed, self-demobilising, sunflower-seed-chewing masses of "khaki-overcoats." The date, October 25, which has now become historic, was conditioned partly by the approaching Second All-Russian Congress of Soviets (October 26),

[1] *Krestyanskoe Dvizhenie*, p. 269. [2] Ibid., p. 269.

but fundamentally by Lenin's realisation of the peasant insurrection then proceeding irresistibly in the villages of the countryside.

The policy of punitive expeditions which with other favourable factors (e.g. the crushing of a potential Soviet power in the capital led by Hrustalev Nosar, and the different international situation) had been successful in December 1905 and the early months of 1906, did not have any success in 1917. The unity of the urban centres, which crystallised in favour of the old Imperial Government at the end of 1905, and enabled it to subdue the peasant risings, had now, in 1917, given place to a strange coalescence of forces termed "proletarian" which in its own interests had no desire to check the rural revolution. That concatenation of circumstances explains the comparatively bloodless *coup d'état* of October 25 with its epilogue the "Land Decree."

Returning to the Tambov Province, one finds that eight estates were devastated in the Lipetsk district. The old peaceful, pseudo-legal, control was rapidly assuming this form of direct annexation of the squires' territories to those of the respective villages. Troops were sent to Kirsanov district. By September 25 order had been restored everywhere—as subsequent events showed, only temporarily. Three acts of mob law were reported, one of which ended in the death of the victims. The Aladinsk Committee's president was the object of an armed attack (September 26).[1]

Events in Voronesh gave indication of the local committees' power as exerted against owners of enclosed farms and commissioners. Even food committees were ignored in some cases. That affairs were growing more embittered was revealed by the killing of an estate manager, his daughter and a watchman. G. Shkarin, an estate-owner, was killed during the same period (September 13). Another owner whose estate was robbed was simultaneously wounded (September 21).

The local state of mind was clearly expressed in

[1] Ibid., p. 270.

a village militia's demand for the removal of the inscription on the office of N. A. Svegintsev's steward, such inscription being considered counter-revolutionary (September 22).

Lynchings of thieves occurred in Simbirsk. If peasants' ideas of law and property with regard to the estates and houses of squires seemed peculiar, there was nevertheless a rigid communal spirit which checked any criminality among the villagers themselves. The food question grew keener. Famine threatened. Interference began to take place, on the part of the local soviet and the peasant congress, with the food supply organs. To collect surplus grain, military force had to be used. Land seizures were reported from *otrubs* and purchased areas. Peasant conferences were proceeding generally to decide the land and food questions and to consider the elections of candidates for the Constituent Assembly (September 16).

An invasion of forest areas by peasants from Kazan was opposed by arms and one of the timber-cutters was jailed. On September 22, a district peasant congress expressed its lack of confidence in the district commissioner, his assistant, the head of the militia and the acting-president of the *Zemstvo* board. New officials were then elected. In this way the Provisional Government and the Social Revolutionary Party were left increasingly "in the air" (October 2).

Another province of the Middle Volga—Saratov—was also giving signs of the current collapse of central power. Estates were being raided. Owners and servants were being driven out. Haystacks were being burned. Hardly any counter-action was being taken. The provincial congress of peasant delegates was violently turning leftwards. This was explained as being due to the unsatisfactory determination of land and food supply questions. The congress insisted upon the legislative prohibition of the sale of all land, its transfer to land committees for equalised use, the establishment of the old fixed prices for grain, the transfer of all surplus grain to the needs of the Army, and its free marketing. The Social Revolutionaries were exerting exclusive influence upon the Assembly (September 16).[1]

Attacks by mobs on mansion houses were becoming frequent. The landowners' "soviet" was of the opinion that "someone or other is organising terrorist societies and the peasants are being summoned to attack rich people." A local committee caused the plundering of the estate and house of Baroness Cherksova (September 23). Sedition was caused in a district by the influence of the provincial congress resolution as to the abolition of the right of ownership in land.[2] *Otrubs* (privately owned peasant farms) continued to be subject to communal attack. *Otrubshchiki* (private holders) were by force invited to receive allotments instead of their separate holdings. The attitude in the province regarding the rioting in other provinces was menacing. The provincial commissioner appealed to the people to cease plundering and rioting (September 25). But it was of no avail. Robbing and burning of buildings continued. Authority was non-existent. One district desired a new cantonal *Zemstvo* to control all resumed estates (September 30).

Similar events were chronicled for Penza. Transport of rye for Army and Town had been prevented by the peasantry from August 9 to September 15. The Census was held up. A member of a food board was expelled after he had tried to settle disputes arising out of the Grain Monopoly. Burning of manor-houses, secret distilling, the weakness of the militia presented the usual and familiar scene. It was suggested that cavalry brigades should fight illegal distilling and, if necessary, counter-revolution. The cantonal *Zemstvo* elections were not yet finished and were evidently unpopular. "Free apples" from squires was a demand from Penza district which led to a riot and some casualties. Troops were required if the Grain Monopoly was to be enforced (September 18).

Serdobsk and Kozlov districts of adjoining provinces

[1] *Krestyanskoe Dvizhenie*, p. 273.   [2] Ibid., p. 274.

were having a bad effect upon Penza Province.[1] A village assembly went as far as to arrest a president and three members of a food board who were afterwards, however, released.

A famine in food and necessary articles caused alarm in Kazan. Food riots were frequent. In one canton the president of the food committee was killed and all documents and census returns destroyed. The position was admitted to be serious. Troops to the number of 2,275 had been sent to various places in the Province. Some troops however were useless. On one occasion "when the peasant women rushed out, the troops ran away" (September 17).[2] There were clashes between troops and mobs leading to fatal results. Telephone communication was cut in one locality. A mob of 200 demanded the abolition of food and land organisations "which had eaten the people's money." It was decided to abolish those organisations and thus to hamper the Grain Monopoly. Food committees, including those of the province, had not, it was alleged, justified their appointment and the province was on the eve of famine (October 1).

Nizhegorod Province was in the same parlous position as far as food was concerned. Cantonal "self-determination" was now prevalent. Grain transfers from one canton to another required force—what better indication of economic and political dissolution could one have than that? Bakunin's idealisation of the sovereignty of the village community was now, in effect, realised, though under catastrophic conditions. A truly *smutnoe vremya* (troubled time) was at hand. The people were openly hostile to the food administration, and that hostility was to be fatal to Kerensky.

The progress of the rural revolution is partly revealed by the very composition of the October reports in *Krestyanskoe Dvizhenie*. They are usually brief. The Central Agricultural and Middle Volga Provinces were filled with blazing *usadbas* (residences). Reserve regi-

---

[1] *Krestyanskoe Dvizhenie*, p. 277. [2] Ibid., p. 278.

ments stationed in various parts of the country even participated in the general disorders. Brigandage made life unsafe. The prevalence of armed deserters and men on leave, besides the complete collapse of military discipline and the feebleness of militia, made the village, or cantonal, or sometimes, the district, committee the sole residuary legatee of law and order. And that law and order differed from that to which Russia had been accustomed. The chronic disorganisation of food and fuel supply, the collapse of the internal market, the Provisional Government's dying endeavour to enforce the unpopular Grain Monopoly, all gave evidence that what afterwards was known as "Bolshevism" was there before a definite party-creed could cover it with a name. The "peasant movement" was definitely now a "movement" in physical fact as well as ideology.

Prince Volkonsky, a member of a small aristocratic circle, owner of 12,000 acres round his Pavlovka residence near Borisoglebsk, Tambov Province, had the good fortune to gaze unharmed upon the surrounding chaos. He was to live as a politically innocuous personage for four years under the approaching Soviet rule. Fate had played him a strange trick in enabling him to be elected president of a Social-Revolutionary committee in the earlier days of the February changes. It had even been whispered that his estates would be left to him owing to his benevolent management of them. Such days were now over. Class compromise was dead. The peasantry were stirred by wilder passions. The breakdown of government had led to the complete decay of central authority.

Mention has already been made of the fact that Volkonsky had paid a visit to the Volga Kama Bank at Novocherkask in the autumn of 1917. He found that his return via the Rostov-Harkov route was impossible owing to the seizure of Rostov. He returned via Tsarytsin, which, he was told, meant a dangerous journey. Before he reached Tsarytsin, news was passed round that the Borisoglebsk wine cellars had been looted—an occurrence becoming not infrequent in other parts of the country at this date.

> At the next station [he stated] there were a few drunken people, but in Tsarystin we already saw the disgusting picture of several drunken soldiers with their overcoats unbuttoned, their fur caps falling over their ears and cigarettes in their mouths, stopping before two officers in a mockingly threatening pose.[1] ... We arrived [at Borisoglebsk] in the night. You cannot imagine what the station was like: it was a drunken occupation; a sea of staggering overcoats; the barefaced impudence of the human herd that was ashamed of nothing. I made my way through the mob with my travelling bag in one hand and my typewriter in the other. Why was I not robbed? My star. ... I came into the porch: there was not a single cab. Mud, the mud of the black soil, impassable mud, and still I had to go home. It was quite two miles to my house. My goloshes stuck in the mud, they made a smacking noise as I drew them out. ... It was dark and sloppy and difficult to walk; the dry rattle of rifle volleys in the dark town came to my ears from time to time. ... I at last reached the part of the town where the asphalt began. ... I stopped. ... I looked round. ... On the asphalt there were papers, broken glass and empty paper boxes lying about. The shop windows were broken. That proved that there had been a "pogrom."

Proceeding, he met three militiamen, who had concealed their armbands to avoid the attentions of the mob. He at last reached his house where, in a state of complete exhaustion, he was given coffee, even at that time sugarless.

Next morning he went to a special *Zemstvo* Sanitary Board meeting where the events of the preceding night of storm were described to him. He understood why the people had not slept.

> The cisterns and casks were ablaze and the mob, regardless of the flames, ladled out the spirit, drank it and got drunk. Men, women and children, and even old women, all wanted to have their share of the fête. ... They were drunk before they drank anything: they were drunk from desire. They climbed on the cisterns, and pressing their breasts to it—drank. Some fell into the burning alcohol:

---

[1] Volkonsky, op. cit., p. 174.

human fat floated on the surface, but they continued to drink. They carried away the burning liquid in pails. . . .

Soldiers from a hospital near by had participated, with the result that the building was set on fire and the wounded were saved with difficulty. Whether the record is more vivid than reality in Volkonsky's description one cannot say, but it is interesting to have a contemporary account of the social disintegration which reached its climax in October.

It appeared to Volkonsky that after the "pogrom" of the wine cellars it was impossible to live in Borisoglebsk. It was also difficult to live in Pavlovka, his country house. The control of the district board had begun to assume "offensive dimensions." Besides, to remain was not without danger. A brigand named Churilov had made his appearance in the neighbourhood and was causing terror to the whole district.

Five miles distant from us, on the estate of the former General Bunin, where his daughter and her husband were living, Churilov had killed the husband, and, ordering the wife to pray for her soul, had shot her in the shoulder. I went to see her on the following day.[1] In Pavlovka [continued Volkonsky] we had the windows of the lower storey boarded up. A whole system of signal cords was attached to the bell, which was worked by the clock. . . . In consequence reports went round that Pavlovka was impregnable, that it was surrounded by electrical conductors.

To such straits was a member of the old influential governing class of Russia now reduced. Despite the precautions, he deemed it wiser to depart. In the first days of November he removed to town and on the next day departed for the Cossack village of Uryupino which, until January, provided an oasis of comparative calm in the inhospitable human desert around.

The scope of this work is limited to 1917. Consequently one cannot follow Volkonsky's fortunes further save to say that he spent four years unharmed under

[1] Volkonsky, op. cit., p. 178.

Soviet rule. His autobiography in 1917 was typical of many other *pomeshchiki*. The peasant insurrection of October did not herald a *pugachovshchina* (slaughter of the squires). Whether it was because, as in 1905, the squires did not remain to gamble with fate upon their estates, or whether it was because the Russian peasantry is not naturally bloodthirsty, the fact remains that few of them lost their lives at this period. The chronicle of *Krestyanskoe Dvizhenie v 1917g.*, embracing the months of March–October, contains little evidence of personal violence towards landowners of large estates.

Robberies and murders were becoming a more frequent phenomenon in Kursk during October. The militia as usual was found wanting. Military force was inadequate, even if only by such means could the insurrection be localised. Cavalry in the newly organised punitive expeditions was demanding 2 roubles 50 kopecks per day for troopers and 15 roubles a day for officers. The railway staffs were terrorised and surrounding provinces were sending agents to obtain grain for removal. Peasant action was general in regard to timber. District land committees ignored provincial orders. Such was the situation that had been attained on October 19.[1]

Horse artillery was applied for by Orel. Timber, as elsewhere, was being illicitly cut. Grain was stopped from transport to town. Men from Kaluga had illegally taken grain away to their own province. The agrarian movement had "assumed an elemental character." In other words, persuasion and argument were of no avail in checking the local supremacy of the respective cantonal committees. Peasants refused to send grain to depôts. They were supported by cantonal and food boards. The towns of Russia were threatened with a food crisis. Local authorities, now helpless, saw their only hope in the application of force. "Anarchy was assuming in the province the proportions of a public calamity."[2] Seizures of land, spoliation of forests, breaking into houses, robberies, prevention of grain transport, and

[1] *Krestyanskoe Dvizhenie*, pp. 320–1.   [2] Ibid., p. 321.

home distilling of spirit had "caused general demoralisation among the people and exposed the towns and the Army to famine." Such was the complaint of the provincial landowners' league which awaited from the Provisional Government "the firm assertion of its orders" (October 10). Robberies and destruction of sugar-factories were symptomatic of the universal weakening of the old order (October 16). A committee was formed to fight anarchy. It resolved to ask the Minister for the Interior to send cavalry or Cossacks (October 19).

Tula notified the presence of widespread Bolshevik propaganda—a fact largely to be explained by the industrial character of the centre of the province. Bolshevik propaganda was, it is well known, primarily industrial. Yet this month was to see a coalition of extreme industrial and agrarian elements, whereby the Social Revolutionaries, as a party, inevitably lost the leadership of the peasant masses—that is, if they had ever really "led" them to the extent they themselves believed.

A district congress of peasant delegates carried a resolution for the transfer of all private and treasury land into the land committees' hands, and providing for the transfer of land to the cultivating population, without waiting for the Constituent Assembly. That was a condensed expression of Lenin's advice delivered on May 22 preceding, at the Peasant Congress in Petrograd. In the Province of Tula, no less than in Orel and Kursk, timber-cutting was a continual feature. The militia was here also unreliable. Its ammunition and revolvers were inadequate. It was in effect an unarmed civil guard, and could not play the part which the old time "gendarmerie" had executed before February. Anarchy was everywhere. Since the provincial commissioner Dzyuin had departed, there was no one to replace him in asserting the Central Government's power. "For the successful struggle against disorder, a new commissioner should be appointed and cavalry despatched." This request was forwarded on October 8 by the combined unions of landowners, priests and trading industrialists.[1] Efremov district described the destruction of private estates as reaching the number of 10–20 per day, the militia commander and the district commissioner being inactive. An Austrian subject Dzhulin was giving orders in their place (October 21). The whole province was disturbed. Moscow military district was asked for aid on October 18. By the 19th of the month more than 30 estates had been broken up. Cavalry was again desired. Divisions of estate-land were being effected (October 19) and railway officials, as elsewhere, were being terrorised (October 21).[2]

In Ryazan, the Ranenburg district still deserved its old reputation as a point of especial tension. Authority was lacking which might prevent raids upon estates. Fuel was extremely scarce. Within a distance of 8 *versts* (0·66 miles) from the town of Ryazan destruction of estates was uninterrupted for four days. Timber reserves were removed, even children participating. On October 2 Ministers were warned that "if measures were not taken to quell disturbances, mob rule, hunger and civil war would occur." Ranenburg witnessed rioting and incendiarism. The spirit stores were in danger (October 3).[3]

In Dankov and Skopin districts the peasantry, "under the influence of local leaders and Baltic agitators, began to arrest local landowners, and to cause them to abandon estates and self-contained farms." They demanded the transfer of land and property to local organisations. They burned various estates, cut timber and pillaged grain, cattle and farm implements. Local authorities, which were believed to sympathise with the movement, did nothing to check such activities. Rioting was increasing and threatened to involve districts in the neighbouring provinces of Tambov and Tula (President of Dankov landowners, October 7).[4]

[1] *Krestyanskoe Dvizhenie*, p. 322.   [2] Ibid., p. 323.
[3] Ibid. On pp. 324–5 is a catalogue of estates attacked.
[4] Ibid., p. 325.

A continual growth of anarchy was evident in Dankov. Landowners desired martial law and cavalry to re-establish order (October 10). Mihaylov district was being involved in a series of riots. It was reported that determined measures were needed to stop them (October 11). In response to the provincial commissioner's requests, Ryazan received a half-squadron of dragoons, Ranenburg, a squadron and Skopin a half squadron (October 13). To stop rioting, a Dankov district estate was handed over to a land committee. The Volkonsky estate in Sapozhok district was burned. (This is not the estate of the Prince Volkonsky already quoted.) Two other estates were subject to depredations (October 17). A district *Zemstvo* assembly, on the same date, resolved to place private estates under the control of cantonal land committees.

Shatov, provincial commissioner for Tambov, reported on October 10 that, for the fortnight preceding, all was quiet in the province. Did this indicate that Tambov was an especially conservative and law-abiding area? Some light is thrown on that question by the statement that, to avoid agrarian disorders, the provincial land board had arranged to take an inventory of all estates, with an instruction concerning the possibility of their transfer to land committees. Such a peaceful victory of peasant aims made much direct attack unnecessary. Prince Volkonsky's words already quoted have given the contemporary history of one estate (Pavlovka) of the Borisoglebsk district of the province. It has been shown that Pavlovka was quietly evacuated by its owner, at the beginning of November, when the district authorities' power was becoming too obvious to be pleasant. Nevertheless, that the province did not enjoy complete calm, was revealed in the same telegraphic despatch, which intimated the existence of disorder in 14 cantons of the Kozlov district. Manor-houses and enclosed farms had suffered to the number of 54, of which 16 had been burned, wholly or in part, and the rest broken up and pillaged. Further, it is interesting to note that "about one-third of the sufferers were peasants, whether *hutoryane*, *otrubniki* or petty owners."

The executive committee of the Kozlov soviets and the food board were, according to their own statement (October 12),[1] being besieged daily by peasants belonging to the famine-stricken provinces. The committee and the board desired that an announcement should be made to all food boards, defining their responsibility for the issue of permits allowing purchase of grain. This announcement should include information as to the provincial and district distribution of foodstuffs. The requisition measures adopted at the Kozlov Railway Station in order to counteract speculators, caused a natural resentment among peasants of the foodless provinces who possessed food permits. The purchase of grain by the very peasants of the famine-stricken provinces raised grain prices to incredible figures and diminished the volume of its transport to collecting points. There was imminent danger that Kozlov district would, in December, be without bread.

The above statement reveals a situation now characterising Russia, which had long since lost such economic unity as it had previously possessed. With economic disruption between consuming north and producing south, political cleavage inevitably followed. That is the secret of October.

On October 13, the power of the Tambov provincial land committee enabled the peasantry to seize an estate in Elatovsk. Its store barns were sealed and there was no possibility of feeding the stock on the estate. The staff of the estate was also without means of sustenance.

Violent invasions of estates were occurring in Spassk where timber-cutting and removal of wood were general.[2]

In Voronesh, divisions of private land were being effected by peasants, relying upon cantonal land committees.

The revival of the *mir* (land-commune) as a socio-economic force was once more in evidence in Simbirsk

[1] *Krestyanskoe Dvizhenie*, p. 327.   [2] Ibid., p. 327.

(Middle Volga) where the Sengiley cantonal land committee and the *skhod* (assembly) resolved to resume any land under spring wheat, whether of *otrubniki* or *obshchinniki*, and to conduct a general redivision (*obshchy peredel*). This decision was adopted on October 2 and was supported by the district and provincial committees.

Similar action tending to annihilate the work of the pre-revolutionary *zemleustroistvo* (land-settlement) occurred in the village of Chukal (Simbirsk Province) where 23 *hutoryane* (private holders) witnessed the seizure of their land, which was subjected to general redivision, their farm-buildings also being threatened with removal (October 7).[1]

The vitality of the land commune seemed especially noticeable in the above province. Ozersk village community in the Kurmysh district divided up land belonging to peasant owners. On the 13th of the same month two village communities of Syzran district destroyed buildings, gardens and stock belonging to fellow-villagers who were *otrubniki*. Similarly, on the 3rd, a *hutor* (private farm) had been attacked by unknown individuals carrying arms. Certain individuals who had left the commune of Chukal, mentioned above, were deprived of their land and also threatened with the removal of their farm-buildings.

Hostility of peasant executive committees in Sengiley district resulted in a refusal of those bodies to transfer their powers to the newly-elected all-class *Zemstva* in that area. In the same part of the province, a food board president was thrashed, after grain had been distributed to the peasantry (October 8).

Saratov Province reported that a conference, on September 29 in Serdobsk district, had decided that the new cantonal *Zemstva* should control estates. This news caused discontent, and to prevent riotous behaviour in Saratov district, 150 Cossacks were summoned. The commissioner's dilatoriness in giving information of disorders in the town and environs of Serdobsk, and his inactivity with regard to wholesale cattle-lifting, resulted in his dismissal (October 5).[2]

[1] Ibid., p. 328.   [2] Ibid., p. 329.

Establishment of communal use of all land, in the Treskinsk cantonal assembly on October 3, heralded seizures and destruction of separate peasant owners' holdings. There was also a case where an individual peasant owner lost 2,300 roubles, besides his other property.

One of the most prominent features of Russian life that was to help to change the country's history, was the steady breakdown in military discipline. The old Army was dissolving and, in its dissolution, brought down the whole edifice of state. The provincial commissioner of Saratov told the Central Government that it was desirable to diminish the population of the town by removing the majority of the infantry and machine-gun regiments. By that means it would be easier to combat rioters who were frequently clothed in military uniform (October 5).

Balashov district, already well known since 1905, when Stolypin himself had been its Provincial Governor, provided a case of communal wood-cutting on peasants' private land. Open attacks upon estates were frequent. Stock and property were being pillaged. Grain could not be sent away. Village communities were demanding its transfer to them. *Otrubshchiki* (private holders) were being expelled from their holdings. Mob violence was prevalent. It was suggested by the provincial commissioner that order should be restored, if necessary, by armed force. When one remembers the opinions expressed by Stolypin in his report as Governor of Saratov (1904–5) after he had quelled disturbances in this very area, one cannot but remark the collapse of the attempt which he was called upon to inaugurate to effect a drastic reorganisation of the functions of the *mir* (land-commune).

Further cases of active hostility towards holders of individual farms occurred in Petrovsk district, according to reports of October 12 and 21. Landowners were afraid to adopt decisive measures against village depredations, owing to intimidation. A mob of troops invaded the Vasilchikov estate and demanded wine and vodka from the spirit store. The garrison commander refused to afford any protection. The town *duma* (council) of

Petrovsk at a combined session, in which all social organisations participated, declined to allow Cossack forces to be sent for. It was arranged that special infantry and cavalry detachments should be formed to guard the town and its environs. Several village assemblies in Saratov district decided to distribute the livestock and implements on three large estates. On four other estates there were destructive raids.

On October 4 the Penza commissioner stated that a district land committee had divided up all Treasury land, as far ahead as 1920. This land was handed over to the necessitous sections of the population for their fuel supply and for building material.

The reason for the prevalent general timber-cutting by peasants was said to be the high prices which private owners had fixed for its sale (October 4).[1] Mills were also being seized. Two cantons—Dertevsk and Lipyagovsk—were mentioned as being prominent in the most dangerous district—that of Penza. Squires and servants were being expelled and farm-buildings dismantled. Even a stone dwelling—an infrequent feature of Russian rural life—was not free from similar treatment.

Throughout the whole province of Penza a census of grain reserves was being conducted, and such reserves were being requisitioned with the aid of troops. The belated cantonal *Zemstvo* was being universally rejected by the peasantry as a governing organ. Sometimes the local soviet organised attacks upon it and, at other times, there was dissatisfaction with elected representatives, who were removed from office in consequence (October 5).[2] Undeterred by threatened punitive expeditions, the local peasantry (as in Narovchat) continued to break up the farms of those who had taken advantage of the Stolypin Legislation to leave their communes (October 12). Not only such *otrubs* but also the private estates, which it had been hoped they would guard, were being rapidly destroyed as economic entities. Local authorities could do nothing to stay the general anarchy.

[1] *Krestyanskoe Dvizhenie*, p. 331.   [2] Ibid, p. 331.

Such anarchy implied the general "sacking" of large estates and the removal of their stock. The food question was acute. Townsmen and troops were creating disturbances. Further attacks were expected upon private estates. A disquieting atmosphere reigned in many parts of the Province of Penza (October 21).[1]

So unpopular had food boards become in Kazan that many of them were actually destroyed. Much trouble had been caused by the rise in prices. The surrounding famine-stricken provinces were consequently ready to pay three times as much as the official amount. It was requested that such fixed prices should be abolished and that the Grain Monopoly should cease. It was asked that the closure of the provincial boundaries against the movement of foodstuffs should be revoked. Here, too, illicit timber-cutting was incessant, the militia useless, and secret distilling endemic. Within the province there were no goods and no food reserves. Land committees were distributing free fuel, allegedly without consideration for the need of the receivers. Speculation had become frequent (October 7).[2]

According to President Melnikov of the Kazan Farmers' Union, mass depredations of forest property, compulsory sale of live- and dead-stock, removal of grain, hay and fodder together with the expulsion of staffs were general phenomena throughout the province (October 13).[3]

To combat the prevalent anarchy, the acting commissioner summoned a conference of local authorities and democratic organisations and also district commissioners. This conference decided to support the Provisional Government and to fight any criminal manifestations, no matter whence they proceeded (October 16). As events showed, this optimism was not justified.

Nizhegorod was hardly in better case. To struggle against anarchy in that province, its provincial commissioner deemed it necessary to obtain immediately 500 cavalrymen. Secondly, he desired definite legislation

[1] *Krestyanskoe Dvizhenie*, p. 332. [2] Ibid., p. 332. [3] Ibid., p. 333.

providing for the peasantry's needs—in particular he advocated the speedy transfer of all land, including forests, to the land committees' control "in order thereby to be able to protect general interests and not those of the squires" (Commissioner Sumgin, October 12).

Meanwhile a wave of riotous destruction had enveloped Lukoyanov district, involving the breaking up and burning of 8 estates. This movement showed signs of spreading (October 12).

In the last communication from this province more than 20 estates were described as having been broken up. This figure included a *Zemstvo* farm with an agricultural college. Cavalry once more were demanded to check disorder (October 20).[1]

The *Krestyanskoe Dvizhenie v. 1917g.* ceases its record on the eve of the fall of the Provisional Régime. The Central Agricultural and the Middle Volga regions have been considered in detail. These two areas certainly merit such detail, not only because they provided a numerical preponderance of peasant discontent, but also because they were the groundwork upon which the new revolutionary powers consolidated their authority. The permanence of the October upheaval was secured by the loyalty of the provinces represented therein to the new Government, first in Petrograd, and eventually in Moscow, the change of capital being a recognition of the fact. In the provinces along the old War Front, the disintegration of the Army, whether in Bessarabia, Volynia, Minsk, Pskov, Petrograd or Esthonia, even sharpened the social antagonism. Disorderly regiments were not a moderating factor in the West where the presence of *hutoryane* (self-contained farmers) and the absence of communal tenure (as for instance in the Baltic States) did not save the former squires. It was mutinous soldiery which sacked Prince Svyatopolk Mirsky's residence in Kovno and caused the death of a squire, Sangushko, in the Ukraine.

Meanwhile, in the Capital, Petrograd, a keen political

[1] Ibid., p. 334.

observer was watching events and was preparing to hitch his party's waggon to the widespread peasant risings that had brought authority to naught. What had been Lenin's tactical and mental evolution since his speech in May? How did he adapt his industrial policy to the needs of a war-weary peasant soldiery, a food-hungry urban populace and a land-hungry peasant countryside?

CHAPTER VI

LENIN AND THE LAND DECREE OF OCTOBER 26, 1917 (o.s.)

THE Bolshevik leader's speech at the Peasant Congress in May did not seem to create an immediate impression. Indeed, the assembled delegates are reported to have laughed at his suggestion that power should be directly seized.

The "July Days" compelled the leader of the steadily growing party to seek refuge in Finland, a region of the old Empire now virtually independent. There was a chance that the new Kerensky Administration might lay violent hands upon him. That however was not his destiny. He spent his time in hiding completing his *State and Revolution*, wherein *inter alia*, he emphasised his anti-Bakuninism by asserting that "Revolution is the most authoritative thing in the world." Anarchy in the sense of a loose federation of communal villages—the goal of many of the early *narodniki*, and of Bakunin himself, was not his aim. But that certainly did become the situation of Russia during 1917, when the "State" actually died away temporarily. Lenin, as a devotee of the principle of a workers' dictatorship, could not admire such an invertebrate system. Yet, to secure his final objectives he had to postpone their immediate adoption. One article in the newspaper *Rabochy* (August 1917) is strangely apposite in its indication of the way Lenin effected his displacement of the Social Revolutionary "general staff." In his examination of the draft of the 242 *nakazy* (instructions) compiled by local peasant deputies for the Peasant Congress of May–June, he wrote as follows:

Let us remind the reader what Engels said about the peasant question, not long before his death. Engels emphasised that socialists have no idea of expropriating small peasants, and that only by the force of example will the advantages of mechanised socialist agriculture be made clear to them. The War has placed before Russia in practice a question of precisely similar type. Farm-stock is inadequate. Confiscate it, but do not divide up the highly-cultivated farms. The peasants have begun to understand that policy. Necessity has made them understand. The War has made them understand, for it is impossible to get stock anywhere. There is need to preserve it. But as for large farming—that means economy of labour on stock, as on much else.

It is a striking fact that, in approaching the goal of his life's work—the establishment of a Dictatorship of the Proletariat upon the ruins of the Autocracy of the Squires, Lenin—the Marxian *par excellence*—finds no direct guidance from his Western mentor, but quotes only Marx's twin-soul, Engels. Engels' advice, one imagines, would have better suited Menshevik Maslov, who feared the effects of an expropriation of the peasants' quasi-property—the *nadel*. The remainder of the paragraph is strangely reminiscent of Chernov's discourse to the May Congress. There he had deprecated "a kind of 'cottage-industry,' local seizure of land," despite his agreement with the idea, supported by Lenin, that "the actual preparation of all land projects must come from below."[1]

This statement of doctrine also re-echoes Chernov's Ministerial Decree of July 16, prohibiting interference with well-organised and highly developed farms.

Proceeding to register in August his attitude to practical agrarian problems, the Bolshevik leader admitted that the peasants wanted to retain small-farming, to "level it in an equalised fashion, and periodically to equalise it anew." "Let them do so," proclaimed Lenin, the Marxian materialist, bowing before old peasant custom and its reflex in *narodnik* theory. No intelligent socialist would dissociate himself (he thought) from peasant

---

[1] *Zemel. Vop. Doklady Ministra Zemledeliya Chernova Vseross. Sovet Krest. Dep.*, pp. 31, 34.

poverty on that account. . . . The transfer of authority to the proletariat—that was the point. And then all that was substantial, basic and fundamental in the programme of the 242 *nakazy* would (he asserted) become effective. "But," significantly added the Marxian, sceptical of *narodnik* idealisation, "life will show with what changes of aspect it will occur."

Then, in what is the most pregnant passage in the article, Lenin proceeded:

> As for us, we are not doctrinaires. Our teaching is not dogma, but a guide to reality. We do not claim that Marx or Marxists know the road to Socialism in all its concreteness. That would be nonsense. We know the direction of the road. We know what class-forces lead along it; but a concrete and practical means will be shown only by the experience of millions when they take up the work. . . . Only in a close alliance with the workers, will you be able to commence to accomplish in fact the programme of the 242 *nakazy*. . . .
>
> And when, in alliance with the urban workers in relentless warfare against capital, you begin to accomplish the programme of the 242 *nakazy*, then all the world will be secure. . . . Then will commence the reign of Socialism, the reign of peace, the reign of those that labour.

Few would, one suggests, be prepared to minimise the value of the above words as evidence of Lenin's socio-political evolution on the eve of October. To link his ideas upon the ideal government of mankind with the actualities of Russia's contemporary problems, he was prepared to jettison, temporarily at least, much of what many had considered to be orthodox Marxian theory. Prince Volkonsky (quoted elsewhere) has stated his conviction that there would have been Bolshevism, even without the Bolsheviks. Presumably the author of this opinion implies that peasant insurgence could not have been checked in 1917, even had Lenin and his party been non-existent. The whole question involves the rôle of personality in history. The writer, while not wishing to be fantastic, would like to ask, "What would have happened if there had been no Lenin at this date?" The very Bolsheviks, inclined by Marxian theory to minimise personality, obviously regarded their leader as more than a simple *primus inter pares*. It must have been a matter for conjecture to many as to how a Cromwell came to lie in Westminster Abbey, or a Napoleon "the little corporal" in the *Invalides*. Stranger still, surely, was it for the leader of a party that revered impersonal *ananke* to attain popular apotheosis and Pharaonic mummification in the Kremlin—the nucleus of the Muscovite race! Would he have reached this apotheosis as a Marxian "diehard" who sneered at the backwardness of the Russian village? One must doubt it.

On September 14, Lenin announced that "this dictatorship of the proletariat and the poorest peasants would give land to the peasants and complete power to the peasant committees in the villages." [1]

"Theory and practice are two different things and to determine the questions (of the proletariat and the peasantry) theoretically and practically is not one and the same thing." [2] It is certain that, long before this statement, it had become clear to him that so-called "orthodox" Marxism could not without adaptation prevail in a country whose problems were largely due to deficiency of urban amenities, rather than to their decadence.

What was Lenin's own post-revolutionary estimate of October 1917?

> Our constructive work in the village [he asserted] passed through two principal phases. In October 1917, we seized power, together with the peasantry as a whole. That was a *bourgeois* revolution in so far as the class struggle in the village had not yet developed. Only in the summer of 1918 did the present proletarian revolution begin in the village. If we had not been able to support that revolution, our work would have been useless. The first step was the seizure of power in the town, the establishment of the Soviet form of government. The second step was . . . the separation, in the

---

[1] Cf. *Rabochy Put*, Sept. 14, 1917. "Vlast Sovetam," *Marxism i Leninism*, p. 24.
[2] Iz rechi na 3 kongresse Kominterna, June 1921, *Marxism i Leninism*, p. 91.

village, of the proletarian and semi-proletarian elements, and their alliance with the town proletariat to fight against the village bourgeoisie.[1]

The Bolshevik Party's seizure of power "with the peasantry as a whole" in support, was based fundamentally on the "Land Decree." What was this Decree? An analysis of the outstanding achievement of the Second All-Russian Congress of Soviets of Workers', Soldiers' and Peasants' Delegates of October 26 (November 8), 1917, reveals interesting features, some of which are less surprising when the organisation of peasant life is remembered.

The first article categorically asserts that "the landowners' right to property in land is herewith abolished without compensation." The second declares that landowners' estates, lands of the Imperial Family, of monasteries and of the Church with all their live- and dead-stock, buildings and appurtenances, are placed in the charge of Cantonal Land Committees and District Soviets of Peasants, pending the decision of the Constituent Assembly on the land question.[2] The orderly transference of formerly private or public lands to the local committees was to be carefully regulated. "Strictest revolutionary control" was to be exercised over buildings, implements and farm-stock generally. Damage to what was to be public property was to be punished as a criminal offence in revolutionary courts (Art. 3). Under Article 4, guidance in carrying out the land reform, pending the Constituent Assembly's final decision, was to be derived from a summarised version of 242 local peasant "Instructions" arranged by the Editorial Committee of the Journal of the All-Russian Soviet of Peasants' Delegates and published on August 6 (19), 1917.[3] Lands of peasants and Cossacks of private army rank were to be untouched.

[1] VIII siezd R.K.P., March 1919, *Marxism i Leninism*, p. 89.
[2] The final forcible dissolution, in January 1918, of the short-lived Constituent Assembly was to render nugatory this important proviso. But Russia's ill-fated Parliament had not yet met, and was still regarded as the symbol of democracy by all the advanced parties, including the Bolsheviks.
[3] *Izvestya*, No. 88, Aug. 6 (19), 1917.

In the *Land Instruction of the Peasants*, it was written that "the problem in its entirety can only be solved by a popular Constituent Assembly." The first section of the *Instruction* announced that "the right of private property in land is to be abolished for all time." "Land shall not be bought, sold, leased or otherwise alienated." Consequently the idea of the old *nadelnaya zemlya*, or peasant "allotment-land," as existing before 1906, embraced the whole area of the country. All lands, regardless of previous ownership or tenure, were to be resumed without compensation, to become the property of the entire people and be placed at the disposal of those who tilled them for use (i.e. *Trudovoe zemlepolzovanie* [Labour land-user]). Those suffering by the new situation could claim public support, pending their readaptation to the new system. By Section 2, mineral wealth, forests and also waters possessing national importance, were to be at the exclusive disposal of the State. Lesser objects of public utility were to be administered locally by district organs of self-government. Valuable cultural plots (Sec. 4) were to be preserved as model farming undertakings by public authorities. Land attached to houses, and any adjacent cultivated garden plots, were to remain under their existing ownership—the area of such lands, and their taxation, to be subsequently fixed. Stock-breeding farms were to become publicly-owned, compensation to be reserved for the Constituent Assembly to decide. The entire farm property to be confiscated—live- and dead-stock—was to become public property, either local or national, without compensation. But peasants who possessed inadequate holdings were exempt from such confiscation.

Article 6 is significant of the ideas which were now coming to the surface in the peasant mass, and had been crystallising in party programmes during the previous decade.

The right to use the land shall be given (regardless of sex) to all citizens of the Russian State who desire to work it by their own hands, i.e. by the labour of their respective families or on co-operative principles, but only for such periods as they are able to do so.

Hired labour was not to be permissible. Should a member of a village community become disabled, then, for a period not exceeding two years, the community was obliged to assist him until his recovery, arranging for the public tillage of his land. Agriculturists, who through old age or permanent incapacity had ceased to be able to work their own lands were to forfeit the right to use them but were, instead, to receive a State pension. It is interesting to see the re-emergence, under stress of revolutionary change, of the old Russian system of working family land-tenure—a principle which had stood at the base of the *mir*, which it had been the aim of Stolypin's Legislation 1906–11 to destroy. To this extent the Revolution of 1917 was a resurgence of old customary land-tenure, or (as Professor Milyukov expressed it, in estimating the forces behind the Russian Revolution) of the "insufficiently 'de-tribalised' nature of the bulk of the Russian People."

Such an inference is strengthened by the contents of the following Section 7 which reads:

> The lands shall be distributed among those who use them on the principle of equalisation, that is on the basis, as determined by local conditions, of the normal labour or food units. No restrictions shall be placed on the mode of land-tenure, the separate village-communities determining whether it shall be household, individual, communal or co-operative tenure.

In this section arises the full implication of the Great Russian, redistributory, levelling commune which the *narodniki* (peasant socialists) of the 'seventies had looked upon as the solution of the chief social problems of the country.

Plekhanov had passed from the *narodnik* fold to the fatal inevitability of Marxist dialectic. Lenin, his successor, spurning this fatal inevitability (when it appeared to imply inertia), by adopting this peasant programme, returned to the old earthen base of the earlier native Russian socialists. If he was an internationalist in his regard for the security of the communist revolution which he led, his strategy made him watch keenly his village communal groundwork. That is the secret of his power and the explanation of the apparent paradox of the Russian Revolution, when viewed through Western European spectacles.

Consider the following:

All lands [Sec. 8] after their confiscation form the land-fund of the entire people, its distribution among the labouring classes being effected by the local and central organs of self-government, from the democratically organised non-class village and urban communities to the central regional institutions. The land-fund shall be periodically redivided in accordance with the changes in the population and the growth of productivity and the improvement of agriculture, provided that the original allotment nucleus remains intact. The lands of those who cease to be members of their respective communities shall revert to the common land-fund; nearest relations of the previous users, or persons designated by them, being entitled to preference in any new allotment of them. The value of permanent improvements as well as the cost of fertilisers applied to such lands shall be repaid whenever they have not been consumed during the reversion of the allotment to the land-fund.

The old *narodnichestvo* (peasant socialism) with its anticipated *cherny peredel* (equalised redistribution) is here attained in unexpected perfection. Provision was of course made for migration of surplus population at the cost of the State. The order of transfer included:—willing peasants possessing no land; undesirable members of the community; deserters, and lastly, those agreeing to voluntary transference or selection by lot.

The above *Instruction* being, in its own words, "the expression of the absolute will of the overwhelming majority of thinking peasants throughout Russia," was to have the force of provisional law and, pending the meeting of the Constituent Assembly, was to be carried out "with as little delay as possible" and, in some parts, "with the inevitable gradation determined by the District Soviet of Peasants' Delegates."

The above Proclamation was followed by the "Decree on Land Socialisation" of February 19, 1918, which, however, did not close an epoch, as did its predecessor, but simply amplified the original idea. The Civil War which lasted from 1917–21 was, as far as general peasant support of the new Administration was concerned, a struggle to consolidate the ground won in the October Land Decree.

In conclusion, what can be more interesting than the Bolshevik Leader's own estimate of what had resulted from the "Peasant Movement" of 1917?

"The Russian village has been 'levelled out.' The medium peasantry has increased. Our village has become a still 'pettier *bourgeois*' place. The medium peasantry is a self-sufficient class—the only one which after the obliteration and expulsion of squires and capitalists remains capable of opposing the proletariat. Therefore, (continued Lenin, referring to a notice he had seen when entering the hall where he spoke in March 1921, before the All-Russian Conference of Transport Workers), it is ridiculous to write on placards that 'to the reign of the Workers and Peasants there will be no end.'" These words revealed the revolutionary leader's consciousness, sharpened after the Kronstadt Rising of 1921, that his Socialist objectives still depended upon the vagaries of the peasant mass.

> One of the last and most determined struggles which we shall conduct is against the "petty *bourgeois*" peasantry, because we have not conquered that "petty *bourgeois* anarchic element, and upon the victory over it immediately depends the destiny of the revolution in the very near future.[1]

It was left for a successor to take up the challenge implied in the revolutionary leader's words.

Of Stalin and the policy of collective farming this is not the place to speak.

But neither he nor his treatment of the post-revolutionary peasant problem would have been politically possible without the development of the Peasant Movement which reached its crisis in 1917.

[1] March, 1921, *Marxism i Leninism*, p. 101.

GLOSSARY

ARTEL. A workers' fellowship or guild.

BARSHCHINA (cf. *corvée*). Compulsory service on estate of squire.
BATRAKI. Agricultural labourers in Russian Baltic Provinces.
BOLSHEVIKI. ("Majority" section.) Extreme wing of R. Soc. Dem. Party (1903) under Lenin's leadership.
BORBA (V DEREVNE). Class struggle (in village).
BOURGEOIS, as Russian socialist term, implied one believing in private profit, an anti-socialist.
BOURGEOISIE. Class of persons with above beliefs.

CHERNY PEREDEL. General redivision of land.
CHETVERT. 5·77 imperial bushels.
CHREZPOLOSITSA. System of intermingled strips of land, i.e. open field cultivation.

DESYATINA. 2·69 acres.
DUMA. (GOSUDARSTVENNAYA). Imperial Parliament estab. in 1905.
DUSHA. Literally, "soul." Term applied to an individual Russian peasant for taxation purposes under serfdom.
DVOR. Peasant family household.
DVORYANIN. Member of gentry class.
DVORYANSTVO. Gentry.

FUNT. Measure of weight equivalent of 0·90 lb. (avoirdupois).

GUBERNIYA. Administrative Province.
GRAZHDANIN. Citizen.

HOLOP. Slave.
HUTOR. An enclosed farm with its owner's residence inside it.
HUTORYANIN. Peasant owner of farm separated from village holdings.

KOPEIKA (KOPECK). $\frac{1}{100}$ of rouble.
KREPOSTNIKI-POMESHCHIKI. Serf-owning squires.
KREPOSTNOE PRAVO. Bondage Right (or serfdom).
KRESTYANIN. Peasant.
KRESTYANSTVO. Peasantry.

Glossary

KRUGOVAYA PORUKA. Mutual guarantee by peasants for taxation or debt burdens.
KULAK. Originally a village usurer who thrived on the poverty of his neighbours. Later a political term of abuse applied to any peasant who was more prosperous than his fellow-villagers.

LATIFUNDIA. Political term of attack applied to large estates mainly dependent for cultivation upon peasant competition for leases. These estates usually employed peasant livestock and implements.
LATIFUNDIARY CULTIVATION OF ESTATES. Employment by estate-owner of peasant labour and livestock instead of his own.

MENSHEVIKI. "Minority" section of R. Soc. Dem. Party (1903). Politically moderate compared with "Bolsheviki." ("Majority" section.)
MIR. Communal Assembly of village. See OBSHCHINA.
MUZHIK. Peasant.

NADEL. Peasant land-allotment upon Emancipation (1861).
NAKAZY. Instructions.
NAROD. The common people; more specifically, the peasantry.
NARODNICHESTVO. Peasant Socialism popular in the 'seventies of the nineteenth century.
NARODNIK. Supporter of above.

OBROK. Rental payment in kind or money.
OBSHCHESTVO. Society or community.
OBSHCHINA. Land commune.
OBSHCHINNIKI. Members of land commune.
OBZOR. Review.
OTHOZHIE PROMYSLY. Outside earnings.
OTKAZ. Right of giving notice of intention to leave estate.
OTRABOTKI. Land leases in return for labour as rent.
OTREZKI. Lands "cut off" from peasant holdings at Emancipation (1861).
OTRUB. An enclosed farm with its owner's residence still in the local village.
OTRUBNIKI (or OTRUBSHCHIKI). Owners of individual holdings not yet separate from those of fellow-villagers.

PEREDEL (CHERNY). Redivision of land (general).
PODVORNIKI. Household (family) owners of heritable land.
PODVORNOE VLADENIE. Household (family) tenure.
POGROM. Riot.
POLOZHENIE. Act or Statute (e.g. of Emancipation).
POMESHCHIK. Member of landed gentry class.
POMESTYE. Estate originally held on service tenure.
PRIRESKI. Supplementary land grants for peasants.

Glossary

PUD. 0·32 cwt.
PUGACHOVSCHINA. General rising against (involving murder of) Russian Squires.

RAZVERSTANIE. Dividing up of village lands under Stolypin Agrarian Legislation (1906).
RAZVERSTSKA. Revolutionary redivision of all land.
ROUBLE. Nominal value 2*s*.

SELSKY. Pertaining to village.
SKHOD. Local peasant assembly under Code of Laws.
SMUTNOE (VREMYA). Troubled (time); i.e. time of troubles.
SMYCHKA. Term used to describe peasant-proletarian co-operation as basis of Communist Government.
SOBSTVENNOST. Ownership.
SOKHA. Peasant's wooden plough.
SOVIET. Council.
SOYUZ SOYUZOV. Congress of Unions.
SVOD (ZAKONOV). Code (of Laws).

TRUDOVAYA SOBSTVENNOST. Cultivator-ownership.
TRUDOVIKI. Peasant Labour Party.
TRUDOVOE POLZOVANIE (TRUDOVOE ZEMLEPOLZOVANIE). Cultivator-ownership.
UKAZ. Imperial Decree.
USADBA. A residence.
USTAVNAYA GRAMOTA. Charter of land-allotment for village-community at Emancipation (1861).
UYEZD. Administrative District below Guberniya (Province).

VERST. 0·66 miles.
VLADENIE. Ownership.
VOLOST. Group of village communities (canton).
VOLOSTI (CHERNYE). Originally free settlements, directly responsible to Tsar.
VOLYA. Freedom.
VOSPOMINANIYA. Reminiscences.
VYKUPNAYA OPERATSIYA. Redemption Payment System instituted after the Emancipation of Russian Peasants.

ZEMLEUSTROISTVO. Land Settlement (1906–17).
ZEMSKY NACHALNIK. Land Captain. An appointed official possessed of judicial, administrative and police powers over peasants.
ZEMSTVO. A provincial or district council based upon limited franchise and possessed of limited powers.

BIBLIOGRAPHY

Agrarnoe Dvizhenie v 1917g. The Agrarian Movement in 1917, Vol. I (XIV), pp. 182-226, 1926. Krasny Arhiv. (Red Archives).
ANTSIFEROV, BILIMOVICH. *Russian Agriculture during the War*, Carnegie.
BESELOVSKY, B., FRICHE, V. M., and PICHET, V. I., *Argarny Vopros v Sovete Ministrov v. 1916g.* (*The Agrarian Question in the Council of Ministers in 1906*, Central Archives R.S.F.S.R., 1924).
BRANFOOT, MISS, "A Critical History of the Narodniki" (unpublished).
CHERNOV, V. M., *Zemelny vopros.* Doklady Ministra Zemledeliya V. M. Chernova Vseross. Sov. Krest. Dep. (May 1917.) (*The Land Question.* Reports of the Minister for Agriculture, V. M. Chernov, to the All-Russian Soviet of Peasant Delegates [May 1917].)
——, "Agrarny vopros i sovremmeny moment," *Zemlya i Volya*, No. 44, Moscow, 1917. ("The Agrarian Question and the Present Moment," lecture by V. M. Chernov delivered on April 30, 1917, at Shanyavsky University, Moscow, 1917. Social Revolutionary Party, *Land and Liberty*, No. 44, Moscow, 1917.)
—— *Novy Zakon o zemle v Uchred. Sobran. Petrograd, 1918.* (*The New Law concerning Land in the Constituent Assembly, Petrograd, 1918.* President of the Constituent Assembly, V. Chernov's Land Socialisation Scheme.)
DRAGE, G., *Russian Affairs*, 1904.
DUBASOV, PANTELEEV, *Agrarnoe Dvizhenie v 1905g. Doklady.* The Agrarian Movement in 1905. (Reports of Dubasov and Panteleev, Vols. IV–V [XI–XII], pp. 182–92, 1925, K.A.)
DUCKWORTH. *Letters of the Tsaritsa*, 1924.
DUMA. Stenographicheskie otchety Gosudarstvennoy Dumy. Imperial Duma. Shorthand Reports.
DZHANSHIEV. *Epokha velikikh reform.* (*Epoch of the Great Reforms.*)
ENGELMAN, I., *Istoriya Krepostnovo Prava v Rossii.* (*The History of Bondage Right [Serfdom] in Russia.* Translated from German into Russian by V. Shcherb, ed. A. Kizewetter, 1900.)
FARIE, R., tr. by, *The Russian People, Institutions and Resources.*
HRULOV, POTOTSKY. *Iz istorii agrarnovo dvizheniya 1905–6.* (Reports of Hrulov and Pototsky, Krasny Arhiv.)
HYNES, A. L. *Russian State Papers, 1915–18.* Selected and edited by A. L. Hynes; introd. C. T. Hagberg-Wright. London, 1929.

Itogi Zemleustroistva, Graficheskoe izobrazhenie deyatelnosti Zemleustroitelnykh Kommissii za pervoe pyatiletie, Izd. 1912, St. Peter. (*Stages in Land Settlement*. Graphical Representation of the Activity of the Land-Settlement Commission for the first Five Year Period, edit. 1912, S.P. Through the courtesy of A. Safonov, formerly of the Department of Land Settlement.)

KACHOROVSKY, "The Russian Land Commune," *Slavonic Review*, March 1929.

KENNARD, H. P., and PEACOCK, N. *Russian Year Book, 1911–14.*

KLYUCHEVSKY, V. O. *Kurs russkoy istorii*. (*Course of Russian History*.)

KOEFOED, A. A. *Borba s chrezpolositseyu v Rossii i za granitseyu.* (*The Struggle with the Intermingled Strip System in Russia and Abroad,* A. A. Koefoed, 1906.)

—— *Zemleustroistvo*, 1914, 2e izd., St. P., 1914. (*Land Settlement, 1914,* A. A. Koefoed, 2nd edit., S.P. 1914.)

—— *Hutorskoe Razselenie.* (*Settlement on Separate Farms*, A. A. Koefoed, 1906.)

Komissiya dlya sostavleniya polozheniy o krestyanakh vykhodyashchikh iz krepostnoy zavisimosti, 2e. izd., *Materialy Red. Komm. S.P.B.*, 1859–60. (The Commission for the Drafting of the Act concerning the Peasants emerging from Serfdom. 2nd Edit. of the *Materials of the Editing Commission*, S.P., 1859–60.)

KORNILOV, A. A. *Modern Russian History.*

KOVALEVSKY, M. M. *Russian Political Institutions.*

Land Decree of Second All-Russian Congress of Soviets of Workers', Soldiers' and Peasants' Delegates, October 26 (November 8), 1917.

LAZAREV, G. "Kak krestyanam dali volyu," *Zemlya i Volya*, No. 43. ("How the Peasants were given Freedom," *Land and Liberty*, No. 43, G. Lazarev, Moscow, 1917.)

LENIN, "The Land Revolution in Russia," Speech on Land Question in December 1918 with the two fundamental land decrees of Russian Soviet Republic, I.L.P., London. (Speech upon the Agrarian Question.)

—— Rech po agrarnomu voprosu. (Speech on the Agrarian Question). (All-Russian Soviet of Peasant Deputies, May 22, 1917.) Moscow, 1917.

—— Iz rechi na VIII Siezd R.K.P. (March 1919). (From a Speech at 8th Session of Russ. Comm. P. [March 1919].)

—— *O prodovolstvennom naloge*, doklad na siezde R.K.P. (*Concerning the Food Tax*. Report to the Session of the Russian Comm. P. [March 1921].)

—— "Brestky Mir." ("The Brest-Litovsk Treaty," 7th Party Congress [March 1918].)

—— "Vlast Sovetam" (article in *Rabochy Put*, September 14, 1917.) ("Power to the Soviets." [Article in *Labour Way*, September 14, 1917].)

LENIN. "Krestyane i Rabochie." ("Peasants and Workers.") (Examination of 242 Peasant Deputies' Instructions presented to the All-Russian Peasant Soviet in May 1917. *The Worker*, August 1917.) For above, see *Works*, Collected Edition, or Marxism and Leninism, S. Semkovsky, Proletarian Press, 1925, Leningrad.
—— *Agrarnaya Programma Russkoy Sotsial-Demokratii* (February 1902). Pervonachalny tekst rukopisi s zamechaniyami avtora (N. Lenina), G. V. Plekhanova, P. B. Akselroda, V. I. Zasulich i Y.O. Martov pod red., L. V. Kameneva, *Leninsky Sbornik III*, Gosizdat, Leningrad, 1925. (*The Agrarian Programme of Russian Social Democracy* [February 1902]. Original Text of MS. with the notes of the author [N. Lenin], of G. V. Plekhanov, of P. B. Axelrod, of V. I. Zasulich and Y. O. Martov, under editorship of L. V. Kamenev. *Lenin Collection III*. State Publishing Dept. Leningrad, 1925, Leningrad.)
—— "Agrarnaya Programma S. Demok. v Russk. Rev." (June 18, 1908), zhurnal polskoy s.d. *Przeglad*, s.d., No. 6, 1908. ("The Agrarian Programme of Social Democracy in the Russian Revolution" [June 18, 1908]. Journal of Polish Social Democratic Party, *Przeglad*, No. 6, 1908. Collected Works, Russ. edit., Vol. XX, Part I, pp. 273–303. [N.B. A Report to Polish Comrades on his own Book, written 1907: not actually published until 1917].)
—— *The State and Revolution.*
—— *The Proletarian Revolution.*
—— *Razvitie Kapitalisma v Rossii.* (*The Development of Capitalism in Russia*, 1898, Lenin.)
LEROY-BEAULIEU, A. *L'Empire des Tsars.* (*The Empire of the Tsars* [in French].)
LITOSHENKO. "Landed Property in Russia." *Russian Review*, Vol. II, No. 4.
LOBANOV-ROSTOVSKY. "Psychological Undercurrents of the Russian Revolution," *Slavonic Review.*
LYALL, R. *The Military Settlements of Arakcheyev.* Historical Tracts, London, 1824.
LYAZAREVSKY, N. *Zakonodatelnye akty* (1904–1908). (*Legislative Acts* [1904–1908]. Edited by N. Lyazarevsky.)
MACKENZIE, WALLACE D. *Russia.*
MAKLAKOV, BASIL. "The Peasant Question and the Russian Revolution," December 1923, *Slavonic Review.*
MANUILOV. "The Stolypin Reforms." *Russian Review*, Vol. I, No. 4, 1912.
—— *Kursi po Kooperatsi*, i, Tom. II. (*Courses on Co-operation*, Vol. II, edited by Manuilov.)
Materialy dlya istorii uprazdneniya krepostnovo sostoyaniya (*Alek. II*), (Materials for the History of the abolition of Serfdom [Alexander II].)

Materialy Red. Kom. po krest. del. 1859. (*Materials of the Editing Commission on Peasant Affairs, 1859.*)
MASARYK, I. *Spirit of Russia.* (Trans. Eden and Cedar Paul, 1919.)
MASLOV, P. *Agrarny Vopros v Rossii.* (*The Agrarian Question in Russia,* S.P., 1905–8.)
MAVOR, J. *An Economic History of Russia.*
MELNIK, J. *Rüssen über Russland* (ed. J. Melnik, 1906). (*Russians upon Russia.*)
MEYENDORFF, DR. A. F. "Soviet Family Law," *Slavonic Review,* March, 1927.
MEYENDORFF, BARON A. F. *Background of Russian Revolution.* Colver Lectures in Brown University, U.S.A., 1928. Baron A. F. MEYENDORFF, formerly Vice-President of Imperial Duma.
MILYUKOV, P. N. *Russia and its Crisis.* Crane Lectures for 1903.
—— "Krestyane" ("The Peasants"), (*Encyclopædia of Brokhaus and Ephron,* Vol. XVI, S.P., 1895.)
—— *Russia To-day and To-morrow,* 1922, London.
MITRANY. *Land and Peasant in Roumania.*
Le Monde Slave, Paris.
Narodnoe Delo (*The People's Task*). Weekly Paper of Peasant Co-operators of Yeniseisk Province, Siberia. Nos. 1–29, June 4–December 24, 1917.
NOLDE, BARON B. *L'Ancien Régime et la Revolution Russes,* 1928. (*The Old régime and the Russian Revolution.*)
OGANOVSKY, N. P. "Revolutsiya naoborot (Razrushenie obshchiny)," *Zemlya Narodu,* No. 6, 1911. ("Revolution in Reverse [The Destruction of the Commune]," *Land for the People,* No. 6, 1911.)
—— "Obshchina v Rossii (statistichesky ocherk)," *Zemlya Narodu,* No. 6, 1917, Petrograd. (The Commune in Russia [A Statistical Essay], *Land for the People,* No. 6, 1917, Petrograd.)
—— *Zemlya Narodu,* No. 1, "S nebes na zemlyu." Sbornik statey N. P. Oganovskavo i N. N. Sukhanova, Moscow, 1917. "Kesarevo-Kesaryu," N. Sukhanov; "Revolutsia naoborot" (1911). (No. 1, "From Heaven to Earth." Collection of Articles by N. P. Oganovsky and N. N. Sukhanov, Moscow, 1917. "Render unto Cæsar," N. Sukhanov; "Revolution in Reverse" [1911], N. P. Oganovsky.)
—— "Otkuda poshla krestyanskaya zemelnaya nuzhda" (1st. zemel. vopros so vtoroy poloviny 18vo veka.), N. P. Oganovsky, *Zemlya Narodu,* No. 4, Izd. 2e, Zadruga, Moscow, 1917. ("Whence Sprang the Peasant Need for Land?" [History of the Land Question from the Second Half of the Eighteenth Century], N. P. Oganovsky, *Land for the People,* No. 4, 2nd ed., "Fellowship," Moscow, 1917.)
Personal Report to the Tsar Nicholas II upon Turkestan by Senator Count Constantine Pahlen (1910) (in Russian).

PARES, SIR BERNARD. "The Stolypin Reforms. *Russian Review*, Vol. I, No. 3, 1912.
—— "Conversations with Stolypin," *Russian Review*, Vol. II, No. 1, 1913.
—— *Cambridge Modern History*, Vol. XII, Chaps. 12 and 13.
—— *My Russian Memoirs*.
—— *History of Russia*.
—— "The Second Duma," June 1923 (*Slavonic Review*).
—— "Rasputin and the Empress," *Foreign Affairs*, N.Y., January 1928.
—— "A Peasant Meeting, August 1905," *The Contemporary Review*, Jan. 1906, London.
PAVLOVSKY, G. *Agricultural Russia on the Eve of Revolution*, 1930.
POBEDONOSTSEV, K. P. *Reflections of a Russian Statesman* (1898).
POKROVSKY, M. N. *Krestyanskoe Dvizhenie v 1917*. v dokumentakh i materialakh pod red., M. N. Pokrovskovo i Y. A. Yakovleva: podgotovili k pechati K. G. Kotelnikov i V. L. Meller. (The main original source material for that year including all telegraphic reports from and to the Central Government relating to the peasant disturbances.) Gozidat, 1927, Mosk., Lening. (*The Peasant Movement in 1917*. Documents and Materials under editorship M. N. Pokrovsky and Y. A. Yakovlev: prepared for publication by K. G. Kotelnikov and V. L. Meller, 1927, Moscow, Leningrad.)
—— *Oktyabristkaya Revolutsiya*. Sbornik statey. (*The October Revolution*. Collection of Articles.)
Politicheskoe Polozhenie Rossii nakanune Fevralskoy Revolutsii v zhandarmskom osveshchenii. (okt. 1916), Tom. IV (XVII), 1926, K.A. (The Political Position of Russia on the eve of the February Revolution according to Police Information [October 1916]. Vol. IV (XVII), 1926, Kr. A.)
RAMBAUD, A. *Histoire de la Russie*. (*History of Russia* [in French].)
ROCHER, M. *La Russie à la fin du XIX siècle*. Trans. M. Rocher 1900. (*Russia at the end of the Nineteenth Century*.)
RODICHEV, F. Duma member for Tver. "Liberal Movement in Russia, 1855–1917" (*Slavonic Review*) June and December, 1923.
ROMANOV, P. *Mart-May 1917g. Obzor polozheniya*, Tom. XV, 1926, Kr.A. (*March–May 1917. Review of the Position*. Vol. XV, 1926.)
Russian Local Government during the War, 1929, Carnegie.
Sbornik Zakonov i Rasporyazenii po Zemleustroistvu (1908). (*Collection of Laws and Decrees upon Land-Settlement* [1908].)
SEMENOV, N. P. *Osvobozhdenie krestyan v tsarst. Imp. Alek. II*. Khronika deyateln. kom. po krest. del. (*The Emancipation of the Peasants in the Reign of Alexander II*. Chronicle of the Transactions of the Committee on Peasant Affairs, N. P. Semenov [1889–98].)
SEMEVSKY, V. *Krestyane v tsarstvovanie Ekateriny II*. (*Peasants in the Reign of Katherine II*.)

SEMEVSKY, V. *Krestyansky vopros v Rossii vo vtoroy polovine XVIII i pervoy polovine XIX veka.* (Krestyansky stroy S.P.B. 1905.) (*The Peasant Question in Russia in the First Half of the Eighteenth and the Second Half of the Nineteenth Century.* [The Peasant Situation, S.P.B., 1905.])
SERGEYEVICH, V. *Drevnosti russkavo prava.* (*Antiquities of Russian Law.*)
SEVIN. "Chastnaya sobstvennost na zemlyu i obshchinnoe zemlevladenie," *Zemlya i Volya*, 1917. ("Private Ownership in Land and Communal Land Tenure," *Land and Liberty*, 1917.)
SHESTAKOV, A. *Krestyanskaya Revolyutsiya 1905–1907gg. v Rossii*, Mos., Lenin., 1926. (*The Peasant Revolution of 1905–1907 in Russia*, Moscow, Leningrad, 1926.)
SHIDLOVSKY. "The Stolypin Reforms," *Russian Review*, Vol. I, No. I, 1912.
"Shto nuzhno narodu," *Zemlya i Volya*, No. 42, Moscow, 1917. ("What the People Need," *Land and Liberty*, No. 42, Moscow, 1917.)
STALIN. *Leninism.*
STOLYPIN, D. A. *Ob organizatsii nashevo selskavo byta*, Moscow, 1892. (*Concerning the Organisation of our Rural Life.*)
STOLYPIN, P. A. *K istorii agrarnoy reformy Stolypina.* (*Concerning the History of the Agrarian Reform of Stolypin.* Stolypin's Report as Government of Saratov, 1904, Vol. IV [XVII], pp. 89–90, Kr. A.)
—— *Perepiska N. A. Romanova i P. A. Stolypina 1906–11g.*, Tom. V, str. 102–8, 1923. (*The Correspondence of N. A. Romanov and P. A. Stolypin* [1906–11], Vol. V, pp. 102–8, 1923, Kr. A.)
—— *Iz perepiska P. A. Stolypina s Nikolaem Romanovym*, Tom. XIII, str. 83, 1928. (*From the Correspondence of P. A. Stolypin with Nicholas Romanov*, Vol. XIII, p. 83, 1928, Kr. A.)
—— Pismo Balasheva k Stolypinu, Tom. II (IX), str. 291–4, 1925. (Letter of Balashev to Stolypin, Vol. II [IX], pp. 291–4, 1925. Kr. A.)
—— Razgon Gosudarst. Dumy, Zased. 53 (1907), Tom. XLIII, str. 65, 1931. (The Dissolution of the Imperial Duma (53rd Sitting, 1907), Vol. XLIII, p. 65, 1931, Kr. A.)
—— *Svod Zakonov*, Tom. II, str. 2042 *et seq.* (*Code of Laws*, Vol. II, pp. 2042 *et seq.*, Stolypin Legislation 1906–10–11.)
STRUVE, P. B. *Food Supply in Russia during the War*, 1929.
—— "A Great Russia," *Russian Review*, Vol. II, No. 4, 1913.
—— *Ocherki doreformennovo hozyaistva.* (*Essays upon the Pre-Emancipation Economy*, P. Struve, October 1913, Moscow.)
TCHERKINSKY. "Agrarian Policy in Soviet Russia," *International Review of Agricultural Economics*, October–December, 1924.
TROTSKY, L. *1905* (1924).
—— *1917.*
—— *Lenin* (1924).
—— *From October to Brest-Litovsk.*

Bibliography

TYUMENEV, *Ot revolyutsii k revolyutsii*, Leningrad, 1925. (*From Revolution to Revolution*.)

VINOGRADOV, P. *Outlines of Historic Jurisprudence*, Oxford, 1920.

VOLKONSKY, PRINCE S. *Vospominaniya*, 1924 (trans. A. E. Chamot). (*Reminiscences of Prince S. Volkonsky*, 1924.)

VOLKOV, N. T. *Novy Zakony o Zemleustroistve. Sbornik*, St. Petersburg. (*New Laws upon Land-Settlement. Collection*.)

WILLIAMS, H. W. *Russia of the Russians*.

WITTE, S. J. *Krestyanskoe Dvizhenie v 1905g.* (*The Peasant Movement in 1905*. Report to S. Witte, Vol. II (IX), pp. 66–93, 1925, Kr. A.)

—— *Borba S. J. Witte s agrarnoy revolyutsey*, Tom. VI (XXXI), str. 81–102, 1928. (*The Struggle of S. J. Witte with the Agrarian Revolution*, Vol. VI (XXXI), pp. 81–102, 1928, Kr. A.)

—— *Vospominaniya (1849–1915)*. (Memoirs of S. J. Witte [1849–1915].)

YERMOLOV, A. S. *Zapiska A. S. Yermolova Nikolayu II v 1905g.* (*A. S. Yermolov's Report to Nicholas II in 1905*. Necessity for National Representation, Vol. I (VIII), pp. 49–69, 1925, Kr. A.)

ZAITSEV, C. *The Agrarian Question in Russia* (1931).

INDEX

Abolition of serfdom (1861), xv
Absenteeism, 7–8
Act of Emancipation (Polozhenie, 1861), 26
Agitation against land and food committees, 218
Agitators, Baltic, 230
Agrarian Bill (1906–7), 105
Agrarian Commission of 1st Duma (1906), 39
Agrarian Law (projected) (1917), 193
Agrarian policy of Lenin, 88, 91, 92–3, 120, 124–5
— programme of Social Democratic Party (1902), 92
— — of Tsar's Government (1906), 35–7, 42–4
— upheaval, essence of, 101
— — radical bourgeois nature of, 123
Agricultural labourers, 7
— societies, 16
Agriculture, conditions of (1906), 39
Aims of Bolshevist land-policy, 124–5
Alexander II, xvi
Alexander III, coronation declaration, xvi, 3
Allotment-land, 6, 108
Anarchy, 212, 228
Appeal to people by 1st Duma (1906), 40–1
Army and peasant disturbances (1905–6), 23–4
Arrest of food-board members, 224
— of members of 2nd Duma (1907), 41

Article 87 (emergency powers), 41
Aspect of countryside after Stolypin legislation, 74
Assemblies of peasants (1905), 16–17, 155
—, cantonal (1917), 233
Attacks upon manor-houses, 231
Autocracy, Lenin's view of, 91–5

Bakunin, views of, 239
Baltic agitators, 230
— provinces, 7, 49–50
Bank, Peasant, 67
— reform of, 25
— purchases of land under, 67–8
— policy of (1905), 67–8
— regional distribution of work of, 69–70
— success of, 70–1
"Banquet period," xvii
"Betting on the strong" (*stava na silnikh*), 58
Bezobrazov, 22
Bill of 104 (1906), 31–4
Bill of 33 (1906), 34
Bimetallism, Agrarian, 114
Black-Earth regions, land-settlement, 72–6
Bolsheviks and Social Revolutionaries, 181
— and seizure of power, 220–1
Bolshevism and peasantry, 89–91
— versus Social Revolutionary movement, 91
— peasant support of, 137–8, 143–4
Bolshevist policy, 88, 124
— propaganda, 159, 229

259

Bondage, relics of, 2–5, 59–60, 90–93
— conditions under, 2–5
— *see also* Serfdom
Bourgeois nature of Russian Revolution, 118
Bourgeoisie of 1789, Lenin's view of, 93
Breach between consuming and producing provinces, 203–4
Breakdown of fundamental relationships, 173–6
Break-up of estates, 230–1, 236
Burning of manor-houses, 216, 218–19, 237

Cantonal assemblies, 219–20
— self-determination, 224
— Zemstvo election, 216
Capitalism and agriculture, 107–8
— in Russia, two paths for, 100–1, 108
Casualties, war, 135–6
Cavalry, intervention of (1917), 217, 219
Censorship, 15
Census of agriculture and land (1917), 202
Central Agricultural Region, 138–40, 224
Central Industrial Region, 142
Central Russia, leadership of, 117
Character of dissidents from land-commune, 64
Chernigov, Province of, 51
Chernov, V. (Minister of Agriculture), 89, 144, 159–62, 196, 240
Chrezpolositsa (intermingled strip-system). *See* Stolypin.
Class-war in village, 95, 97, 143–5
Cleavage, economic, in Russian village, 92
Clergy, influence of, 11
Closure of provincial boundaries, 236
Code of 1649, xv

Colleagues' views of Lenin's Agrarian Policy, 89–90
Collective ownership of land, xvi
Colonisation, regions of recent, 142
Commissioner of Province, departure of, 229
Committees of peasants, 165, 171, 180–2
Commune, land, 27
— capitalism in, 109
— disruption of, 82–3, 110, 144
— inequalities in, 109
— strength of, 109
Confiscation of land, Government's attitude (1906), 37–40
Congestion, rural, 75–7
Congress of Peasants (Moscow, Aug. 1905), 16–17
Congress of Provincial Assemblies (*Zemstva*), xvii–xviii
Congress of Soviets (2nd) (1917), 220
Congress of Town and Provincial Officials (July 1905), 15
Constituent Assembly, xviii
— advocacy of, 16, 21
— postponement of, 220
Constitutional Democrats, policy of, 30–1, 41, 101–2, 120, 185–6
Continental enclosure movement (outside Russia), 49
Contrast between 'seventies and 1905, 13–14
Council of Ministers (1906), 25–7
Cultivable area, 102
Cultivator-ownership, 4–5, 91, 100–1, 196
Cultural differences between Society and peasantry, 178
— improvement, lack of, 10–11

Dankov district, 230–1
Débâcle, military, 132
Debt-bondage, xv
Decree concerning land of Oct. 1917, 31, 34

Index

Decree of Nov. 9, 1906, 41–2, 77–80
Decrees of July 12 and Aug. 23, 1917, 210
Denmark, enclosure-movement, 49
Dictatorship of peasant and proletarian, 116
Differentiation in land-commune, 68, 110
Diminishing returns, law of, 113
Disorder, agrarian, 206–7
Disruption of land-commune, 60–1, 70–2
Dissolution of 1st Duma, 28–9, 40–1
— of 2nd Duma, 41–2
Distilling, illicit, 177–8
Disturbances, peasant (1902 and 1905), 8
Dividing up of land (1917), 218–19
Dubasov, 34
Duma, Imperial, xix, 4–5, 18, 19, 21, 28–31, 35–46, 105, 134–136
Durnovo (Minister of Interior), 23

Economic background of peasant actions (1917), 192
— development of Russia, 100–2
— difficulties during disruption of land-commune, 74–5
— disruption (1917), 173–7
— distinctions among peasants, 83–4
— significance of peasant revolution, 103–4
— strength of land-commune, 56–57
Education system, weakness of, 10–11
"Elemental" character of peasant movement, 228
Emancipation Act (*Polozhenie*, 1861), 1–6, 9, 26
Emergence of real peasant movement, 225
Emergency powers (Article 87), 41

Emperor, Russian. *See* Tsar
Employer and employed, relationship of, 96–7
Empress, Russian. *See* Tsaritsa
Enclosure-movement, 46–56, 60–1
Engels and peasant-problem, 240
England, land conditions in, 107
English enclosure-movement, comparison with, 46–8
Engrossing of peasant-land, 62, 68
Enterprising class of peasantry, 66
Estates, burning of, 237
Ethical code of peasantry, 192–3
Excesses, local control of, 171–2
Exile of 2nd Duma members, 41–2
Expropriation of "latifundia" (large-estates), 39–40, 98
— — — pseudo-legal, 165, 192
Expulsions of squires, 218–19
Extensive farming, xvi

Famines, xvi
Farming, non-capitalistic, 6–7
— technical level of, 6–7
February, (March) Revolution of 1917, 135–6
Financial basis of land-commune, 37, 39
Finland, Lenin's flight to (July 1917), 239
— enclosures in, 49–50
"Fiscal-police" stage of serfdom, xvi
Food-boards, destruction of, 236
Food-committees, 174, 201–4, 217, 222
Food-crisis, 136, 216–17
Food-question, 173–4, 228–9
Food-riots (Sept. 1917), 222
Food-transport, cessation of, 236
Franchise (of Duma), extension of by Witte, 28
Free-allotments, 6–7
French enclosure-movement, comparison with, 49
French Revolution of 1789, comparison with, 38
Fundamental Laws, 29, 42

Gagarin, Prince, report of, 207–8
Gapon, Father, xvii
Garrison-troops, absence of (1904–1905), 18
— disarming of (Tambov), 219
General labour-duty, 130
Golovin, F. A. (Pres. of 2nd Duma), 141
Goremykin, Prime Minister, 28, 35–7
Government, Russian, efforts of to improve peasant conditions, 10, 26
— — land-policy of, 33–7
— — challenge to Duma (1906), 39
— — weaknesses of policy, 71, 170, 220, 222
Grain hold-up, 222–3
— monopoly, 174–5
Grain-removal by peasants, 216
Grain-requisitions, 174–5
Grain-trade, stoppage of, 175
Great Reforms, xvi
Great Russia, 143
Grievances of peasantry, 3
Grounds for upheaval, 120
Gurko, Minister of Interior, 37

"Hereditary war-service" stage of serfdom, xv
Hertsenstein, land-project, 31
Holstein, enclosure-movement, 49
"Hungry years" (1872 and 1891–1892), 9–10
Hutor-system (separate-farming), 70, 73, 80

Imminence of peasant-rising (1905) 18
Incendiarism, rural, 219
Indemnity for land resumed, 106
Independent farmers, percentage of, 84–5
Industrial policy of Lenin, 93, 96
Insufficiency of land, 7
Intelligent farmer and land, 128

Intelligentsia and peasantry, 12–14, 169–170

Japanese War (1904–5), xvi
Japanese War, unpopularity of, 19

Kachorovsky, views of, 109
Kaluga, province of, 228
Katherine II, xvi
Kaufman, Professor A. A. (1906), 26
Kazan, Province of, 157, 168, 187–91, 202–4, 213, 222, 224, 236
Kerensky, A. (Minister of Justice, War and Prime Minister), failure of military offensive of, 191
— effect of peasant movement on, 194–5
Kornilov, Gen., march on Petrograd, 208
Koslov district, 232
Krivoshein, A. V., 27–8
Kryzhanovsky, Lieut.-Gen., 23
Kulak element, 143
Kursk, Province of, 145, 147–50, 162, 191, 206, 215, 228–9
Kusmin-Karavaev, speech by, 40
Kutler, 25, 26, 29

Labour-rent, 80–1, 98–9
Lake region, 142
Land captains, 11–12
— committees, 184–7, 205–6
— Decree of 2nd All-Russian Soviet Congress (Oct. 1917), 31, 34, 243–6
Land Socialisation bill (1906, 31–3
Land-commune, *see also* Commune, 63, 120–1, 245
Land-fund, local control of, 246
Land-question, peasant views of, 104–7
— in 2nd Duma, 117–18
— in May 1917, 173

Index

Land-settlement operations, 83-7
Land-shortage, 75-7
Landless peasants, 70
Landownership, statistics of, 96, 125
Latifundia (large-estates), 98-9
Latifundiary system of cultivation, 98-101
Law of June 14, 1910 (Stolypin), 60-61
— of May 29, 1911 (Stolypin), 61
Layers among peasantry, 109, 112
Leased-land and allotment-land, 109
Leases for labour-rent, 7, 66, 80-1, 99-100
— by State after revolution, 128
Legal status of peasants, 129
Lenin, declaration of, Sept. 14, 1917, 242
— theories of (1898), 38, 144, 206, 238-9
Lessons of 1905, 103
Letters of Tsaritsa, 134-5
Levelling of village, 247
Liberal parties and peasantry, 15
Limitation of holdings, 62
Liquor and troops, 162-3
Local authorities and peasant disorders, 11
— government, distrust of, 117-18
— police, 12
— settlement of land-question, 193
Lvov, G., Prince (Prime Minister), resignation of, 194

Manifesto (Tsar's) of October 1905, 20-2
— — of Nov. 3, 1905, 25
Markov, A., Provincial Commissioner, 215
Marxists and liberal populists, 104-5
Maslov, P., and Lenin, 103
Mecklenburg-Strelitz, Duke of, devastation of estate (1902), 8
Medical side of Great War, 135

Medium peasantry, increase of, 247
Meeting of 1st Duma, 28
Mensheviki, Lenin's breach with, 93, 95
— programme of, 105-6
— criticism of, 108, 113-14
Mentality of peasantry (1917), 156-7
Meyendorff, Baron, devastation of estate (1905), 8
Middle Volga region, 138-41, 221-2
Migulin, Professor, and Duma's land-policy, 25, 28-9
Military force, inadequacy of, 228, 234
— — appeal for, 229
Militia, unreliability of, 205, 217-218
Milyukov, P., 30, 41
Mirsky, P. S., Prince, xvii
Mobilisation, military (1904-5), 18
Mobility of land-holdings under Stolypin Laws, 69
Modern trend, Lenin and, 123-4
Money-rent as interest, 114
Mukhanov, speech in 1st Duma (1906), 39
Municipalisation of land, opposition to, 103, 113
— — — and political restoration, 116-17
Mutinies of soldiers, 237

Nabokov, V., 30, 41
Nakazy (peasant instructions), 239-41
Narodnichestvo (peasant socialism), 121-2, 246
Narodniki (peasant socialists), 5
Nationalisation of land, 16, 17, 93-4, 104-5, 107
— and rent, 113
— and law of diminishing returns, 113
— as *bourgeois* measure, 115

264 Index

Nationalisation, tactical value of, 116–17
— limitations of, 117–18
— implications of, 119
Nicholas II. *See* Tsar
Nizhegorod, Province of, 204–5, 214, 224, 236
Novoe Vremya, article in, 46
Number leaving land-commune, 62–3

Obninsky, report to 1st Duma, 40
October Manifesto (1905), 21, 22, 29
October 1905 and 1917, comparison of, 221
— upheaval, 1917, 237
Orel, province of, 162, 206, 216, 228
Orthodox Marxism, 241
Otreski (lands cut off in 1861), 93
Otrubs (separate-farms), 73

Palitsin, 23
Pantaleev, 34
Paradox of Russian Revolution, 246
Pares, Sir Bernard, at Torzhok cantonal assembly, 19–20
Parties, rise of, in 20th-century Russia, 92
Pasture-land, need of, 6
Pastures, shortage of, 76–7
Payments of peasants, 6
Peasant Congress (May 1917), 239
Peasant disturbances (1902 and 1905), 8
— — (in 1917), areas of, 138–9
— labour party, 105
— — land-socialisation bill of, 31–4
— rising (Oct.–Dec. 1905), 20
— socialism, 91, 105, 121–2
— support of Bolshevism, 143–4
"Peasant," significance of term, 105
Peasant-land, 105–6
Peasants' Union, xviii, 20

Penza, Province of, 147, 155, 157, 167, 172, 184, 201, 223, 235
"Personal-contractual" stage of serfdom, xv
Personality of Lenin, 241–2
Peter the Great, xvi
Peter III, xvi
Peterhof Conference, xviii
Petrazhitsky, speech of, 40
Petrunkevich, I., 75
Petty *bourgeois* element, 247
Petty farming, 95
Pillaging of stock, 219
Plehve (Minister of Interior), xvii
— Trade Union policy of, 22
Plekhanov and Lenin (1905), 91, 93, 103
Pobedonostsev, K. P. (Procurator of Holy Synod), opinion of, 1
Poland, enclosures, 50
Political movement of peasantry, nature of, 136
Poltava, province of, 51
Poor, committees of, 126
Poorer peasants, 70, 75–6, 81, 96
Populists (*narodniki*), 103, 122
Port Arthur, xvii
Post-revolutionary estimate of Oct. 1917, 242–3
Postscript, Lenin's (1908), 123
Prevalence of communal tenure, 56–7
Priests and peasant disorders, 11
Private property versus capitalism, 114
Production, problem of (after revolution), 127
Profit-motive and land-tenure, 113–14
Proletariat, a potential peasant, 116
Propaganda, illegal, 12–14
Property-rights in land, peasant view of, 2–4
— — — decline of respect for, 154–5
Prorogation of 4th Duma, 136
Prosperity, rural, 74

Index

Prosperous peasants and townsmen, 71–2
Provincial Assemblies (*Zemstva*), xvii
Provincial boundaries, closure of, 236
— distribution of land-settlement, 85
Provisional Committee of members of 4th Duma, 136
Prussia, enclosure-movement, 49
Public Communication of Government, June 1906, 39
Punitive expeditions against peasantry, 23–5, 34, 219, 221, 222
Purchase of land by peasants, 68–9

Rabochy (Aug. 1917), 239
Radical *bourgeois* nature of peasant, 115, 123
Ranenburg district, 197, 230
Rasputin and Tsaritsa, 134, 135
— influence on Court, 134
— conspiracy against, 135
— murder of, 135
Redemption payments, abolition of, xv–xvi, 20–6
Redistributions of land, 3, 56–7
— machinery of, 82
Redivision of all land, 93, 112
Registration of peasants, xv
Relativity of revolutionary legality, 117
Rent, burden of, 8
— as interest, 114
— question of, 113–14
Republic, need for, 118
Restoration of old conditions, 116
— of peasant rights, 124
Result of peasant movement, 247
Revolution of 1905, xvi
Revolutionary aspect of peasantry, 88–90, 98, 116, 123
Riman, General, 34
Rising, peasant (Oct.–Dec. 1905), 20

Rodichev, opinions of (1906), 75
Rural revolution, inevitability of, 107
Russian revolution as *bourgeois* phenomenon, 115
Ryazan, Province of, 146, 150, 164, 179, 197, 207, 218

Saratov, Province of, 155, 183, 200, 212, 222
Seasonal migration of labour, 14–15
Seizure of land by peasants, right of, 20
— — — — — Lenin and, 124
— — — — — effect on troops, 126
— — — — — on cultivation, 127
Self-determination, cantonal, 224
Semi-bondage relationships in Russian Centre, 9, 98
Semi-proletarian peasant-class, 64
Separate farms, 69–72
Serfdom, abolition of (1861), xv
— phases of, xv–xvi
Shingarev (Minister for Agriculture, 1917), 184
Significance of term "peasant", 105
Simbirsk, province of, 146, 155, 167, 179, 182, 200, 211, 222, 232
Skopin district, 230
Smychka (peasant-proletarian union), 122
Social Democratic Party, exile of members of, 42
— — — programme (1902), 92
Social Revolutionary Party, 13, 38, 89, 154, 179, 181, 202, 206
— — — in Second Duma, 112
Socialisation, meaning of, 101
Socialisation Decree (Feb. 1918), 246
Socialism (early Russian), 91–2
— rise of (1917), 169

Socialist parties and nationalisation of land, 104–5
Southern Russia, land-settlement, 70, 72
Soviet, as workers' organisation, 22, 23
— arrest of members of (St. Petersburg, 1905), 28
Soviet of Peasant Delegates (May, 1917), Lenin's Address, 124, 193
Special Commission of 1st Duma, 39
Squires, schism among (1905), 22
— enterprise among (1906), 66
— as agents of change, 108
— attacks on (1917), 146–7
— expulsions of, 219
Stakhovich, views of, 41
Stalin and Lenin, 90
State and Revolution (Lenin), 239
Statistical result of land-settlement operations, 84–7
Stock-farming, difficulties after 1906, 76
— Lenin's views on, 130
— pillage, 219
Stolypin, A., article by in *Novoe Vremya*, 46
Stolypin, D. A., theories of (1892), 35
Stolypin, P. A. (Prime Minister), 28, 30, 35, 37, 40–1, 46, 58–9, 73, 121, 141, 185
  Laws, 28, 42–6, 55–6, 57–62, 66–87, 144–5, 185, 196
Stratification (social) in land-commune, 64
Successful revolution, characteristics of, 116
Supplementary incomes, need of, 7
— land-allotments, need of, 17
— — abandonment of hope of, 63
Supremacy of local committees, 126
Surplus population, 246

Tambov, Province of, 146, 151, 164, 180, 198–9, 207, 219, 221, 230
Tambov, town of, 207–8
Technical level of agriculture on *latifundia* (large-estates), 99
— progress among farmers leaving land-commune, 73, 77
— weaknesses of land-settlement, 80–4
Tenure and efficiency, 99–100
Timber, need of, 6
— cutting of, 172
Tolstoy, L. N., Count, protection of former house of (1917), 218
Torzhok cantonal assembly (1905), 19–20
Trade Unions, 15, 22, 23
Transport, breakdown in, 136, 173–4
Trepov, General, xvii, 25
Trotsky, L., and Lenin, 89
Trudoviki (peasant labourites), 30–34
Tsar Alexander III, coronation declaration, 3
Tsar Nicholas II, declaration, 3
— — — faith of peasants in, 13
— — — Decrees of 1904–5, 16, 18, 22, 25
— — — letter to Stolypin, 34, 45–6, 130–1, 134–5
Tsarevich (heir-apparent of Nicholas II), 134
Tsarina. See Tsaritsa
Tsaritsa (consort of Nicholas II), 134–5
Tsereteli, motion of, in 2nd Duma (1907), 41
Tsushima, Battle of, xvii
Tula, Province of, 146, 163, 192, 197, 207, 217–18

Uncontrollable peasant movement, 214
Union, Peasants', 17, 20

Vasilchikov, Prince, speech of, 59–60
Village-unity (in 1917), 242–3
Violence caused by resistance to land - settlement operations, 82–3
— of Stolypin, 58, 121, 124
Volkonsky, Sergius, Prince, 164, 180, 208–9, 214, 225
Voronesh, Province of, 152, 166, 179, 181, 199–200, 210–11, 221, 232

Wages, advance-payment of, 8
— level of, 8
War, Great (1914), 132–3
Well-to-do peasants and disturbances, 10
— — after 1906, 71
Western European upheaval, 117
Western Russia, enclosures in, 50
White Russia, 139–40

Witte, S. J. (Prime Minister), 23, 28, 29
— correspondence of, 1
— report to Tsar (Jan. 1906), 27

Yakushkin, speech at elections (1906), 30
Yanson, Y. E., Prof., 6
Yermolov, A., Letter to Nicholas II (1905), 22

Zemstva (Provincial Assemblies) and peasantry, 12
— — — conferences of, 15
— — — meetings, 17
— — — Congress (June 12, 1905), 17
— — — cantonal elections to (1917), 202
Zemstvo, Moscow, xvii
Zinovyev and Lenin, 89
Zubatov and Trade Unions, 22